Nix Mastery

Reproducible Systems and Functional Package Management

Robert Johnson

Published by HiTeX Press

For permissions and other inquiries, write to:
P.O. Box 3132, Framingham, MA 01701, USA

Contents

Introduction

In the rapidly evolving landscape of technology, the need for robust, reliable, and reproducible systems has never been more pressing. As organizations increasingly rely on complex software environments, the tools and methodologies used to manage these systems must evolve to meet new demands. This book, "Nix Mastery: Reproducible Systems and Functional Package Management," introduces readers to Nix, an innovative approach to system configuration and package management that stands out for its unique functional properties and focus on immutability.

Nix is a powerful package manager that fundamentally changes how software is managed and deployed. Built on the principles of functional programming, it offers a declarative and immutable model that ensures precise control over software environments. It introduces a paradigm shift from traditional package management systems by tracking the dependencies and binary identities of packages, allowing for consistent and repeatable builds. This ensures that environments can be exactly reproduced, a critical feature for both development and production systems aiming for high reliability.

The Nix ecosystem, which includes the Nix package manager, the Nixpkgs repository, and NixOS, a Linux distribution based on Nix, caters to a wide range of use cases, from individual developers seeking reliable tooling to large organizations aiming to streamline their infrastructure. Nix's reproducible build system prevents "it works on my machine" problems, while its declarative approach allows configurations to be managed efficiently across entire fleets of machines, irrespective of scale.

This book aims to provide a comprehensive guide to mastering Nix, covering everything from its basic concepts and scripting language to advanced topics like custom package management strategies and continuous integration workflows. It will delve into the specifics of building and customizing environments, leveraging Nix's capabilities to automate infrastructure management, and ensuring security and isolation in contemporary computing landscapes.

Whether you are a software developer, systems administrator, or IT professional, "Nix Mastery: Reproducible Systems and Functional Package Management" will equip you with the knowledge and skills needed to harness the full potential of Nix. Each chapter is carefully structured to build on the foundational concepts of Nix's functional model, providing detailed insights and practical examples to solidify understanding and application.

The journey through this text is not just about learning a new tool; it is about adopting a new way of thinking about software development and systems management–one that prioritizes precision, reliability, and reproducibility. By embracing Nix, you join a community committed to building software environments that can meet the highest standards of modern software practices.

This book sets out to demystify Nix, guiding you through its logical constructs, nuanced configurations, and powerful integrations. Let's embark on mastering the art of reproducible systems and functional package management with Nix, and discover how it can transform your software infrastructure into a model of consistency and efficiency.

Chapter 1

Introduction to Nix and Functional Package Management

Nix represents a paradigm shift in package management by utilizing the principles of functional programming to achieve deterministic, reproducible software environments. Unlike traditional systems, Nix manages packages in a purely functional way, which means builds are isolated, dependencies are version-controlled, and state does not interfere across installations. This approach enhances reliability and simplifies configuration management by allowing entire environments to be rolled back, rebuilt, or replicated with precision. The underlying philosophy and benefits of Nix provide a robust foundation for dealing with modern software complexities, making it an essential tool for developers and system administrators who demand consistency and transparency in their workflows.

1.1 The Philosophy Behind Nix

The innovative philosophy behind Nix derives its core principles from functional programming, applying them to system and package management. This underpinning philosophy of immutability and declarative configuration offers a stark contrast to conventional package managers, where statefulness and mutable configurations often lead to inconsistent environments and dependency hell. Nix employs a purely functional approach, which provides several decisive advantages: it ensures reproducible builds, eliminates side-effects, and enables atomic upgrades and rollbacks.

Central to Nix's philosophy is the concept of *immutability*. In computing, immutability refers to the inability to modify a data object after its creation. In the context of Nix, this means software packages and configurations are never altered once they are built. Each package is associated with a unique identifier, derived from applying a hash function to its source code and all its dependencies. This approach ensures that identical builds always produce identical outputs, leading to reproducibility across systems.

The immutability principle is visually and functionally represented by the Nix store, typically located in /nix/store. Each package in the Nix store is stored in a directory named with its hash and its name in the format:

/nix/store/<hash>-<name>-<version>

The Nix store provides isolation between the files of different packages. This unique architecture allows multiple versions of the same package to coexist without conflict, as they are encapsulated within their respective store paths. As a result, users can maintain multiple versions of software, resolve dependencies with precision, and transition between package versions seamlessly without interference.

Immutability, therefore, provides a fundamental layer of reliability. By ensuring builds are consistent and repeatable, Nix alleviates many of the deterministic failures encountered with traditional mutable systems.

Another cornerstone of Nix's paradigm is its use of *functional pro-*

gramming principles. Functional programming, a paradigm mostly attributed to its emphasis on mathematical functions and immutability, aligns succinctly with Nix's goal to foster predictable and maintainable system configurations.

Within Nix, the configuration of packages is defined using the Nix Expression Language (NEL). The NEL is a lazy, purely functional language that simplifies the representation of packages as composable pieces, ensuring build descriptions remain clear and deterministic. Below is an example of a simple Nix expression to build the GNU Hello package:

```
{ stdenv, fetchurl }:

stdenv.mkDerivation {
  pname = "hello";
  version = "2.10";

  src = fetchurl {
    url = "http://ftp.gnu.org/gnu/hello/hello-${version}.tar.gz";
    sha256 = "0ssi1wpaf7plaswqqjwigppsg5fyh99vdlb9kzl7c9lng89ndq1i";
  };

  buildInputs = [ ];

  meta = {
    description = "A program that produces a familiar greeting";
    homepage = "http://www.gnu.org/software/hello/";
    license = licenses.gpl3;
  };
}
```

In this expression, the mkDerivation function composes various attributes to define the package. Attributes such as pname, version, and src are declarative statements that contribute to the build output. This declarative style, contrasted with imperative scripting often used in other systems, facilitates clear and verifiable configurations.

Nix inherently avoids side-effects. Traditional package managers often execute builds directly within the global system directories, risking the contamination of environments and undeterministic interference between separate package dependencies. However, in Nix's functional paradigm, dependencies are explicitly defined and confined within isolated environments. Builds occur in chroot, sandboxed environments, which guarantee an absence of external influence.

Moreover, the atomicity inherent to Nix's operation allows for seamless upgrades and rollbacks. Each change to a Nix system is atomic, meaning it is either fully completed or not applied at all. If an upgrade fails or introduces issues, users can instantly revert their systems to a previous state with complete assurance that no partial changes reside within the infrastructure. This robust mechanism of rollback empowers greater security and confidence in system state transitions.

To further elucidate, consider an upgrade scenario within a traditional package manager that may partially apply and then fail due to a broken dependency. This would often leave the system in an inconsistent state, requiring manual intervention and troubleshooting. Nix circumvents this problem through its atomicity and immutability by ensuring the entire system reverts precisely to its pre-upgrade state without residue or corruption.

In addition to maintaining a pristine system environment, Nix contributes to a global effort towards sustainability in computing. Its deterministic builds consume fewer resources by eliminating the need for rebuilds that characterize many mutable systems plagued by state drifts and dependency conflicts. Through efficiency and reusable configurations—where environments can be deployed across multiple systems precisely as specified—Nix fortifies not only practical development pipelines but also encourages environmentally conscious computing practices.

The philosophical alignment of Nix with immutability and functional paradigms is further exemplified in its sophisticated handling of *garbage collection*. Unlike traditional systems where obsolete or redundant dependencies often accumulate, leading to bloat, Nix can precisely identify and safely remove unreferenced packages within the store. Commands like nix-collect-garbage expunge unnecessary artifacts without risking active dependencies or user configurations.

The philosophy driving Nix integrates well into the broader field of *infrastructure as code* (IaC), where system infrastructure is managed through codebases rather than manual workflows. Nix lends itself exceptionally well to IaC through its declarative language, orchestrated to define intricate system setups reproducibly. This empowers DevOps professionals and software developers to maintain full systems in version control, equivalent to maintaining application source code.

Additionally, the principles of reproducibility and atomicity are echoed in Nix's deployment practices with *NixOps*—a tool for deploying NixOS configurations to physical or virtual machines. With NixOps, the same declarative configurations specified for local development can be deployed across diverse environments, whether clouds, containers, or bare-metal systems. This capability underscores the Bernoulli efficiency theorem prevalent in computer science where minimizing needless variance and focusing on functional purity optimizes overall performance.

The philosophy underpinning Nix represents a modern approach to tackling perennial issues of software reliability, dependency management, and environmental consistency. By aligning with functional programming principles and embracing immutability, Nix offers a compelling solution to the hindrances of traditional package and configuration management. Its contributions to sustainable computing, clearly defined package ecosystems, and reproducible configurations champion an era where deterministic control over software environments is feasible, efficient, and precise.

1.2 Overview of Functional Package Management

Functional package management represents a paradigmatic shift in how software systems and environments are managed, particularly in terms of how they handle packages and their dependencies. This approach leverages principles drawn from functional programming, notably immutability and pure functions, to enhance the reliability, consistency, and reproducibility of software and systems. This section provides a comprehensive exploration of functional package management as exemplified by Nix, comparing it to traditional package management systems and elucidating its benefits for developers and end-users.

Traditional package management systems such as APT (Advanced Package Tool) for Debian-based systems or RPM (Red Hat Package Manager) for Red Hat-based systems have long been the standard. These systems work by installing, upgrading, configuring, and removing software packages. They typically manage a central database that keeps track of installed packages and their relationships, maintaining system consistency by resolving dependencies so that packages function correctly.

In traditional systems, package managers are often procedurally script-driven, meaning that the installation and configuration of software rely on executing a sequence of procedural steps. While effective for many scenarios, this model frequently encounters challenges, including, but not limited to, dependency conflicts (commonly referred to as dependency hell), mutable state issues, and non-reproducible environments due to side-effects and system drift over time.

Functional package management, by contrast, fundamentally breaks away from these challenges by introducing immutability and stating explicitly that software builds should produce the same results given the same inputs, a concept analogous to a mathematical function. Packages in a functional package management system are immutable and typically stored in a dedicated location, ensuring that installations do not alter the existing environment.

A core element of functional package management is the use of *unique identifiers* and *hash functions* to manage packages and their dependencies. In Nix, for example, when a package is built, a unique path in the /nix/store is created, identified by a hash that results from its source code and dependencies. This characteristic necessitates a careful construction of dependency graphs, ensuring that all paths leading to a particular package build are deterministic and reproduce identical outputs.

The Nix Expression Language (NEL) is utilized to describe package build recipes succinctly. It follows a declarative approach, as opposed to procedural scripting methods, to define software builds and environments. This emphasizes a higher level of abstraction and promotes a clearer intention in expressing system characteristics. A basic Nix expression defining a hypothetical package might look as follows:

```
{ stdenv, fetchurl, myLibrary }:

stdenv.mkDerivation {
  pname = "my-package";
  version = "1.0";

  src = fetchurl {
    url = "http://example.com/my-package-${version}.tar.gz";
    sha256 = "0abhghwpaf7whatever255r9kdsjfh0per";
```

```
  };

  buildInputs = [ myLibrary ];

  meta = {
    description = "A custom package for demonstration";
    homepage = "http://example.com/my-package";
    license = licenses.mit;
  };
}
```

This expression illustrates several key features of functional package management, notably the absence of side-effects. The source and any build dependencies are fetched based on exact hash codes, guaranteeing that external changes to the source do not inadvertently affect the build. The exactness in specifying inputs means that builds are isolated, forming the basis for reproducibility and minimizing system drift.

Benefits and Improvements over Traditional Systems

Functional package management provides numerous benefits that address the deficiencies inherent in non-functional approaches:

- **Reproducibility:** Since builds are defined functionally with explicit dependencies, the same build environment can be recreated effortlessly on different machines. This is vital for scenarios like continuous integration, where environments need to be consistent across multiple test and build agents.
- **Co-existence of Multiple Versions:** Unlike traditional systems where upgrading to a newer version of a package could override the current version, functional package managers can store multiple versions of the same package concurrently, thanks to their hash-based identification.
- **Atomic Transactions and Rollbacks:** Functional package systems manage changes atomically. If an update fails, the system can swiftly return to its prior state without partial updates lingering and causing inconsistent behavior. This rollback functionality is a substantial advantage in maintaining the stability of production systems.
- **Progressive and Declarative Configurations:** Functional

package managers allow users to define configurations declaratively which are akin to writing code that specifies what the system should look like, rather than how to achieve it. This approach simplifies complex configurations and ensures precise control over system state.

To illustrate the configurability and reproducibility, consider the setup of a Python development environment with specific package dependencies in a traditional vs. a functional package management system:

Traditional Approach:

A typical setup might involve manually installing Python packages using pip with a requirements file:

```
$ pip install -r requirements.txt
```

This can lead to issues across different setups due to mutable state and varied configurations.

Functional Approach:

In contrast, Nix would handle this by defining a comprehensive environment in a single declarative Nix expression:

```
{ pkgs ? import <nixpkgs> {} }:

pkgs.mkShell {
  buildInputs = [
    pkgs.python3
    pkgs.python39Packages.requests
    pkgs.python39Packages.numpy
  ];
}
```

This expression creates an environment ready to use with specified versions of Python and libraries, eliminating variability between environments.

Impact and Use Cases

Functional package management has broader implications and applications across various fields:

- **Software Development:** Developers benefit from deterministic build environments. With the ability to mirror the same environment across development, testing, and production, functional package management reduces the classic "it works on my machine" problem.

- **DevOps and System Administration:** DevOps practitioners can leverage functional systems to define infrastructure as code (IaC), ensuring that deployments are predictable and consistently configured across cloud and on-premise environments.

- **Research and Data Science:** In academic and data science domains, where replicating environments is crucial for experiment verification, functional package management ensures precise reproduction of computational experiments.

- **Security and Compliance:** Functional systems inherently promote transparency and traceability by maintaining complete build and dependency information, enhancing security audits and compliance checks.

Despite numerous advantages, functional package management introduces a learning curve as users become accustomed to its model. It reshapes traditional workflows to embrace immutability and declarative configurations profoundly. In this evolving landscape, the need to understand functional paradigms extends beyond pure system management, venturing into holistic development practices that emphasize reliability and sustainability.

As more practitioners realize the significance of reproducibility, consistency, and the ability to manage systems and software with mathematical precision, the adoption of functional package management systems like Nix continues to grow. These systems represent a forward-thinking approach to overcoming historical limitations, offering a robust, efficient, and pragmatic solution to modern software management challenges.

1.3 Understanding the Nix Ecosystem

The Nix ecosystem encompasses a suite of tools and concepts that offer a revolutionary approach to managing software packages and configurations, based on functional programming principles. It is a comprehensive environment built around the Nix package manager, extending its functionality beyond mere package management to include a reproducible Linux distribution—NixOS—and flexible deployment toolchains. Understanding the Nix ecosystem requires a detailed examination of its components: Nix itself, Nixpkgs, NixOS, and auxiliary tooling such as NixOps and Hydra. These components work seamlessly together, making the ecosystem a highly efficient and deterministic choice for package management and system configuration.

At the heart of the Nix ecosystem is the *Nix package manager*, which distinguishes itself through its functional approach. Rather than managing packages as mutable entities that can be changed in place, Nix treats them as immutable builds—unique products specified entirely by their dependencies and build instructions. Nix emphasizes reproducibility and isolation, allowing for conflict-free coexistence of packages and their specific versions. These qualities are crucial for maintaining consistent environments across different machines and use cases.

A key feature of the Nix package manager is its use of a *store*, typically the /nix/store directory, which holds all installed packages. Packages are stored in paths determined by hashing their build instructions and dependencies, ensuring that identical configurations always yield identical paths. This thorough approach prevents impromptu modifications or interferences, offering a robust foundation for any reproducible build system.

Nixpkgs functions as the collection of packages for the Nix package manager, representing a vast repository maintained by a dedicated community of contributors. This collection is organized using the Nix Expression Language, providing formality and precision in declaring packages. Each package defines its build process through a declarative syntax, facilitating the generation of consistent binary outcomes across any supported platform.

Consider the definition of a common package, such as *wget*, within Nixpkgs:

```
{ stdenv, fetchurl, openssl }:

stdenv.mkDerivation rec {
  pname = "wget";
```

```
  version = "1.21.1";

  src = fetchurl {
    url = "https://ftp.gnu.org/gnu/wget/wget-${version}.tar.gz";
    sha256 = "0lgm82gghwpaf7plaswqqjwigppsg5fyh99vdlb9kzl7c9lngasf";
  };

  buildInputs = [ openssl ];

  meta = {
    description = "Internet file retriever";
    homepage = "https://www.gnu.org/software/wget/";
    license = stdenv.lib.licenses.gpl3;
  };
}
```

This Nix expression succinctly defines *wget*, specifying its version, source, checksum, and dependencies. The systematic form of such definitions underscores the functional nature of Nixpkgs, suitable for reproducible and verifiable builds.

NixOS, an integral part of the Nix ecosystem, is a Linux distribution built atop the principles of Nix. NixOS utilizes the Nix package manager to manage its entire system configuration, making it uniquely declarative and immutable. Through NixOS Configuration files, whole systems—from boot loaders to user services—are defined in a replicable manner.

Consider a simple NixOS configuration file setup:

```
{ config, pkgs, ... }:

{
  imports = [ ];

  boot.loader.grub.device = "/dev/sda";
  networking.hostName = "nixos";
  fileSystems."/" = {
    device = "/dev/sda1";
    fsType = "ext4";
  };

  services.httpd.enable = true;
  services.sshd.enable = true;

  environment.systemPackages = with pkgs; [
    wget
    vim
  ];
}
```

Here, a NixOS configuration specifies critical components such as the boot loader, network settings, file systems, and enabled services alongside default system packages. NixOS's ability to efficiently rollback changes if updates fail makes it highly suitable for mission-critical applications by favoring robustness and stability.

Complementing NixOS's reproducibility is *NixOps*, a tool designed for deploying and managing NixOS configurations across various infrastructures. NixOps supports diverse deployment platforms like cloud services or physical hardware, enabling cross-environment consistency seamlessly.

To deploy a simple pre-defined configuration using NixOps, you might execute:

```
$ nixops create ./network.nix ./network-ec2.nix -d my-deployment
$ nixops deploy -d my-deployment
```

Here, a deployment is created and instantiated using declarative network configurations, ensuring each node reflects the coordinated NixOS state.

In conjunction with NixOps, *Hydra*, the Nix-based continuous integration (CI) server, automates the building, testing, and deployment of software or system configurations. Hydra continuously evaluates changes to the Nix expressions, providing feedback by rebuilding affected packages and configurations to ensure correctness and stability. This integration ensures the Nix ecosystem aligns tightly with modern DevOps practices, enhancing continuous delivery pipelines' effectiveness.

The Nix ecosystem's application stretches beyond DevOps and system administration to software developers, research computations, and academia. Its deterministic nature is invaluable for reproducibility in scientific computations and experiments. Researchers can safely release experiments with complete environment setups as Nix expressions, ensuring they are faithfully recreated by peers irrespective of underlying hardware or software discrepancies.

Despite the extensive benefits, adopting the Nix ecosystem presents notable challenges. Learning functional configurations diverges significantly from conventional imperative processes, necessitating a paradigm shift in how developers specify environments and software. However, as infrastructure-as-code paradigms gain adoption, the transition becomes increasingly seamless for informed practitioners.

Moreover, the multitude of dimensions that the Nix ecosystem operates upon results in non-mutable paths that limit some forms of immediate system profiling. Nevertheless, this limitation dovetails into Nix's core strengths: consistency and reproducibility.

Advancements in the ecosystem over recent years have addressed iterative challenges, with innovative contributions continually extending its usability. Improved tools aim to refine user experience specific to onboarding processes, while community contributions enhance configuration libraries, ensuring they cater to a broader range of applications and environments.

As developers and administrators increasingly require precise control and transparency over computations and deployments, the Nix ecosystem's draw becomes imperative. It demystifies complexity through its steadfast adherence to functional principles, enabling comprehensive and transparent management across build pipelines, system infrastructures, and intricate software dependencies.

Interplays within the Nix ecosystem also cultivate software sustainability, where systems effectively minimize redundancy and leverage existing builds to reduce resource consumption. Efforts such as the Binary Cache utilize pre-built packages, saving computation time and power that would otherwise be spent on recompiling entire derivations locally. Consequently, the ecosystem not only optimizes development lifecycles but fosters ecological stewardship by reducing carbon footprints and computational waste.

In summary, a robust understanding of the Nix ecosystem involves appreciating the intrinsic harmony it nurtures between functional design and system efficacy. It champions reproducibility and determinism as foundations upon which modern systems can operate more reliably and securely. Through Nix, Nixpkgs, NixOS, NixOps, and Hydra, the ecosystem demonstrates a meticulous balance of power and precision, suited to the demands of an ever-evolving technological landscape. The Nix ecosystem epitomizes the future trajectory of package management, defining pathways where clarity, confidence, and computational integrity converge.

1.4 Why Choose Nix for Package Management

Selecting an appropriate package management system is a pivotal decision for developers, system administrators, and organizations aiming to maintain efficient, reliable, and scalable software environments. Nix offers a unique and compelling approach to package management through its foundation in functional programming principles. This section explores the distinctive advantages of Nix, contrasts it with traditional package management systems, and highlights scenarios wherein Nix emerges as an optimal solution.

Nix differentiates itself by treating package management as a mathematical function, where builds are defined by inputs such as source code and dependencies, and outputs are immutable and precisely reproducible software packages. This functional approach guarantees that given the same set of inputs, builds will consistently generate the same output—a promise that directly results in environments that are dependable and free of the erraticism often found in traditional systems.

- **Reproducibility and Consistency**

  One of the primary reasons to prefer Nix is its unparalleled commitment to reproducibility. In traditional package management systems like APT or YUM, builds and installations can subtly change due to mutable state and external updates, leading to environments that are hard to replicate. This issue becomes evident in situations involving:

  - **Continuous Integration and Deployment (CI/CD)**: Ensuring that conditions in development, testing, and production pipelines are identical is crucial. Nix allows pipelines to define environments as strict derivations of code, ensuring predictability in results.
  - **Scientific Research and Experimentation**: Researchers need to guarantee that software environments for complex simulations or analyses remain consistent over time to validate results. Nix ensures repeatable

build environments, fostering precise peer replication and collaboration.

Nix achieves this through its package descriptions and build processes encoded in Nix expressions. These expressions specify everything needed for building packages declaratively, devoid of side-effects, promoting environments that are resource-efficient and states that resist unexpected drift.

- **Isolated and Conflict-Free Environments**

  Traditional package managers often wrestle with version conflicts and dependency hell—a situation where certain requirements of software versions are incompatible with one another. Nix eschews these challenges through its immutability and isolation by:

  - Allowing **Multiple Versions**: Nix can coexist seamlessly with multiple versions of the same software without interference due to its unique hashing mechanism of the Nix store (/nix/store). This indexing ensures that identical source code and dependencies consistently lead to the same package path.
  - Enabling **Environment Isolation**: Each Nix package is built in a sandboxed environment, removing any unwanted interference from global system states or dependencies. This isolation extends even to runtime, where distinct environments can be configured for specific applications.

  Consider a scenario where multiple projects require distinct Python versions. With Nix, users can define each project's environment independently using shell derivations, ensuring each project integrates the correct dependencies and Python version:

```
{ pkgs ? import <nixpkgs> {} }:

pkgs.mkShell {
  buildInputs = [
    pkgs.python39Packages.numpy
    pkgs.python39Packages.pandas
    pkgs.python38
  ];
}
```

This setup runs a shell with Python 3.8, isolating all necessary inputs without affecting the wider system.

- **Atomic Upgrades and Reliable Rollbacks**

  Nix introduces atomicity to package management—ensuring updates are fully applied or not at all. If an error occurs during a transaction, Nix safeguards against partial or corrupt states by allowing instantaneous rollbacks, a feature not as easily attained in traditional systems.

  An enterprise deploying critical operations can leverage Nix's rollback functionality to safeguard against unexpected disruptions. For instance, through the command:

  ```
  $ nix-env --rollback
  ```

  Admins can revert swiftly to the previous application state without compromising continuity. This robustness is especially valuable in production-level systems where downtime could result in significant loss.

- **Nix Channels and Binary Caches**

  Nix channels enhance flexibility and convenience, grouping sets of reusable dependencies, thereby streamlining access to specific sets of packages over time. By subscribing to a channel, users ensure environments keep pace with ongoing updates and improvements, automatically integrating the latest compatible package versions.

  Alongside channels, Nix makes efficient use of binary caches—repositories containing pre-built binary results of derivations. Binary caches reduce compilation times and resource use by allowing builds to use pre-compiled binaries rather than recompiling locally, offering significant performance efficiencies.

  Users can integrate a binary cache in their configuration, reducing build times:

  ```
  {
    substituters = [
      "https://cache.nixos.org/"
    ];
    trusted-public-keys = [
  ```

```
    "cache.nixos.org-1:1VNdRj+Pv2kYkvMEJe..."
  ];
}
```

This configuration snippet allows the system to fetch already built packages from a trusted binary cache, limiting the necessity to rebuild large packages from the ground up.

- **Sustainability and Ecosystem Benefits**

  Nix's flourish across the open-source landscape entails community synergy achieving steadfast strides toward more 'eco-friendly' software practices. By promoting reproducibility, reducing waste through shared binaries, and fostering clear, modularized package expressions, Nix contributes toward scalable and sustainable software solutions.

  Moreover, the Nix ecosystem's encompassing tools like NixOS, NixOps, and Hydra expand its applications beyond typical usage paradigms:

  - **NixOS** provides a tightly coupled operating system where settings and configurations are version-controllable, replicable, and manage system state inclusively—a hallmark of robust infrastructure-as-code paradigms.
  - **NixOps** offers sophisticated deployment capabilities across multiple infrastructure boundaries, ensuring consistent application delivery across virtual, cloud-based, and physical systems.
  - **Hydra** acts as a continuous integration service to automate and verify changes within systems managed by Nix, presenting an efficient mechanism to enforce reliability over extensive, intricate deployments.

- **Real-World Case Studies and Community Success**

  The efficacy of Nix in production environments can be attested through numerous case studies and community endorsements:

  - **Research Institutions**: Academic institutions leveraging Nix for large-scale simulations report success in replicable research environments that hold steadfast across various hardware configurations, crucial in collaborations that span multiple institutions globally.

- **Enterprise-Level IT Operations**: Companies engaging in large-scale continuous integration and delivery employ Nix's robust mechanisms to reduce system downtime and enhance the reliability of development pipelines.
- **Open Source Community Collaborations**: Numerous open-source projects utilise Nix for environment consistency across development teams, reducing time spent addressing configuration errors and letting developers focus on innovation and core problem-solving.

In essence, choosing Nix as a package management partner represents embracing an era where consistency, precision, and clarity form the bedrock of modern computational environments. While transitioning to Nix may demand initial adaptation, its alignment with the demands of reproducible systems, environmental sustainability, and collaborative development summarily proves Nix as an indispensable ally in navigating the complexities of contemporary software ecosystems.

Chapter 2

Core Concepts of Nix Language

The Nix language is central to leveraging the powerful capabilities of Nix for package management and system configuration. It employs a functional syntax, focusing on immutability and purity to ensure that code execution remains consistent and free from side effects. Nix expressions are the building blocks of this language, enabling the precise definition of packages, dependencies, and configurations. Mastery of the Nix language involves understanding its core constructs, such as functions, lists, and attribute sets, which facilitate modular and reusable code. Through Nix, users can achieve predictable outcomes across diverse computing environments, making it a critical component for enhanced software reproducibility and reliability.

2.1 Nix Syntax and Basic Types

The Nix language, primarily employed for package management and system configuration, rests upon a foundation of clear and concise syntax coupled with fundamental data types. It is imperative to grasp these elements as they serve as the building blocks for crafting more advanced expressions. The language emphasizes functional programming paradigms, ensuring immutability and purity, and provides a robust syntax to encapsulate these concepts effectively.

The lexical structure of Nix syntax exhibits a prefix notation, differing from more conventional languages. Every Nix script is essentially a valid Nix expression, allowing users to evaluate it directly. Given the importance of evaluating expressions, a deep understanding of its data types and basic syntactical rules is essential.

Whitespace and Comments

In Nix syntax, whitespace generally delineates tokens, ensuring that expressions are read and interpreted correctly. Various forms of whitespace—spaces, tabs, and newlines—function as token separators. However, their presence or absence does not inherently influence the logic or output of a Nix expression unless explicitly required.

Utilizing comments is another aspect of writing pristine and comprehensible Nix code. Nix supports both single-line and multi-line comments. A single-line comment is initiated with a hash symbol #, while multi-line comments are enclosed within /* and */. These comments are essential for documenting code, elucidating intricate logic, or providing context for complex expressions.

Example:

```
# Single-line comment
let
  /*
    Multi-line comment
    explaining a complex logic
  */
  x = 10;
in x + 2
```

Basic Types

Nix provides a succinct set of primitive data types that form the core of the language's operations. These include integers, floating-point numbers, strings, path names, booleans, null, and functions. Understanding these types is crucial as they facilitate manipulation of more complex structures like lists and attribute sets.

- **1. Numbers:** Nix supports both integral and floating-point numbers. Numbers in Nix follow typical arithmetic operations but without an explicit need for declaration; they are simply inferred by usage.

  Example:

```
let
  a = 5; # Integer
  b = 3.14; # Floating-point
in
  a * 2 + b / 0.5
```

- **2. Strings:** Strings in Nix are sequences of characters enclosed within double quotes. They support interpolation, enabling the insertion of Nix expressions within a string by wrapping expressions in ${}.

  Example:

```
let
  name = "Nix";
  version = 2.3;
in
  "The version of ${name} is ${version}"
```

- **3. Paths:** Paths are strings referencing files or directories on the file system. Paths can be absolute or relative and are wrapped in angle brackets for Nix search paths. Nix specifically supports native handling for paths to ensure effective package management.

  Example:

```
let
  myPath = /home/user/.config/nixpkgs;
in
  "${myPath}/config.nix"
```

- **4. Booleans:** Boolean data types include true and false, which facilitate conditional logic within Nix expressions.

  Example:

```
let
  condition = true;
in
  if condition then "It's true" else "It's false"
```

- **5. Null:** The null type represents an undefined or uninitialized value, functioning similarly to the null in other programming languages.

  Example:

```
let
  value = null;
in
  if value == null then "No value" else "Has value"
```

Operations on Basic Types

Manipulating these basic types is a routine necessity when operating within Nix. Arithmetic operations can be performed on numerical types, while strings allow concatenation and interpolation. Logical operations are typically employed with boolean values.

- **1. Arithmetic Operations:** Nix supports the standard arithmetic operators: addition +, subtraction -, multiplication *, division /, and modulo %. These operations are straightforward, with traditional precedences.

  Example:

```
let
  x = 10;
  y = 3;
in
  x + y * 2
```

- **2. String Operations:** Strings primarily support concatenation, achievable through the use of the plus + operator. More advanced operations frequently involve interpolation or function manipulation of strings when used within expressions.

  Example:

```
let
  part1 = "Hello, ";
  part2 = "world!";
in
  part1 + part2
```

- **3. Boolean Operations:** Boolean expressions leverage logical operators such as && for conjunction, || for disjunction, and ! for negation. These operators are valuable for constructing conditional logic.

  Example:

```
let
  a = true;
  b = false;
in
  a && !b
```

Type Conversion and Type Checking

The dynamic nature of Nix allows flexible handling of different data types, but there are instances where type conversion plays a crucial role. Although Nix automatically manages types as needed, one must sometimes perform explicit checks or conversions to ensure the proper functionality of expressions.

Type checking often depends on usage scenarios. Given the implicit type inference, the language doesn't require explicit casting, yet errors may occur if types are unexpectedly mismatched within expressions.

To prevent such errors, type validation and careful construction of expressions, taking type expectations into account, are necessary. Functions may be explicitly designed to accommodate certain types, thus avoiding potential runtime errors.

Error Handling and Debugging

Despite Nix's straightforward data representation, it is crucial to possess robust mechanisms for error handling and debugging. Understanding error messaging and applying appropriate debugging techniques enhances the reliability and maintainability of Nix expressions.

Debugging usually involves inspecting expressions step-by-step. The language provides facilities through built-in functions such as assert and trace, which allow preemptive evaluation of specific conditions or logging of values during expression evaluation.

Example of using assert:

```
let
  value = 5;
in
  assert value > 0; # Ensures the value must be positive
  value * 2
```

Example of using trace:

```
trace: output the trace with the given message
```

These tools are integral for a developer to diagnose issues effectively and ensure that Nix expressions perform precisely as intended or provide informative feedback when encountering unexpected scenarios.

Attributes and Variables

Nix's approach to handling variables is rooted in its core principles of immutability. Variables are typically bound using let expressions, allowing for temporary assignments within the scope of an expression block.

Attributes add another layer to handling complex data structures. Attributes are essentially key-value pairs capable of constructing more hierarchical data models. They play a pivotal role as configuration parameters in Nix.

Example of let and attribute bindings:

```
let
  config = {
    locale = "en\_US";
    timezone = "UTC";
  };
in
  "Current configuration: ${config.locale} / ${config.timezone}"
```

Advanced users often employ a combination of these techniques alongside sophisticated functional constructs to architect and manage more intricate Nix expressions.

This section encapsulates the essential syntax and data types of Nix, offering a robust foundation for writing more complex and dynamic expressions.

2.2 Functions and Variables in Nix

The Nix language is built to employ functional programming paradigms, and it does so with graceful simplicity. At the heart of this paradigm are functions and variables. Understanding these core elements is fundamental to mastering the Nix language. Functions provide the reusability and modularity often necessary in package management and system configuration, while variables facilitate easy management of data.

Variables in Nix

In Nix, variables are used to store values, which can then be reused in expressions or passed as arguments to functions. Variables are immutable in Nix, meaning once a value is assigned to a variable within a scope, it cannot be changed. This immutability aligns with the functional programming ethos, ensuring predictability and reliability of Nix expressions.

Variables are introduced using let expressions which create local bindings. These bound variables are only available within the context they are defined, helping to manage scope effectively and avoid polluting the global namespace.

Example of variable binding with let:

```
let
  x = 42;
  y = "Hello, Nix!";
in
  "${y} The answer is ${x}."
```

In this example, once the expression is evaluated, it produces a string by interpolating the values bound to x and y into it. Variables are fundamental for creating understandable and reusable expressions.

Function Definitions in Nix

Functions in Nix are first-class citizens, similar to many functional programming languages, meaning they can be passed as arguments to other functions, returned as results, and assigned to variables. They are defined using a streamlined syntax involving an input argument list and a function body expression.

The function declarations follow this generic structure:

```
arg1: arg2: ...: expression
```

For example, a simple function that adds two numbers:

```
let
  add = a: b: a + b;
in
  add 5 3
```

On evaluation, this expression returns the sum of 8. The function add takes two arguments, a and b, computes their sum, and returns the result.

Functions can encapsulate complex operations and be consequently utilized as a fundamental building block for composing sophisticated expressions.

Anonymous Functions

Anonymous functions are frequently used in Nix to quickly define short-lived functions that are immediately applied to arguments. These functions do not need explicit naming, which can be advantageous when the association of a function with a specific operation is unnecessary.

Example with an anonymous function:

```
let
  square = x: x * x;
in
  (x: x + 1) (square 4)
```

This example evaluates first the square of 4, passing 16 to the subsequent anonymous function which increments the value by 1, resulting in 17.

Higher-Order Functions

One of the powerful aspects of Nix is its ability to handle higher-order functions—functions that can take other functions as arguments or return them as results. This paradigm allows for building abstract operations that can operate on functions of varying complexity.

Consider a higher-order function that accepts a function and an integer, returning the result of applying the function twice:

```
let
  applyTwice = f: a: f (f a);
  addOne = x: x + 1;
in
  applyTwice addOne 5
```

This returns 7, because the function addOne is applied twice to the integer 5. Such structures enable substantial reuse and composition in Nix.

Default Arguments and Optional Parameters

Nix functions can also support default argument values, which can be defined at the time of function declaration. This aids in constructing flexible functions that can handle optional parameters without requiring explicit specification from the function caller.

A function showcasing default parameters would be:

```
let
  greet = name ? "World": "Hello, ${name}!";
in
  {
    defaultGreet = greet {}; # Uses default argument
    personalGreet = greet { name = "Alice"; };
  }
```

The function greet produces "Hello, World!" when no argument is provided, leveraging the default value, and "Hello, Alice!" when given an argument. The optional parameter syntax is immensely useful in various contexts requiring defaults.

Recursive Functions and Let-In Constructs

Nix permits the definition of recursive functions, utilizing them self-referentially within their body. This feature is indispensable in constructing iterative computations or traversing data structures such as lists and sets.

Implementing a factorial function utilizing recursion:

```
let
  factorial = n:
    if n == 0 then
      1
    else
      n * factorial (n - 1);
in
  factorial 5
```

Recursive functions exploit the power of repetition with elegance and minimal state, maintaining a concise approach while managing complex operations effectively.

Combining Variables and Functions with Let-Expressions

Variables and functions in Nix integrate seamlessly within the let-in pattern, facilitating more sophisticated scripts without surrendering readability or maintainability. The let binders in Nix provide robust encapsulation, vital for developing modular scripts.

Consider an example where variable and function contexts are managed together:

```
let
  addPrefix = prefix: name: "${prefix}${name}";
  prefix = "Mr. ";
in
  addPrefix prefix "Smith"
```

Here, a function addPrefix utilizes a local variable prefix, demonstrating how user-defined variables can interact with functions cohesively.

Scoping and Closure

Nix enforces lexical scoping, which means that the scope of a variable is determined by its position in the code. This principle governs the visibility of variables in nested scopes and ensures that their bindings do not leak into unrelated sections of code.

Such scoping is central to the conceptual model known as closure, where a function retains the context in which it was created. This powerful feature enables functions to carry around their environment, augmenting the expressiveness of the language.

Example illustrating lexical scoping and closure:

```
let
  addClosure = n:
    let
      increment = x: x + n;
    in
      increment;
in
  (addClosure 10) 5
```

In this example, the function returned by addClosure remembers that n is 10 even when applied later as increment on the argument 5. It computes 15 as the result.

This feature accentuates the power of using lexical scoping and closures in the Nix language for handling complex variable interactions with reduced side effects.

The intricacies of functions and variables form an indispensable segment of the Nix language's syntax. Understanding their interaction offers developers and users alike the flexibility to construct scalable and maintainable configurations and compositions, contributing significantly to the declarative power of the Nix ecosystem.

2.3 Nix Expression Structure

The structure of Nix expressions serves as the foundation upon which its functional and declarative programming paradigms are built. By composing expressions with precision and care, developers can harness Nix's capabilities for package management and system configuration. At its core, a Nix expression is a recursive structure that can encompass values, functions, conditionals, lists, and attribute sets, all of which can be nested within one another to define sophisticated logic.

General Expression Syntax

A Nix expression is everything it contains—a Nix file is essentially a Nix expression. At the highest level, a Nix expression may be an atomic value, such as an integer or a string, or a complex structure composed of lists, functions, attribute sets, or conditional expressions.

Each element within a Nix expression can be succinctly described using a consistent syntax that embraces:

- Atomic values: These include integers, floating-point numbers, strings, booleans, paths, and the null type.
- Operations and comparisons: Arithmetic operators, concatenators, logical operators, and comparisons applied to atomic values.
- Complex structures: Attribute sets, lists, conditionals, and function definitions that enable abstraction.

Example:

```
let
  path = /etc/nix/config.nix;
  flag = true;
in
  if flag then
    "File path is ${path}"
  else
    "No file path defined"
```

In this example, the top-level expression is a conditional expression that evaluates to one of two string values based on the boolean flag.

Expressions with Attribute Sets

Attribute sets are key-value pairs that provide a straightforward method for structuring data within Nix. They serve as dictionaries or associative arrays and are central to managing configurations and defining packages. The syntax for defining an attribute set involves enclosing attributes in braces and assigning values using an equals sign.

Basic Attribute Set Example:

```
let
  attributes = {
    name = "example";
    version = "1.0";
```

```
    enabled = true;
  };
in
  "Package: ${attributes.name}, Version: ${attributes.version}"
```

When evaluated, the expression extracts and interpolates the name and version attributes into the output string.

Nested Attribute Sets:

Attribute sets can be nested, forming a hierarchy that allows complex data structures to be represented naturally. This nesting closely mirrors the organizational structures often required for detailed configurations.

```
let
  project = {
    metadata = {
      title = "Project Title";
      authors = "Author Name";
    };
    settings = {
      optimization = true;
      outputDir = "/var/project/output";
    };
  };
in
  "${project.metadata.title} by ${project.metadata.authors} stored at ${project.
      settings.outputDir}"
```

In this example, attributes are grouped under metadata and settings, reflecting a logical data organization that simplifies access and modification.

Modifiers and Inheritance

Attribute sets in Nix can leverage concepts like inheritance and overriding, facilitating powerful mechanisms for reuse and customization without redundancy. When one attribute set is combined with another, values in the second set can effectively override those in the first.

Example of attribute overriding and inheritance using rec for recursion:

```
let
  baseConfig = rec {
    os = "linux";
    version = "1.0";
```

```
    path = "/usr/local";
  };

  customConfig = baseConfig // {
    version = "2.0";
    // Modify baseConfig with additional settings
    customFeature = "enabled";
  };
in
  "Running on ${customConfig.os} version ${customConfig.version}"
```

The // operator merges two sets, where customConfig inherits from baseConfig while providing an updated version and adding a customFeature. This strategy underlines flexibility in hierarchical data handling.

Lists and Iteration

Nix expressions accommodate lists as a critical part of managing collections of data. Lists are defined by enclosing a sequence of values in square brackets, which can subsequently be processed collectively or individually.

Example of lists:

```
let
  items = [ "apple" "banana" "cherry" ];
  totalItems = length items;
in
  "There are ${totalItems} items in the list."
```

This example initializes a list of strings and evaluates its length using the length function, highlighting list manipulation.

Working with List Comprehensions:

Nix supports iterating over lists directly within its expressions, allowing transformations and filters to be applied. This process is often executed with the aid of the map function and list comprehensions for functional-style transformations.

Example using the map function:

```
let
  items = [ 1 2 3 4 5 ];
  addOne = x: x + 1;
  incrementedItems = map addOne items;
in
  incrementedItems
```

The map function applies addOne to each item in the list, demonstrating Nix's ability to succinctly express list-based transformations.

Conditional Logic

The control flow in Nix is predominantly managed through conditional expressions. Basic conditional logic utilizes if-then-else, ensuring decisions can dynamically alter output or control pathways based on evaluated conditions.

Example of an if-then-else expression:

```
let
  number = 42;
in
  if number > 10 then
    "Greater than ten"
  else
    "Less than or equal to ten"
```

The result of the condition dictates which string is returned, underscoring how effectively Nix can incorporate logic into its expressions.

Conditional expressions can incorporate logical operations to handle more complex scenarios, combining expressions effectively to form nuanced logic constructions.

Integration of Functions and Expressions

The combination of functions in Nix with expressions allows for effective code reuse and modularity, ensuring that projects remain scalable and maintainable.

Functions are seamlessly integrated into the structure of Nix expressions, transforming complex computations into manageable, reusable operations. Their applications in real-world Nix configurations range widely from simple utility calculations to managing intricate configuration setups via hierarchical combinations.

Example of a structured configuration function:

```
let
  config = { os, version ? "1.0", features ? [] }: {
    system = "${os}-${version}";
    enabledFeatures = features;
```

```
  };

  mySystemConfig = config {
    os = "linux";
    version = "5.10";
    features = [ "network" "graphics" ];
  };
in
  "${mySystemConfig.system} with features: ${mySystemConfig.enabledFeatures}"
```

Such a configuration function simplifies initialization and management of setups by abstracting common configuration parameters into function calls. This approach not only reduces redundant code but anchors flexibility in reconfiguring parameters at the invocation level.

Recursive Expression Structures:

Nix also facilitates recursive expression structures, generally through the rec keyword, allowing Nix expressions to self-reference. This feature is invaluable when an expression's value is dictated by related expressions or calculations.

Example of recursive expression structure:

```
let
  rec factorial = n: if n == 0 then 1 else n * factorial (n - 1);
in
  factorial 6
```

In the above, factorial is defined recursively, demonstrating how recursion is integrated directly into Nix's lexical model to solve iterative problems effortlessly.

Expression Composition

Ultimately, a well-designed Nix expression exhibits both composability and clarity, allowing developers to express concepts succinctly while maintaining comprehensibility. Employing a combination of higher-order functions, let-bindings, and attribute set manipulations allows for the abstraction of repeated patterns, ensuring that the resulting configurations and builds are both clean and agile.

As Nix's main vehicle for declaration and configuration, a structured approach to Nix expressions unveils a path toward greater programmatic control and efficiency. By leveraging the robust syntax and paradigms provided, developers can address complex tasks with relative ease, a testament to the deliberate design of the Nix language.

2.4 Lists and Sets in Nix

In the Nix language, lists and sets are fundamental data structures that allow developers to organize and handle collections of data efficiently. Understanding these structures is crucial for anyone looking to leverage Nix's capabilities in package management and system configuration as they frequently feature in complex expressions and configurations.

Introduction to Lists

Lists in Nix are ordered collections of elements, where each element can be of any data type including integers, strings, paths, booleans, or even other lists and sets. Lists are integral in scenarios requiring iteration, transformation, and aggregation of data. They are defined with square brackets, and elements are separated by spaces.

Example of a simple list:

```
let
  ingredients = [ "flour" "sugar" "eggs" "milk" ];
in
  "Recipe requires: ${lib.concatStringsSep ", " ingredients}"
```

In this example, a list of strings is created to represent ingredients, and the expression ultimately concatenates these elements into a single string with commas separating them.

Operations on Lists

Nix provides an array of functions to operate on lists, enabling manipulation and traversal without easing up on the functional style. Some common operations include:

- Accessing Elements: Use the elemAt function to access elements at a specific index.

```
let
  items = [ "apple" "orange" "banana" ];
  thirdItem = lib.elemAt items 2;
in
  "The third item is: ${thirdItem}"
```

- Length of List: Retrieve the number of elements in a list using the length function.

```
let
  fruits = [ "apple" "orange" "banana" ];
  numFruits = lib.length fruits;
in
  "There are ${numFruits} fruits in the list."
```

- Concatenation: Combine multiple lists into a single list using the ++ operator.

```
let
  list1 = [ 1 2 3 ];
  list2 = [ 4 5 6 ];
  mergedList = list1 ++ list2;
in
  mergedList
```

Higher-Order Functions on Lists

Higher-order functions enable more elegant and abstract operations on lists by passing functions as arguments. These include:

- Mapping: Applies a function to each element of a list.

```
let
  nums = [ 1 2 3 ];
  double = x: 2 * x;
  doubledNums = map double nums;
in
  doubledNums
```

- Filtering: Selects elements that satisfy a given predicate.

```
let
  nums = [ 1 2 3 4 5 6 ];
  isEven = x: x % 2 == 0;
  evens = filter isEven nums;
in
  evens
```

- Folding (Reducing): Accumulates the elements of a list into a single value.

```
let
  nums = [ 1 2 3 4 ];
  sum = lib.foldl (acc: x: acc + x) 0 nums;
in
  sum
```

Higher-order functions provide a powerful mechanism for list manipulation, endorsing reusability and composition over imperative loops and conditionals.

Nested Lists

In some situations, it's necessary to work with lists of lists, such as representing matrices or nested data structures. Nix supports nesting by allowing lists to contain any type, including other lists.

Example of a nested list:

```
let
  matrix = [ [ 1 2 3 ] [ 4 5 6 ] [ 7 8 9 ] ];
  firstRow = lib.elemAt matrix 0;
in
  "The first row of the matrix is: ${lib.concatStringsSep ", " firstRow}"
```

This structure provides a way to gracefully model complex data scenarios, offering functional methods for processing nested elements effectively.

Introduction to Sets

Unlike lists, sets in Nix—technically referred to as attribute sets—represent key-value pairs similar to dictionaries or hashes in other programming languages. These sets are pivotal for organizing configurations and options in Nix expressions. Sets are defined using braces {}, separating keys from values with an equals sign.

Basic attribute set example:

```
let
  user = {
    name = "Alice";
    age = 30;
```

```
    country = "Wonderland";
  };
in
  "${user.name} is ${toString user.age} years old and lives in ${user.country}."
```

Operations on Sets

Attribute sets offer various functions for accessing and manipulating their data:

- Accessing Values: Retrieve values using the dot notation.

```
let
  settings = {
    resolution = "1920x1080";
    fullscreen = true;
  };
  fullscreenMode = settings.fullscreen;
in
  "Fullscreen is set to: ${if fullscreenMode then "enabled" else "disabled"}"
```

- Union and Overriding: Combine two attribute sets using the // operator, where the right-hand set can override keys from the left-hand set.

```
let
  defaultSettings = { sound = 50; fullscreen = false; };
  userSettings = { fullscreen = true; theme = "dark"; };
  combinedSettings = defaultSettings // userSettings;
in
  combinedSettings
```

- Existence Check: Verify whether a particular key exists using the hasAttr function.

```
let
  person = { name = "Bob"; age = 40; };
  keyExists = lib.hasAttr "age" person;
in
  "Does the 'age' attribute exist? ${toString keyExists}"
```

Nested Sets and Recursive Attribute Sets

Sets can be recursively defined, allowing the abstraction of configurations that reference themselves or depend on hierarchical data.

Example of a nested and recursive attribute set:

```
let
  rec systemConfig = {
    basePath = "/etc";
    extPath = "${basePath}/ext";
    paths = {
      mainConfig = "${basePath}/config.txt";
      extraConfig = "${extPath}/extra.txt";
    };
  };
in
  systemConfig.paths
```

Recursion in attribute sets is a powerful technique for elaborating derived or computed attributes without redundancy.

Combining Lists and Sets

Both lists and sets are often used together within the Nix language to create dynamic and flexible configurations. Lists of attribute sets and vice versa can represent collections of configurations.

Example of combining lists and sets:

```
let
  environments = [
    {
      name = "development";
      active = true;
    }
    {
      name = "production";
      active = false;
    }
  ];

  activeEnvironments = filter (env: env.active) environments;
in
  map (env: "Active environment: ${env.name}") activeEnvironments
```

This example highlights filtering of active environments using list operations on a list of attribute sets, demonstrating how they can be professionally intertwined for advanced logic.

Sets provide multiple levels of customization, adjustment, and inheritance, making them indispensable in building scalable and manageable systems. Their integration with lists allows for creative and practical solutions to complex scenarios.

Practical Applications in NixOS and nixpkgs

In the broader context of NixOS and the nixpkgs repository, lists and sets are pivotal. Attribute sets are fundamentally used to define package attributes, system configurations, service modules, and user settings. Lists facilitate grouping related settings, such as enabled services or package dependencies, and play an instrumental role in providing modular configurability.

Example in NixOS Configuration:

Within NixOS, a configuration file is predominantly structured as sets and lists, involving recursive definitions, customizable modules, service declarations, and more.

```
{
  networking = {
    hostName = "nixos";
    interfaces.eth0.ipv4.addresses = [
      { address = "192.168.1.10"; prefixLength = 24; }
    ];
  };

  services = {
    apache.enable = true;
    nginx = {
      enable = false;
      virtualHosts = [
        {
          hostName = "example.com";
          root = "/var/www/example";
        }
      ];
    };
  };
}
```

Lists and sets allow declarative specifications for system behavior, reducing complexity and promoting clarity and traceability of configurations—a paradigm shift from traditional imperative setup schemes.

Overall, the versatility of lists and sets in Nix underscores their importance as collective data structures, essential for efficient expression design and configuration management. They are the vectors through which functional programming principles empower Nix with systemic elegance and operational flexibility. Through their careful application and combination, Nix users can encode complex software environments and system setups with precision and ease.

2.5 Conditional and Recursive Expressions

Conditional and recursive expressions in Nix are powerful constructs that enable the creation of dynamic and complex logic within scripts and configurations. They allow developers to implement logic that can evolve based on variable data or conditions, making them indispensable in many computational contexts, including package management and configuration designs.

Understanding Conditional Expressions

Conditional expressions in Nix provide the means to execute distinct code paths based on boolean conditions. These expressions make extensive use of the if-then-else construct, which evaluates a condition and returns one of two possible expressions.

A basic structure for a conditional expression is:

```
if condition then
  expression1
else
  expression2
```

The condition must be a boolean, whereas expression1 and expression2 can be any valid Nix expression, such as a number, string, or function.

Example of a simple conditional expression:

```
let
  temperature = 30;
in
  if temperature > 25 then
    "It's a warm day."
  else
    "It's a cool day."
```

This example tests if the temperature is greater than 25; if true, it returns a string declaring a warm day; otherwise, it states a cool day.

Complex Conditional Logic

For more elaborate scenarios, multiple conditional expressions can be nested or combined using logical operators to facilitate complex decision-making processes. Logical operators such as && (and), || (or), and ! (not) are available for combining conditions.

Example demonstrating nested conditionals with logical operators:

```
let
  age = 18;
  hasConsent = true;
in
  if age >= 18 || hasConsent then
    "Allowed to proceed."
  else
    "Permission denied."
```

In the above example, the logical || operator checks if either the age condition is met or the consent flag is true for allowing progression.

Conditional Expressions in Attribute Sets

Conditional expressions can also be seamlessly integrated within attribute sets, providing conditional attribute evaluation—common when defining system configurations or package conditionalities in Nix. This approach ties conditions directly into the data structure itself.

Example of using conditionals in an attribute set:

```
let
  useOptimization = true;
  buildSettings = {
    optimizationLevel = if useOptimization then 3 else 0;
    debugSymbols = !useOptimization;
  };
in
  buildSettings
```

This sets a higher optimization level when enabled and adjusts the debugSymbols flag accordingly, illustrating how conditions intertwine with attributes directly in configuration logic.

Introduction to Recursive Expressions

Recursive expressions in Nix present a method for defining expressions that reference themselves either directly or indirectly. They are quintessential in defining iterations or computations that rely on repetitive procedures until a specific condition is met.

Recursive definitions generally utilize the rec keyword to announce recursive scopes where self-referential bindings are permissible. Primarily, recursive functions are used for operations such as factorial computations or traversals over recursive data structures.

Basic recursive function implementation:

```
let
  rec factorial = n: if n == 0 then 1 else n * factorial (n - 1);
in
  factorial 5
```

This function calculates the factorial of a number by calling itself with decremented values until it reaches zero, at which point the recursion halts, returning an accumulated product.

Recursive Attribute Sets

Recursive sets can define attributes that depend on each other or even recursively expand their values. This feature facilitates data structures that dynamically compute their content based on self-referential logic.

Example of recursive attribute set usage:

```
let
  rec fileStructure = {
    home = "/home/user";
    documents = "${fileStructure.home}/docs";
    projects = "${fileStructure.home}/projects";
  };
in
  fileStructure
```

Here, rec introduces an attribute set that is able to refer back to its definitions, allowing paths to be constructed dynamically while relying on preceding attributes.

Applications and Use Cases

The practical use of conditional and recursive expressions extends well into various domains of Nix applications, ranging from package management, system configuration to infrastructure setup:

- **Conditional package options:** Packages can alternative build paths or dependencies based on conditional expression results. This technique enables significant flexibility in managing different deployment environments or optimization levels.
- **Recursive inventory or data crawling:** Recursive expressions elegantly handle complex data hierarchies or configure interdependent system modules that reference one another.

Example applying conditionals in a package definition:

```
let
  stdenv = import <nixpkgs> {};
  isSystemX86 = stdenv.isx86;
  customPkg = stdenv.mkDerivation {
    name = "custom-package";
    src = ./source;
    archSpecificFlags = if isSystemX86 then [ "-march=x86" ] else [];
    buildInputs = archSpecificFlags ++ [ stdenv.gcc ];
  };
in
  customPkg
```

This definition presents a package whose attributes adjust based on the architecture detected, demonstrating conditional logic woven into package build expressions.

Recursive Pattern Matching and Processing

While Nix lacks pattern matching found in some functional languages, recursion can function as a workaround to iteratively manage data structures breaking complex expressions into simple self-referential computations.

Example of a recursive approach through a list:

```
let
  rec sumList = l:
    if lib.length l == 0 then 0
    else lib.head l + sumList (lib.tail l);

  numbers = [ 1 2 3 4 5 ];
in
  sumList numbers
```

The expression recursively reduces the list numbers into a sum, processing it by dividing it into its head and tail until dequeuing is complete.

Organizing logic to account for conditional or recursive cases within Nix declarations unlocks potential for efficiently handling diverse computation paradigms and configuration requirements. These flexible elements of the Nix expression landscape enhance the expressivity and reach of the entire system. The considered deployment of conditionals and recursive structures establishes a pathway for dynamic and comprehensive scripting solutions, further aligning Nix with functional programming's ethos of clarity, conciseness, and correctness in code design. Through these constructs, developers gain full expressive control over how logic is applied to dynamic environments, ensuring robustness and adaptability in Nix-based ecosystems.

2.6 Modules and Evaluations

In Nix, modules and evaluations are foundational concepts that enable efficient management of configurations and expressions. Modules provide a framework for organizing code into encapsulated and reusable components, while evaluation governs the process by which Nix expressions are processed and resolved into concrete values or outcomes. Both constructs play pivotal roles in achieving modularity, reusability, and clarity within Nix-based systems.

Understanding Nix Modules

In the context of NixOS, a module represents a unit of configuration that can be combined and integrated with other modules to form a complete system setup. Each module typically defines a set of options and specifies behavior that contributes to the overarching configuration.

Modules are described using attribute sets where each key-value pair represents a configuration option or parameter. By leveraging modules, developers can structure system configurations logically, separating concerns, and enhancing maintainability.

Defining a Basic Module

A simple NixOS module might look like this:

```
{ config, pkgs, ... }:

{
  options = {
    services.myService.enable = lib.mkOption {
      type = lib.types.bool;
      default = false;
      description = "Enable or disable my custom service.";
    };
  };

  config = {
    environment.systemPackages = [ pkgs.git ];
  };
}
```

This module specifies an option to enable or disable a fictional service and includes it as part of the system environment packages if enabled. The use of lib.mkOption facilitates defining module options with types like booleans, integers, and strings.

Composition and Inheritance of Modules

One of the strengths of Nix modules is their ability to be composed through inheritance and overriding. This composition allows constructing complex configurations by layering and merging simpler ones. This behavior is typically managed using imports and overlays, permitting customization and extension in a controlled fashion.

Importing Modules

Modules in NixOS can be imported using the imports attribute, allowing developers to include external module files into a current configuration.

Example:

```
{
  imports = [
    ./moduleA.nix
    ./moduleB.nix
  ];
}
```

This configuration incorporates the definitions and options from moduleA.nix and moduleB.nix, combining their contributions into the current configuration scope.

Overriding and Extending Module Options

Modules often facilitate overriding or extending options using a hierarchical approach. Developers can modify default behaviors or integrate new capabilities by redefining keys within module files.

For example:

```
{
  config.environment.systemPackages = old: old ++ [ pkgs.vim ];

  options.services.myService.enable = lib.mkOption {
    default = true;
  };
}
```

The above introduces a modification to append vim to existing system packages and adjusts the default state of myService.enable to be true.

NixOS Module System

The NixOS module system is instrumental in defining the overall configuration of a NixOS system. At its heart, the system is governed by a collection of interrelated modules that define everything from boot settings to additional services.

- Files: Each module is a Nix expression stored in files, commonly located within the /etc/nixos directory for configuration specifics.
- Structure: Modules consist of inputs, options, and configuration attributes that collectively shape behavior contingent on conditions and dependencies.

Example:

```
{
  imports = [ <nixpkgs/nixos/modules/installer/cd-dvd/installation-cd-minimal.nix>
      ];

  boot.loader.grub.device = "/dev/sda";
  time.timeZone = "America/New_York";
}
```

In this setup, the configuration leans on a predefined NixOS module to establish installer settings, specifying a bootloader device and adjusting the time zone.

Evaluations in Nix

Evaluation in Nix refers to the process of interpreting and computing the desired state specified by Nix expressions. The end goal of evaluation is to convert a declarative definition into an actual system or package state that reflects the user's configuration intent.

The evaluation process involves several stages:

- Parsing: Nix interprets the expression syntax into a parse tree.
- Normalization: The tree undergoes normalization where redundancies and simplifications occur.
- Resolution: Referring and resolving external dependencies and imports.
- Output Construction: Generating a result, which might be a series of derivations for packages or a set of configurations for a system build.

Example of Evaluation

Consider an instance where a simple expression needs evaluation:

```
let
  double = x: x * 2;
  result = double 5;
in
  result
```

Through evaluation, the expression double 5 resolves to yield a concrete value of 10.

Lazy Evaluation and Purity

Nix employs lazy evaluation, a strategy where expressions are evaluated only when required. This approach helps in reducing unnecessary calculations, enhancing performance particularly in extensive configurations.

- Purity: Nix ensures purity during evaluations by not permitting side effects, which guarantees deterministic results no matter when or where expressions are evaluated. This characteristic aligns with functional programming approaches, offering reproducible builds and consistent deployment results.

Evaluation Environments

The environment in which a Nix expression is evaluated includes its context of available variables and attributes. These evaluations can oscillate depending on the presence of specific configurations or compositional layers introduced through module imports.

In a typical NixOS setup:

```
{
  environment = {
    systemPackages = [ pkgs.coreutils ];
  };

  services = {
    sshd.enable = true;
  };
}
```

These components will integrate into their respective environments under evaluation, spawning the practical settings and service management policies delineated within their definitions.

Debugging and Tracing Evaluations

Debugging evaluation issues can sometimes be intricate due to Nix's declarative and lazy evaluation nature. It provides built-in tools such as nix-instantiate and nix-build for processing and instantiating expressions, useful for assessing the execution paths and inspecting intermediate results.

- Tracing and Debug Outputs: Nix offers facilities such as the trace function to log output during evaluation.

Example usage of trace:

```
let
  debugInfo = value:
    lib.trace "Evaluating value: ${value}" value;

  foo = 3;
  bar = debugInfo (foo * 2);
in
  bar
```

Here, trace will display the computation path of bar, assisting developers or users in tracing evaluations and understanding data flows or behavioral intricacies.

Module management and evaluation mechanisms significantly influence how Nix environments are constructed and maintained. Through these constructs, Nix empowers comprehensive breakdowns of configurable elements, offering vast modularity and precision by which a user can ascertain, mold, and verify accommodating systems. It epitomizes a rigorous yet flexible paradigm that scales from granular control at the attribute level to vast overarching systems configurations with compositional clarity and peerless consistency.

Chapter 3

Setting Up Nix Environment

Setting up the Nix environment is a foundational step that involves installing the Nix package manager and configuring it for effective usage across various operating systems. This setup process includes configuring user profiles and system settings to ensure optimal integration with existing workflows. Basic command-line operations are introduced to familiarize users with managing packages and environments via the Nix shell. Addressing common installation challenges and troubleshooting tips helps establish a smooth initial experience, providing a stable base for exploring Nix's advanced features and benefits in managing reproducible software environments.

3.1 Installing Nix on Your System

The installation of the Nix package manager lays the foundational groundwork for leveraging its capabilities to manage packages in a reproducible and efficient manner across diverse operating systems. The versatility of Nix, owing to its functional declarative model, facilitates its adoption on Linux, macOS, and Windows systems. This section provides a comprehensive guide to installing Nix, focusing on ensuring accuracy and understanding potential nuances encountered in various system environments.

The installation process begins with Linux, due to its inherent compatibility with the Nix package manager and its widespread use among developers and system administrators. The pre-requirements for installing Nix on a Linux system include basic Unix command-line proficiency and superuser access, as certain operations require elevated privileges. Users should ensure that their system-wide environment is current and a recent iteration of a Linux distribution is in use.

```
$ sudo apt-get update
$ sudo apt-get upgrade
```

The installation leverages the Nix installation script available at https://nixos.org/nix/install. The script automates the installation process, ensuring a seamless setup. Execute the following command in a terminal:

```
$ curl -L https://nixos.org/nix/install | sh
```

Upon execution, the script initializes several steps, including the creation of required directories, fetching binaries, and setting up the user environment. It is critical to monitor the installation for any errors related to permission issues or network connectivity. Access to the internet is essential during this stage, as the script utilizes network resources to download necessary binary files and configuration elements.

Upon successful completion of the installation script, the script outputs instructions for modifying the profile configuration. This typically entails adding the Nix binary directory to the user's PATH. It is recommended to append the following commands to your shell configuration file (e.g., .bashrc or .zshrc):

```
$ export NIX_PATH="~/.nix-defexpr/channels"
$ export PATH="$PATH:/nix/var/nix/profiles/default/bin"
```

It is essential to restart the terminal session or source the configuration file to effectuate these changes:

```
$ source ~/.bashrc
```

The next step involves verifying the installation, which can be accomplished by executing the nix-env –version command to display the current version of Nix installed. A successful output indicates proper installation:

```
nix-env (Nix) 2.x
```

Transitioning to the macOS installation, it mirrors many of the steps used in Linux due to the Unix-based architecture of macOS. macOS users should ensure they have curl and git installed, which can be managed through Homebrew:

```
$ brew install curl git
```

With the prerequisites verified, the Nix installation is initiated using the identical script as Linux:

```
$ curl -L https://nixos.org/nix/install | sh
```

Similar to the Linux process, any adjustments to the shell environment variables should be incorporated into the user's preferred shell initialization file. The macOS installation might necessitate additional steps, such as granting system permissions under System Preferences for making changes to protected directories. Users can address potential security prompts by navigating to Security and Privacy settings to authorize necessary permissions.

Once installed, macOS requires verification which follows the same procedure as Linux, ensuring that the user can ascertain the installation's correctness.

Implementation on Windows environments is markedly different, primarily due to the divergence in the underlying operating system architecture. Windows users need to use the Windows Subsystem for Linux (WSL), which provides a Linux kernel interface within a Windows environment. Users are required to enable WSL through Windows PowerShell with administrative privileges:

```
> wsl --install
```

Following the WSL installation, users must install a Linux distribution, such as Ubuntu, from the Microsoft Store. Upon launching the installed Linux distribution, users can perform typical Linux-based installations as described earlier in this section. The installation within WSL mimics the setups for Linux, adhering to the same script and configuration file adjustments.

User familiarity with PowerShell commands and WSL environment management becomes paramount. For a streamlined experience, continuous updates to the WSL environment and prompt management of Linux distribution updates are recommended to maintain system integrity:

```
$ sudo apt-get update && sudo apt-get upgrade
```

A successful installation on Windows via WSL will allow users to run Nix commands seamlessly. An important aspect is to ensure the NIX_PATH variable is correctly initialized and persistent across all sessions in the WSL environment.

Throughout the installation process across all platforms, common issues that could arise include network connectivity errors, filesystem permission limitations, and environmental conflicts. Users should verify system compatibility and available space on the storage subsystem, as Nix and its store can be disk-intensive processes.

The installation process concludes with the validation of a basic Nix command execution to ensure full operability within the chosen operating environment. An example test might involve installing a trivial package using Nix to affirm functionality:

```
$ nix-env -i hello
```

Expected output upon successful installation and execution is:

```
installing 'hello-2.x.x'
```

Post-installation, users are encouraged to maintain their Nix installation by regularly upgrading the Nix package manager and any installed Nix packages to take advantage of updates, security patches, and performance optimizations. This can be accomplished via:

```
$ nix-channel --update
$ nix-env -u '*'
```

Current Nix implementations are constantly evolving, with contributors across the software community driving enhancements that support a growing array of system environments and integration tools. Successful mastery of this section equips users with the capabilities to explore the broader Nix ecosystem, facilitating experimentation with advanced features and collaborative software management strategies.

3.2 Configuring the Nix Environment

Configuring the Nix environment is an essential step following the installation of the Nix package manager, enabling users to tailor their system for optimized performance and usability. This section focuses on the configuration aspects of Nix, which include setting system variables, modifying user profiles, and addressing any nuances that arise during the setup process. A clear understanding of these configurations impacts the functionality of the Nix ecosystem deeply, ensuring a streamlined experience across diverse operating conditions.

The configuration process begins with understanding the fundamental concept behind the Nix store and profiles. The Nix store, located at /nix/store, is a core component that holds all installed packages. This directory is maintained by Nix and should not generally be modified manually. Within this store, packages are uniquely identified by cryptographic hashes that make package management reproducible and prevent file conflicts.

The user environment is configured using Nix profiles, which allow for multiple vendor environments and configurations, each accessible independently. This flexibility is crucial for developing isolated environments for different projects, a key advantage of using Nix. Profiles are typically located in ~/.nix-profile for user-specific configurations. To configure the Nix environment, it is crucial first to ensure that the PATH variable includes the Nix profile:

```
$ export PATH="$HOME/.nix-profile/bin:$PATH"
```

This line ensures that binaries installed via Nix are prioritized when executing commands from the terminal, effectively overlaying these installations over system defaults without overriding them permanently.

Another key aspect of Nix configuration is setting up channels—these are collections of Nix packages that users can subscribe to for accessing software. By default, the Nix channel points to the current stable distribution of Nix software packages, or nixos-unstable. Users can customize their channels by adding alternative repositories, which is especially useful for accessing experimental or niche packages. Managing channels involves commands such as:

```
$ nix-channel --list
$ nix-channel --add https://nixos.org/channels/nixos-unstable
$ nix-channel --update
```

Each channel update operation fetches the latest package definitions, which users can then implement into their environments. Unlike traditional package managers, Nix retains previous software versions, facilitating rollback if necessary.

Configuring the .nixpkgs file, located in the user's home directory, provides advanced users with customization options that enforce a particular environment state or preferences, such as specifying binary cache locations, setting proxy settings, or enabling certain Nix features. This file, which can sometimes be absent by default, can be created and edited to include configurations like:

```
{
  allowUnfree = true;
  binaryCaches = [
    "https://cache.nixos.org/"
  ];
}
```

Here, allowUnfree is a configuration often set by users needing to access proprietary software that Nix packages. Enabling binary caches also significantly reduces build times, as precompiled binaries are fetched instead of compiling software from source.

In addition to user-specific configurations, /etc/nix/nix.conf is a system-wide configuration file that dictates overarching environmental settings. Some environmental variables that might typically be modified include max-jobs to control parallel builds and cores to designate CPU core usage:

```
max-jobs = 4
cores = 2
```

Adjusting these variables is essential for optimizing performance, especially on multi-core systems or when engaging with resource-intensive builds.

An essential feature of the Nix environment configuration is the ability to define environment variables within Nix shells, which are temporary, isolated environments created by Nix. To define a Nix shell configuration, users need to create a shell.nix file within the project directory:

```
{ pkgs ? import <nixpkgs> {} }:
pkgs.mkShell {
  buildInputs = [ pkgs.hello ];
  shellHook = ''
    export MY_VAR="Hello, Nix!"
  '';
}
```

Executing nix-shell in the project directory initiates an environment loaded with specified packages and environment variables, helping maintain a reproducible development environment across sessions. This approach is beneficial for developers aiming to avoid polluting system-wide configurations or when collaborating across teams with specific package requirements:

```
$ nix-shell
```

Inside the Nix shell, running echo $MY_VAR should return the string Hello, Nix!, demonstrating the successful setting of an environment variable specifically within the shell scope.

For persistent, project-specific configurations, users can employ Nix expressions to encapsulate dependencies and configurations, promoting reusability and consistency:

```
{ pkgs ? import <nixpkgs> {} }:
pkgs.stdenv.mkDerivation {
  name = "my-env";
  buildInputs = [ pkgs.python3 pkgs.nodejs ];
}
```

Executing the command:

```
$ nix-build my-env.nix
```

launches a build process, which, when successful, links the defined packages into the result symlink, serving as an entry point to the environment.

NixOS users have additional configuration options available through the NixOS configuration file, /etc/nixos/configuration.nix. This file provides a declarative state for the operating system configuration, allowing users to define system services, network settings, and user accounts in addition to package management:

```
{ config, pkgs, ... }:
{
  imports = [ ];

  boot.loader.grub.device = "/dev/sda";
  networking.hostName = "nixos";
  services.sshd.enable = true;
}
```

To apply changes made in configuration.nix:

```
$ nixos-rebuild switch
```

This command ensures NixOS reflects all declared configuration adjustments, maintaining system stability and consistency, further underlining the Nix philosophy of reproducible environments.

Users are encouraged to engage with community resources, such as forums and repositories, to enhance their understanding and application of Nix configurations. Open collaboration and sharing of configuration best practices contribute significantly to building robust and efficient working environments.

Overall, configuring the Nix environment harnesses the full potential of the package manager, making it adaptable to individual requirements. Mastery of these techniques will equip users with the skills necessary to tackle advanced development workflows, maintain system integrity, and maximize the efficiency of software lifecycle management.

3.3 Basic Nix Commands

Understanding and effectively utilizing basic Nix commands is crucial for managing packages and environments within the Nix ecosystem. These commands form the foundation for performing various tasks, from installing and removing packages to maintaining and querying system environments. This section delves into the key commands available in Nix, providing detailed insights and examples of their application.

The command-line interface is the primary mode of interaction with the Nix package manager. The principal command used for managing packages within Nix is nix-env, a versatile command responsible for package installation, removal, and querying operations.

To install a package using Nix, the nix-env -i command is utilized. For instance, installing a common package such as wget can be achieved with:

```
$ nix-env -i wget
```

Upon execution, Nix resolves dependencies, downloads the required package from the binary cache (if available), and links it to the user's environment. The efficiency of Nix in package management lies in its atomic installations and rollback abilities, ensuring that operations do not inadvertently disrupt existing environments.

Verification of successful installation can be achieved by listing all installed packages using:

```
$ nix-env -q
```

The output will include wget among other installed packages. Each listed package provides details about the package name and version, affirming the active state of each package in the user profile.

Once no longer needed, packages can be removed with the nix-env -e command:

```
$ nix-env -e wget
```

Nix ensures consistency in package removal by verifying all dependencies and preventing the accidental removal of shared dependencies across other packages.

Understanding the status of the Nix environment is pivotal for effective management. The nix-env -q command, used previously to list packages, offers more flexibility with options to filter and format results. For example, to filter packages matching a certain pattern, use:

```
$ nix-env -q | grep git
```

Such queries aid in quickly identifying packages without scanning through extensive lists manually. Detailing packages with versions and derivation attributes can be attained using:

```
$ nix-env -qa --description
```

This command yields a comprehensive list with human-readable descriptions, enhancing the user's ability to understand the repository contents beyond mere package names.

Switching package states without altering configurations is a key aspect of Nix, which is achieved using different profiles. Each profile can be independently queried using:

```
$ nix-env --list-generations
```

The generations represent snapshots of environments at various states of package management, enabling rollbacks or managing divergent configurations.

Restoring a previous environment state is as straightforward as:

```
$ nix-env --rollback
```

This command seamlessly navigates to the last stable configuration, illustrating Nix's commitment to system stability.

Package management in Nix is fundamentally driven by derivations—function-like structures that describe packages, their dependencies, and build instructions. To manually build a derivation, users can employ the `nix-build` command:

```
$ nix-build '<nixpkgs>' -A wget
```

This manually compiles and installs packages from the source, leveraging the complete customizability of the Nix build system. If adjustments to build inputs or processes are necessary, users can modify or rewrite derivation attributes to match specific requirements.

For comprehensive insight into a package's derivation, use:

```
$ nix show-derivation /nix/store/<hash>-<package-name>.drv
```

Analyzing these derivations illustrates the interconnected dependencies and build scripts Nix generates, thus formulating an understanding of each package's build environment.

Channels in Nix delineate curated collections of packages specified by particular versions, essentially resembling repositories in conventional package managers. The command nix-channel allows users to manage these—from listing active channels to adding new ones.

To add a new channel of community-supported packages, execute:

```
$ nix-channel --add https://my-custom-channel.org/custom-channel
```

Maintaining updated channels is necessary for accessing fresh and secure package versions, achieved through:

```
$ nix-channel --update
```

The update propagates new derivations and package definitions to the user's environment, accessible in subsequent package installations or updates.

Effective resource management is an integral function of Nix, achieved through garbage collection—which safely disposes of packages and data no longer referenced by any profile or environment. Invoke garbage collection with:

```
$ nix-collect-garbage -d
```

The -d option deletes old generations, complemented by regular environment profiles, retaining only actively referenced data. This function ensures the Nix store remains clean and efficient.

For comprehensive data cleaning, including clearing unreachable data in the Nix store, users can engage:

```
$ nix-store --gc
```

Such maintenance operations prevent excessive disk usage and contribute to system reliability.

Beyond basic operations, Nix offers commands suited for more advanced use cases, such as nix-shell, enabling reproducible development environments embodying isolated dependency trees, unaffected by other system settings.

To spawn a shell with specific dependencies:

```
$ nix-shell -p gcc hello
```

This function encapsulates project dependencies within an isolated shell, fostering an environment akin to containerization without the overhead.

Advanced users frequently script these commands within nix-shell or shell.nix files for project onboarding simplicity, streamlining environment initialization and documentation.

Harnessing such scripts can lead to project onboarding efficiency and consistency across distributed environments, significantly enhancing development cycles and collaboration.

As users develop familiarity with these basic commands, further exploring the extended functionalities and customization becomes more approachable, empowering comprehensive usage across various domains. Mastery of these commands enables users to seamlessly integrate Nix into existing workflows, ultimately leading to more robust and reproducible software management practices.

3.4 Setting Up a Nix Shell

The advent of the Nix shell has transformed how developers create and manage isolated development environments, offering unparalleled flexibility in handling dependencies and software versions. Setting up a Nix shell involves defining and utilizing ephemeral computing spaces where package versions are controlled and specific to project requirements, all without affecting the host system's global environment. This section delineates the intricate operational framework and benefits of utilizing a Nix shell, alongside comprehensive instructions and examples for effective implementation.

The fundamental principle underpinning a Nix shell is its capacity to instantiate project-specific environments with declared dependencies, which ensures consistent and reproducible configurations across multiple executions and different users. To commence setting up a Nix shell, one typically creates a shell.nix file within the root directory of the pertinent project. This declarative file specifies the environment configuration using Nix expressions.

The basic syntax for a shell.nix file could be succinctly expressed as:

```
{ pkgs ? import <nixpkgs> {} }:
pkgs.mkShell {
  buildInputs = [
    pkgs.gcc
    pkgs.python3
  ];
}
```

In this formulation, pkgs.mkShell creates a development shell where gcc and python3 are available as dependencies, each derivation fetched and set up by Nix on shell invocation. This setup effectively isolates the project-specific tools from the rest of the system ensuring that any package conflicts do not propagate to other areas of development.

Invoking the Nix shell follows straightforward execution of:

```
$ nix-shell
```

Running this command within the project directory containing shell.nix initiates a shell session, scoped by definitions within the file. In this environment, any commands run operate within the confines of the specified dependencies, providing a controlled environment for testing, development, or deployment workflows.

Environment customization and advanced configurations

Beyond simply installing packages, Nix shells allow for environment customization through the inclusion of shell hooks, environment variables, and custom scripts. For instance, to set environment variables or execute scripts upon shell initialization, users can leverage the shellHook attribute available in Nix expressions.

An illustrative shell.nix file with additional customization might appear as follows:

```
{ pkgs ? import <nixpkgs> {} }:
pkgs.mkShell {
  buildInputs = [
    pkgs.nodejs
    pkgs.makeWrapper
  ];
  shellHook = ''
    export NODE_ENV=development
    echo "Node.js development environment activated"
```

```
  ";
}
```

In this instance, NODE_ENV is set to development, signaling any Node.js applications about the current environment context, and the shell emits a console message upon entering the shell to notify the user of the environment's status.

Moreover, advanced users can take advantage of shellHook to automate complex setups, such as initializing databases, downloading additional scripts, or even verifying code integrity through checksum scripts, enhancing productivity and environment reproducibility.

Project-specific dependencies and isolation benefits

The isolation guaranteed by Nix shells ensures that projects maintain consistency devoid of interference from external updates or system-wide upgrades. This setup has profound implications for project integrity, reproducibility, and collaboration. Variability in system environments often results in disparate development outcomes, frustrating both developers and teams wishing to uphold consistent deployment protocols.

Consider a data science team using Python with various libraries like numpy and pandas. The following snippet outlines a potential shell.nix tailored to data analysis:

```
{ pkgs ? import <nixpkgs> {} }:
pkgs.mkShell {
  buildInputs = [
    pkgs.python39
    pkgs.python39Packages.numpy
    pkgs.python39Packages.pandas
  ];
}
```

Creating such a shell file assists teams in maintaining consistent module versions, catering to reproducibility concerns—critical when replicating experiments or results exactly across different stages of research and application deployment.

Integration into workflow and continuous development

Continuous development lifecycles benefit significantly from the introduction of the Nix shell paradigm. Instead of engaging with isolated development practices or leveraging virtual environments that might necessitate distinct management tactics or integration overhead, Nix shells harmonize these necessities into straightforward declarative Nix expressions.

Automated processes such as continuous integration (CI) pipelines can therefore seamlessly incorporate Nix shells, ensuring environments are instantiated precisely as needed, allowing test scripts and builds to rely on identical dependencies. For example, integrating a nix-shell command into a CI script guarantees that each build accesses and operates within a freshly initialized environment, safeguarding against "it works on my machine" scenarios.

```
steps:
  - name: Setup Nix Environment
    run: nix-shell --run "make test"
```

Here, a CI job fetches dependencies and runs tests within the defined Nix shell, encompassing the environment precisely mirrored by the development setups, thus streamlining deployment strategies and accelerating feedback loops.

Limitations and considerations in shell use

While Nix shells provide many benefits from the angle of system stability and dependency management, users should be aware of potential challenges associated with initial configuration overheads and learning curve considerations typical with declarative setups. These setups may require users to invest in understanding the Nix language for crafting effective Nix expressions; however, this investment is generally rewarded through system resilience and reproducibility.

Additionally, drawbacks exist in the nuanced area of binary caches, especially where prebuilt binaries are unavailable. Large package derivations might necessitate extended compile times, which can be mitigated through community caches or locally optimized build settings.

Lastly, accommodating non-standard build processes or dependency bases may occasionally necessitate custom derivations or complex expression definitions, albeit the flexibility afforded by the Nix framework provides significant leeway to resolve such scenarios.

Nevertheless, for most developers and teams, the merits of maintaining isolated, reproducible environments while minimizing global system dependencies far outweigh potential initial configuration friction.

By mastering Nix shell configurations, users empower themselves to achieve project consistency, mitigate environmental drift, deliver faster and more coherent feedback mechanisms in development, and seamlessly integrate reproducible environments into broader CI/CD practices. These capabilities are instrumental in elevating software development practices, particularly in environments dictated by rapid iteration cycles and cross-collaborative frameworks.

3.5 Integrating Nix with Existing Workflows

Integrating Nix into existing workflows presents a compelling opportunity to enhance reproducibility, manage dependencies with precision, and streamline continuous deployment processes. Its functional package management system and declarative nature allow for seamless adjustments to established practices. This section explores how Nix can be incorporated into various workflow scenarios, be it development, deployment, or continuous integration (CI), and presents detailed methodologies alongside practical examples.

The fusion of Nix with legacy systems starts with understanding how the tool's deterministic builds and environment management can augment current processes. Instead of using traditional package managers, Nix offers version-guaranteed builds, ensuring that software behaves consistently regardless of external system changes which often disrupt normalized operations.

Incorporating Nix into the daily development process revolves around creating isolated, immutable environments for each project. This practice mitigates dependency conflicts and environmental inconsistencies typical in concurrent project development. Developers can write shell.nix files for each project, which encapsulate all necessary dependencies, toolchains, and environment variables as follows:

```
{ pkgs ? import <nixpkgs> {} }:
pkgs.mkShell {
  buildInputs = [
    pkgs.python3Packages.django
    pkgs.postgresql
  ];
  shellHook = ''
```

```
  export DJANGO_SETTINGS_MODULE=project.settings
'';
}
```

By utilizing the nix-shell command, developers can enter a project-specific environment free of system-wide changes. This method ensures uniformity among team members' environments, minimizing "works on my machine" dilemmas, particularly in distributed teams or open-source collaborations.

Moreover, the consistent local development environments facilitate swift onboarding processes. New contributors merely need to clone the repository and launch the nix-shell to be up and running with a fully equipped environment.

Nix profoundly influences CI/CD pipelines by providing reproducible builds and environments. Pipelines integrate Nix by leveraging its capability to define build environments that ensure consistent testing conditions against version-pinned packages.

Consider the example of a CI pipeline set up within an organization's building service. Developers might use a pipeline specification akin to the following:

```
steps:
  - name: Configure Nix Environment
    run: nix-shell default.nix --run "make build"
  - name: Run Tests
    run: nix-shell default.nix --run "make test"
  - name: Deploy
    run: nix-shell default.nix --run "make deploy"
```

Utilizing Nix in this deployment procedure ensures that every build and test instance operates within the identical configuration. Variability due to library version changes or dependency updates is eliminated, addressing common integration failures.

The possibility of defining infrastructure services such as databases, caches, or microservices within these Nix environments fosters coherent development and production parity, reducing deployment risk dramatically.

Legacy systems, tightly bound to specific toolchains or dependency versions, can capitalize on Nix to abstract complex environment settings and facilitate shifts towards modern development practices. Through custom nixpkgs expressions, IT departments can encapsulate legacy dependencies:

```
{ pkgs ? import <nixpkgs> {} }:
pkgs.stdenv.mkDerivation {
  name = "legacy-system-env";
  buildInputs = [
    pkgs.gcc8
    pkgs.libxml2
  ];
  src = pkgs.fetchurl { url = "<legacy_project_url>"; sha256 = "<hash>"; };
}
```

Such encapsulation enables legacy software to operate within its precise dependency regime without manual setup, aiding in systematic migrations. Teams can define both internal and external dependencies declaratively, allowing systematic refactoring alongside daily operations.

The native Nix capabilities of breaking dependencies across boundaries aid in containerizing legacy applications, granting further flexibility for cloud migrations or platform agnosticism initiatives, critical in agile environments focusing on modernization and optimization.

Adapting Nix into pre-existing frameworks naturally confronts certain challenges surrounding team acclimatization, learning curves, and system reconfiguration complexities. This transition can entail short-term efforts while investing in long-term operability benefits.

Training programs geared towards literacy in Nix expressions and functional paradigms could mitigate initial friction. Furthermore, incremental adoption in less critical systems facilitates pilot runs to ascertain full-scale benefits without broader operational risks.

Compatibility hurdles may arise due to non-standard systems or bespoke in-house applications. Yet, Nix's flexibility with nixpkgs overlays and unauthorized package channels support the bridging of disparate systems. Developing a collaborative culture enriched with community contributions and insights further expands the Nix ecosystem's applicability.

Beyond conventional applications, Nix supports advanced workflow customizations designed to meet evolving business needs and technical initiatives. Automation scripts—an extremely potent feature of Nix—abound, granting unparalleled capacity to create complex workflows that autonomously manage environments as dynamically as operational requirements dictate.

Nix can be customized to execute automated job scheduling, remote builds, and dynamic environment setups by integrating with lightweight orchestration tools. Examples involve creating custom scripts that adjust compute resources by evaluating performance metrics or extending server capabilities during high-load periods, a critical asset in elastic cloud infrastructures.

To illustrate, consider the following hypothetical script, leveraging Nix and job schedulers for dynamic load management:

```
#!/bin/bash

# Import necessary Nix expressions
source <(nix-shell load-management.nix --pure --run env)

# Check current load balance metrics
if [ $(current_load) -gt $THRESHOLD ]; then
  echo "High load detected, scaling..."
  nix-shell scale-up.nix --run "deploy_increase_capacity"
else
  echo "Load within acceptable parameters."
fi
```

Such dynamic scripting ensures that organizations can scale infrastructure responsively and cost-effectively, matching real-time demand fluctuations.

The integration of Nix into existing workflows provides a compelling advantage: by converging environment management, reproducibility, and deployment automation, Nix fosters agile compliance focusing on development efficiency and operational resilience. Continued exploration and adaptation of Nix expand its robustness as a tool capable of transforming procedural operations across myriad technological landscapes, solidifying its position as a keystone in contemporary DevOps practices.

3.6 Common Installation Issues and Solutions

The installation process of the Nix package manager, despite being streamlined through automated scripts and procedures, can occasionally present challenges that impede successful deployment across diverse operating systems. This section addresses typical installation issues encountered by users and delineates effective solutions, enhancing both understanding and resolution capabilities.

- **Network and Connectivity Problems**

  A frequent issue encountered during Nix installation involves network and connectivity errors, which can hinder or terminate the downloading of necessary scripts and packages. These disruptions often stem from unstable connections or restrictive network configurations, such as firewalls or proxy servers.

  Solution:

  To mitigate such issues, users should first verify their internet connectivity, ensuring no active connectivity disruptions:

  ```
  $ ping nixos.org
  ```

  If connectivity is blocked by a firewall or requires a proxy, configure the terminal session to utilize the proxy by setting environment variables:

  ```
  $ export http_proxy=http://proxy.example.com:port
  $ export https_proxy=http://proxy.example.com:port
  ```

  These adjustments allow the installation script to access requisite network resources through predefined proxy settings, bypassing firewall constraints where applicable.

- **Permission and File System Constraints**

  Another prevalent issue pertains to file system permission constraints, especially on Linux systems requiring root access for certain directories. This can manifest as failed writing or directory creation steps during the installation script execution.

  Solution:

To resolve permissions, ensure that the installation command is executed with sufficient privileges. Using sudo can provide the necessary access:

```
$ sudo curl -L https://nixos.org/nix/install | sh
```

If existing directory structures pose restrictions, verify that the /nix directory is accessible and modifiable. This might entail changing ownership or permissions:

```
$ sudo chown -R user:group /nix
$ sudo chmod -R 755 /nix
```

These commands adjust ownership and alter permissions to provide read and execute access universally while limiting write access to user-specific modifications.

- **Conflict with Existing Software and Dependencies**

  Conflicts between Nix dependencies and pre-installed system applications can lead to failed installations. Pre-existing package versions may not align with those required by Nix, leading to environment instability or failure.

  Solution:

  Conflicts can be preemptively managed by employing Nix in a segregated environment. Disabling conflicting software versions or temporarily prioritizing Nix in PATH variable settings can alleviate immediate issues:

```
$ export PATH=/nix/var/nix/profiles/default/bin:$PATH
```

  For greater isolation, leveraging Docker containers for installation can prevent any direct interference with the host operating system. Create and run a Nix development container with:

```
$ docker run -it --rm --name nix-on-docker nixos/nix
```

  Here, Nix operates within the isolated environment of a Docker container, insulating the underlying system from direct interaction.

- **OS-Specific Issues - macOS and Windows**

  Nix's operation on macOS and Windows (the latter through Windows Subsystem for Linux) occasionally faces unique hurdles, particularly with OS-specific security implementations or system architecture differences.

Solution for macOS:

On macOS, ensure that the Terminal or shell application has permission to access developer tools directories. Adjust system security settings in System Preferences > Security & Privacy to permit actions during installation. Also, utilize a dedicated terminal emulator, such as iTerm2, which may circumvent default terminal restrictions.

Solution for Windows:

For Windows, utilizing WSL requires attention to enabling Linux distribution access and setup. Verify that WSL is activated appropriately:

```
> wsl --set-default-version 2
```

Ensure the chosen Linux distribution is installed and updated from the Microsoft Store and the subsequent installation of Nix proceeds from within this subsystem.

- **Disk Space and Resource Limitations**

  A lack of disk space can hinder the successful completion of the Nix installation, particularly when insufficient storage is allocated to environments where Nix writes packages and dependencies.

  Solution:

  Before installation, ensure that the system has ample free space, typically at least several gigabytes, to accommodate the Nix store and its packages. If storage is limited, consider cleaning unessential files or setting up Nix on external storage through symbolic links:

```
$ ln -s /path/to/external_storage /nix/store
```

  This approach leverages external resources, maintaining system capacity while accommodating Nix's demands.

- **Checksum and Integrity Validation Errors**

During installation, integrity validation errors might arise when package checksums do not match expected values. This scenario involves potential security compromises or package corruption.

Solution:

First, verify network stability to rule out transmission errors. Next, examine the official Nix channels for any recent updates or alterations to package checksums. Consider retrieving the latest nix-channel information before attempting a reinstallation.

```
$ nix-channel --update
```

If discrepancies persist, clearing the existing cache and refetching the package may resolve the issue:

```
$ nix-store --verify --repair
```

These steps are designed to abolish corrupted state perceptions, revalidate package checksums, and resume installation operations securely.

- **Environmental Configuration Anomalies**

  Occasionally, environment misconfigurations obstruct Nix's aptitude for adjusting variables or locating packages in their expected directories.

  Solution:

  Revalidate shell configuration files such as .bashrc or .zshrc to ensure correct environmental variable settings. Ensure path inclusivity:

```
$ source ~/.bashrc
```

  In especially complex environments, initialize a fresh session to eliminate erroneous session-specific variables.

The successful navigation of these common installation challenges into actionable resolutions furnishes users with resilient skills in adapting and employing Nix's installation features. This understanding exploits Nix's potential, enriching deployment outcomes, system stability, and user efficacy across development environments.

Chapter 4

Understanding Nix Expressions

Understanding Nix expressions is pivotal to unlocking the full potential of the Nix package manager, as they define how packages, configurations, and environments are structured and executed. Nix expressions employ a functional approach, using a clear syntax to specify attributes, dependencies, and build instructions necessary for package composition. By comprehending their structure and capabilities, users can create flexible and reusable code modules, import and modify existing expressions, and debug construction processes effectively. Mastery of Nix expressions allows for the development of reliable, reproducible software solutions tailored to specific needs and operational contexts.

4.1 What are Nix Expressions?

Nix expressions are the cornerstone of the Nix package manager, enabling users to define packages, configurations, and computational environments. These expressions represent a functional, declarative language designed specifically to manage the complexities of software installations and system configurations. They offer a high degree of specifyability, wherein each component's build and configuration can be described unambiguously. This section will elucidate the concept of Nix expressions, explaining their purpose and functionality within the Nix ecosystem.

At the highest level, Nix expressions serve to formally describe how individual software components are to be constructed, configured, and deployed. This expressive capability extends to entire configurations of systems, specifying everything from the individual libraries required by a program to the complete configuration required to set up a server environment.

Nix expressions are written in the Nix language, which combines elements of JSON-like syntax with the versatility and precision of functional programming paradigms. This language's primary strengths lie in its immutability, reusability, and ease of reasoning about complex computational dependencies.

A Nix expression can be something as simple as a package specification, which outlines the source from which to obtain the code, any dependencies that need to be available during building, and potentially any patches that need to be applied. Let's consider a basic example:

```
let
  pkgs = import <nixpkgs> {};
in
  pkgs.mkDerivation {
    pname = "hello";
    version = "2.10";

    src = pkgs.fetchurl {
      url = "http://ftp.gnu.org/gnu/hello/hello-2.10.tar.gz";
      sha256 = "sha256:31
            e7e13942b7ceb0ee1014fecf161988bc6f0e6b5b4bcb3ed78e4b256f1777b0";
    };

    buildInputs = [pkgs.gcc];

    meta = with pkgs.lib; {
      description = "A program that produces a familiar, friendly greeting";
      license = licenses.gpl3;
      maintainer = "gnupackages@nongnu.org";
    };
  }
```

The above code demonstrates a simple Nix expression to build the GNU hello package. Each piece of the expression fulfills a specific purpose:

- let ...in: Establishes a local scope for variable bindings, in this case importing the Nix packages from the standard repository.
- pkgs.mkDerivation: A Nix function used to package derivations. A derivation is an abstract representation in Nix of a build action.
- Attributes such as pname, version, and src: These provide metadata and source information for the derivation.
- buildInputs: Lists external dependencies required during the build process.
- meta: Offers additional information, such as a description or licensing details about the package.

Nix expressions emphasize immutability: once an expression is evaluated, its resulting state doesn't change. This assists in ensuring that builds are reproducible independent of changes to the environment in which they are executed. Additionally, the functional nature of Nix means expressions can be composed and transformed systematically, enabling a high degree of reuse and modularity.

The declarative nature of Nix expressions simplifies the process of defining what the system should look like after configurations are applied, as opposed to how to apply them. This aligns with the fundamental principles of modern infrastructure as code, allowing for versions to be managed in the same way they are in source code management systems, facilitating robust CI/CD practices.

To understand further how Nix expressions enable effective package management, let's explore another example where we define a more complex application. Here, we introduce the use of build phases to illustrate additional functionality:

```
{ pkgs ? import <nixpkgs> {} }:

pkgs.mkDerivation {
  pname = "myapp";
  version = "1.0.0";

  src = pkgs.fetchgit {
    url = "https://github.com/user/myapp.git";
    rev = "1a2b3c4d5e6f";
    sha256 = "sha256:somechecksum123456789abcdefghijk";
  };
```

```
  buildInputs = with pkgs; [ python3 nodejs ];

  installPhase = ''
    mkdir -p $out/bin
    cp script.py $out/bin/myapp
    wrapProgram $out/bin/myapp \
      --set PYTHONPATH ${pkgs.python3Packages.numpy}/lib/python3.9/site-
          packages
  '';

  meta = with pkgs.lib; {
    description = "An example application built with Nix";
    license = licenses.mit;
    homepage = "https://github.com/user/myapp";
    maintainers = with maintainers; [ user ];
  };
}
```

In this more elaborate expression:

- pkgs.fetchgit: Facilitates the fetching of source code directly from a Git repository.
- buildInputs: Includes both Python and Node.js as build dependencies, showcasing how multiple environments can be addressed within a single expression.
- installPhase: Customizes how files are setup post-build; the provided script exemplifies copying and wrapping Python files, making use of environment variables to set paths correctly.

Nix expressions can manage not just software packages but also complex environments encompassing many interdependent components. This attribute is essential in contemporary software practices that deploy microservices, containerized applications, and other modular software architectures.

One of the key features of Nix and its expressions is the handling of the build environment in an isolated manner, eliminating the influence of pre-installed packages or environment settings that might overhear external software management tools. It results in clean, precise builds and extensions that mitigate the risks of "it works on my machine" syndrome, where software functions as expected on the developer's system but fails elsewhere.

Let's also consider the extensibility of Nix expressions. They can be composed into more extensive system configurations or embedded within broader composition frameworks designed to orchestrate complex systems. The modular structure of Nix expressions fosters reusability, and sharing allows configurations to be abstracted and reutilized across different projects or team members efficiently.

Nix, with Nix expressions at its core, empowers developers with capabilities similar to those offered by functional programming languages and infrastructure-as-code tools. It systematizes configuration management, reduces environmental drift, and encourages the formulation of elements in a manner amenable to automated tests and constant iteration.

To further illustrate, let us review the integration of Nix expressions into system configuration. Consider a scenario where NixOS, a Linux distribution built entirely on the Nix package manager, is used to declare a full system setup in a configuration.nix file:

```
{ config, pkgs, ... }:

{
  boot.loader.grub.device = "/dev/sda";

  networking.hostName = "mynixos";
  networking.networkmanager.enable = true;

  services.openssh.enable = true;

  environment.systemPackages = with pkgs; [
    wget curl vim git
  ];

  users.users.jdoe = {
    uid = 1001;
    isNormalUser = true;
    extraGroups = [ "wheel" ];
    password = "password-hash-here";
  };

  system.stateVersion = "20.09";
}
```

This Nix expression configures a Linux server. While it bears a resemblance to single-package configuration files, it encompasses aspects crucial to an entire system, including bootloader settings, network management, service executions, and user accounts. Through the Nix language, users can describe detailed and comprehensive states for whole systems, supporting deterministic operations.

Involving Nix expressions in high-level infrastructure decisions presents a unique advantage: everything encapsulated within a Nix expression is reproducible and version-controlled, offering fine-grained control over each aspect of software deployment and system state management.

Practicing the writing and maintaining of Nix expressions invites developers and system administrators to think in terms of declarative specifications and functional dependencies. Once comprehended and correctly utilized, Nix expressions provide an environment of stability and precision, supporting expansive and varied application ecosystems.

4.2 Syntax and Structure of Nix Expressions

Nix expressions are formulated in a declarative, functional language explicitly designed to describe software environments and package definitions. The syntax and structure of Nix expressions can initially appear complex due to their specificity and reliance on functional paradigms; however, once grasped, this syntax provides powerful mechanisms for configuration management and environmental reproducibility. This section delves into the specifics of the Nix expression language, illustrating its core syntax, semantical rules, and the typical structural format employed when writing these expressions.

The fundamental unit of a Nix expression is akin to a syntactic JSON object, known as an attribute set, which consists of key-value pairs. These pairs denote attributes and their respective values, encapsulating everything from simple data types such as integers and strings to complex derivations. Attribute sets utilize braces {} akin to JSON or the dictionary structures found within various programming languages. Attributes are separated by semicolons, and values assign through the '=' symbol.

Consider the following Nix expression in its basic form, exemplifying an attribute set:

```
{
  name = "example-package";
  version = "1.0";
```

```
  dependencies = [ "lib1" "lib2" ];
}
```

The above structure delineates a hypothetical package description, listing attributes for the package name, version, and a dependencies array. Notice the use of square brackets [] to define lists containing multiple values, reinforcing the composability aspect intrinsic to the Nix language.

One of the most potent features of Nix expressions is their reliance on immutable values. Unlike many conventional programming languages where variables are mutable, Nix enforces immutability, ensuring that once a value is assigned, it cannot change. This property is crucial for reproducibility and caching, as it guarantees consistency across builds and installations.

Function definitions and application further enhance Nix's functional nature. Functions in Nix are first-class citizens, promoting modularity and reusability. An essential aspect of functions is the implicit nature of parameter passing, showcased in the following example:

```
{ a, b }:
a + b
```

In this expression, a simple function takes two parameters, a and b, returning their sum. The minimalist syntax underlines reliance on parameter names, with arguments being passed implicitly. To invoke this function, we use the following syntax:

```
let
  sum = { a, b }: a + b;
in
  sum { a = 3; b = 5; }
```

Here, a let binding introduces a local variable sum, which represents our previously defined function. The use of a let expression allows us to encapsulate variables and expressions within a local scope, enhancing modularity and preventing scope pollution.

Nix also provides mechanisms for importing and combining packages or modules, assisting in maintaining structured and organized code. The import keyword loads external Nix expressions or modules, facilitating inclusion and codebase extension. For instance:

```
let
  nixpkgs = import <nixpkgs> {};
  pkgs = nixpkgs.pkgs;
in
  pkgs.hello
```

In the above expression, the canonical nixpkgs package repository is imported, enabling access to a comprehensive pre-defined set of expressions. The latter part of the expression illustrates invoking a specific package, hello, from the imported collection.

Nix expressions support various data types, including integers, strings, booleans, lists, and more complexity through attribute sets. The expression language is markedly type-safe, offering guarantees against type mismatches at runtime—a discipline whose enforcement averts errors common in more permissively-typed environments.

A robust and distinctive aspect of the Nix language is its emphasis on lazy evaluation. Unlike eager or immediate evaluation strategies, lazy evaluation evaluates expressions only when needed. This approach allows Nix to handle large configurations and systems without exhausting resources prematurely. Here's an example to clarify lazy evaluation:

```
let
  x = 1 / 0;
  y = 5;
in
  y
```

In conventional languages following eager evaluation, the expression x = 1 / 0 would result in a runtime division by zero error. However, Nix would successfully return the result, 5 in this case, as x is never evaluated.

Conditionals in Nix are succinctly expressed through if-then-else statements, permitting straightforward choice between expressions:

```
let
  condition = true;
in
  if condition then "This is true" else "This is false"
```

The above expression assesses a condition and returns one or another value contingent upon the boolean evaluation. The explicit structure enhances clarity without requiring cumbersome syntax, further assisted by Nix's inherent immutability.

Moreover, to access attributes from attribute sets, Nix employs the dot notation, akin to accessing properties in JSON or objects in various object-oriented languages. Consider the following nested attribute access:

```
let
  data = {
    user = {
      name = "John Doe";
      email = "john@example.com";
    };
  };
in
  data.user.name
```

The expression yields John Doe, demonstrating dot notation to drill into nested structures effectively. Equally, the property email could be accessed via data.user.email, showcasing the utility of expressive field access.

Nix supports various operators for performing operations on fundamental types such as arithmetic on numerical values, concatenation on strings, logical conjunctions, disjunctions, and negations over Boolean values. These enable comprehensive in-expression operations without the need to fall back to external logic:

```
let
  sum = 10 + 5; # Addition
  difference = 10 - 5; # Subtraction
  product = 10 * 5; # Multiplication
  quotient = 10 / 5; # Division
  isEqual = "same" == "same"; # Equality
  concatenated = "Hello, " + "Nix!";
in
  concatenated
```

The language further incorporates pattern matching facilities via with and inherit constructs, introducing syntactic clarity in scenarios where recurring attributes or paths require repetitive use. Here is a demonstration of its utility:

```
let
  data = { a = 1; b = 2; c = 3; };
in with data; a + b + c
```

Utilizing with data; makes a, b, and c accessible without recurrently employing the data namespace. This facility, grounded in simplicity, progresses into prominence as expressions grow in intricacy.

Nix expressions also describe attributes as derivations, which present an abstract plan for building packages and software environments. Derivations address instructions to compile software from source, manage dependencies, and outline various stages of the software lifecycle (build, install, test, etc.). This aligns with traditional build systems yet persists through the declarative, functional nature:

```
let
  pkgs = import <nixpkgs> {};
in
  pkgs.stdenv.mkDerivation {
    name = "example";
    src = ./.;
    buildInputs = [ pkgs.gcc ];
  }
```

This derivation anticipates standard derivation parameters src and a list of build inputs such as gcc, predicting the expectation of isolated environments entirely helmed by Nix's analytical mechanisms.

While we have unwrapped several layers of Nix expressions' syntax and structure, the complexity lies not solely in understanding the compact syntax, but in conceptualizing the functional paradigm through which Nix facilitates consistent, reproducible, and transparent package management and configuration processes. As we continue, proficiency in Nix expression language will unlock new efficiencies in maintaining robust infrastructures and systems with rigorous precision.

4.3 Attributes and Attribute Sets

Attributes and attribute sets form the foundational data structures in the Nix expression language, allowing for comprehensive representation and organization of data. These constructs are crucial in defining packages, managing configurations, and expressing complex data flows within Nix expressions. This section articulates the role of attributes and attribute sets within the Nix language, how they contribute to the language's declarative nature, and demonstrates their usage in a variety of contexts with illustrative examples.

At its core, an attribute in Nix is analogous to a key in a dictionary-like structure, representing a named entity to which a value can be assigned. These values can span basic types such as strings, numbers, booleans, and can extend to more complex structures like functions, lists, or other attribute sets. The assignment of attributes is fundamental in Nix expressions, serving as a directive for what a specific component, package, or configuration property should represent or equate to.

Attribute sets in Nix carry these attributes as collections of key-value pairs, encapsulated within curly braces {}. They function similarly to objects in JSON or hash maps in other programming languages, providing a hierarchical and modular way to manage collections of interconnected data. Consider this example of a basic attribute set in Nix:

```
{
  name = "simple-package";
  version = "0.1";
  maintainers = ["alice" "bob"];
}
```

This attribute set defines a package with a name, version, and maintainers. Attributes such as name are assigned string values, version also as a string, and maintainers as a list, encapsulating multiple maintainers for the package. The simplicity observed here belies the potential complexity and nested structures attribute sets can entail.

One of the significant advantages of using attribute sets is their ability to organize data cohesively, facilitating clear references and logical grouping of related attributes. This structure allows developers to succinctly define scoped properties and reuse patterns across different parts of Nix expressions, enhancing readability and maintainability.

In more complex applications, attribute sets allow for nesting. By nesting attribute sets, Nix expressions can model sophisticated data schemas akin to namespaces or compartments in other languages. Here, sets of attributes themselves are defined within other attribute sets, promoting clarity through structured hierarchies as depicted below:

```
{
  project = {
    title = "Sample Project";
    contributors = { lead = "Carol"; assistant = "David"; };
    repository = {
```

```
      url = "https://github.com/user/project";
      branch = "main";
    };
  };
}
```

This attribute set defines a project with its title, contributors, and repository details. Each layer belongs to a thematic category, allowing logical partitioning that groups specific properties under respective subsections. Accessing these nested structures requires a dot notation, akin to object property access in other languages, enabling concise and precise references:

```
let
  projectInfo = {
    project = {
      title = "Sample Project";
      contributors = { lead = "Carol"; assistant = "David"; };
    };
  };
in
  projectInfo.project.contributors.lead
```

The above expression retrieves the value "Carol" by navigating the hierarchy to access the lead contributor.

Nix's paradigm promotes immutable data structures, thereby offering predictability and stability. Attribute sets inherit this immutability, ensuring once they are defined, their values remain consistent throughout their lifecycle. Immutable structures dovetail with functional programming principles, facilitating a safe, concurrent processing model devoid of side effects. This model is particularly advantageous when executing complex builds or configurations susceptible to variations in mutable environments.

Beyond simple declarations, attributes in Nix expressions support interpolation. This allows dynamic value generation through string manipulation, embedding expressions within strings yielding computed results. Here's a functional example of attribute interpolation:

```
let
  version = "1.2.3";
in
  {
    package = "mypackage-${version}";
    url = "https://downloads.example.com/mypackage-${version}.tar.gz";
  }
```

The use of $ syntax within strings interpolates the version attribute, constructing the packagename and URL dynamically with each evaluation. This minimizes repetition and errors when managing versions across large projects, as changes automatically propagate throughout usages.

Nix expressions benefit substantially from the functional nature of attribute sets, in particular through the inheritance concepts that build upon existing structures. This is accomplished through either direct inheritance of attributes or the redefinition of existing attributes by overriding them. Importing attribute sets combines data logically, enhancing modular development practices:

```
let
  baseConfig = {
    name = "base";
    features = [ "logging" "monitoring" ];
  };
  extendedConfig = baseConfig // {
    features = baseConfig.features ++ [ "caching" ];
    optimizations = true;
  };
in
  extendedConfig
```

In this expression, baseConfig is defined with a feature set, while extendedConfig inherits and extends this set with additional capabilities. The // operator represents merging, while ++ concatenates lists. extendedConfig thus encapsulates both the logging and caching features, with optimizations enabled, demonstrating how inheritance can adapt existing config attributes.

The operation of overriding is central to customization within Nix, as it allows for tailored derivations and configurations without sacrificing base definitions. This is particularly potent in package management roles where default options may need amendment to suit specific deployment needs or environments without altering the shared foundational structure.

Nix expressions can reach higher complexity in configurations, extending to parameterized attribute sets that accept arguments for customization:

```
{ lib, stdenv, fetchFromGitHub }:

stdenv.mkDerivation rec {
```

```
  pname = "enhanced";

  inherit (lib) version;
  src = fetchFromGitHub {
    owner = "example";
    repo = "repository";
    rev = "v${version}";
    sha256 = "0wi3ak0d1sje9109afd12sdf13f6ae4dui3";
  };

  buildInputs = with stdenv; [ gcc openssl ];

  meta = {
    description = "An enhanced package";
    maintainers = [ "Contrib" ];
  };
}
```

Here, attributes are parameterized through a function that accepts libraries and actions as arguments, promoting scalability and reusability. The use of inherit allows for properties from other sets (like lib) to be brought into scope without explicitly redefining them.

Furthermore, attribute sets operate across the full breadth of NixOS configurations, defining system services, user configurations, hardware settings, and entire system states. This enables state descriptions at the server or even data center level, wrapped within the convenient, immutable structure of attribute sets. Imagine defining a NixOS configuration that orchestrates system services, similar to:

```
{ config, pkgs, ... }:

{
  imports = [ ./hardware-configuration.nix ];

  boot.loader.grub.device = "/dev/sda";

  networking.useDHCP = false;
  networking.interfaces.eth0.useDHCP = true;

  services.sshd.enable = true;

  environment.systemPackages = with pkgs; [
    vim
    git
    curl
  ];

  users.users.alice = {
    isNormalUser = true;
    home = "/home/alice";
    extraGroups = ["wheel"];
  };
```

```
}
```

This configuration file defines a NixOS system with boot settings, network interfaces, services, system packages, and user accounts, crucially organized and manipulated through attribute sets.

The coordination of these components through attribute sets grants comprehensive control over the machine's state, all determined declaratively within the configuration files. This organization aids in predicting system behavior across various runtime environments, allowing reproducible deployments irrespective of when or where the expression is evaluated.

Overall, attributes and attribute sets form the bedrock for building versatile, powerful expressions in Nix. Their inherent design aligns with Nix's paradigm of managing software and configuration through declarative, functional constructs, enabling safe, repeatable alteration and expansion of systems and packages. As users become conversant in crafting and deploying attribute sets into complex schemata, they gain a formidable toolset that scales from discrete microservices to comprehensive data center operations with foresight and meticulous efficiency.

4.4 Writing Custom Nix Expressions

Creating custom Nix expressions is a powerful and flexible way to specify packages, configurations, and entire computational environments within the Nix ecosystem. The process of writing custom Nix expressions involves an understanding of the language's declarative and functional paradigm, as well as an ability to effectively leverage the myriad capabilities inherent in the Nix package manager. This section will provide a detailed exploration of the approach to crafting custom Nix expressions, including the syntax, structure, intricate patterns, and expressive capabilities while showcasing practical examples to support the learning experience.

Nix expressions are primarily built using a blend of attribute sets, functions, operators, and constructs that allow users to specify exactly how software should be built and configured. Writing custom expressions requires more than following a set format; it involves informed decisions about dependencies, environments, and the final usage scenarios that the expressions are meant to accommodate.

To begin writing a custom Nix expression, one typically starts with a clear definition of the package or configuration requirement. A basic example of a custom Nix expression could be constructing a simple derivation for a package not found in the standard Nix package repository. Consider the following straightforward example of a template for a custom package:

```
let
  pkgs = import <nixpkgs> {};
in
  pkgs.stdenv.mkDerivation {
    pname = "custom-tool";
    version = "1.0.0";

    src = pkgs.fetchurl {
      url = "https://example.com/custom-tool-1.0.0.tar.gz";
      sha256 = "1y2d6f5ef9086ac4234437e2d99e287748b18ee2b61c9ba9c93d19c57648f53c
           ";
    };

    buildInputs = [pkgs.gcc];

    makeFlags = [ "install" ];

    meta = {
      description = "A tool for custom operations.";
      homepage = "https://example.com/custom-tool";
      license = pkgs.lib.licenses.gpl3;
    };
  }
```

In this expression:

- A derivation is defined using ‘pkgs.stdenv.mkDerivation‘, which is a standard package definition utility provided by Nix.
- ‘pname‘ and ‘version‘ specify the package name and version.
- ‘src‘ uses ‘pkgs.fetchurl‘ to retrieve the source code from a specified URL, and the ‘sha256‘ field ensures the integrity of the downloaded file.
- ‘buildInputs‘ lists any packages required for building, in this case, the GNU Compiler Collection (GCC).

- 'makeFlags' specifies additional make commands if necessary, here directing the build process to an 'install' target.
- 'meta' sets metadata such as description, homepage, and license information.

Each attribute in the derivation corresponds to a specific part of the build or configuration process, and understanding these nuances empowers developers to craft precise and efficient build scripts. It's crucial to match the Nix language's conventions with native build scripts, so an existing build process can be mirrored or adapted with the tooling and mechanisms offered by Nix.

The Nix ecosystem also supports build phases, allowing for the customization of build processes beyond the default configure-make-install pattern. Developers can define, override, or extend phases using shell script-like syntax embedded within Nix expressions. Here's an example illustrating a customized build phase tailored to more specific needs:

```
let
  pkgs = import <nixpkgs> {};
in
  pkgs.stdenv.mkDerivation rec {
    pname = "advanced-tool";
    version = "2.0.0";

    src = pkgs.fetchFromGitHub {
      owner = "example";
      repo = "advanced-tool";
      rev = "v2.0.0";
      sha256 = "0abc123dedef456ghi789ijkl987mno123pqrstuvwx456yza1bc2def3g4hi5j6
          ";
    };

    buildInputs = [ pkgs.make ];

    preBuild = ''
      echo "Executing pre-build steps"
    '';

    buildPhase = ''
      make all
    '';

    preInstall = ''
      echo "Preparing installation"
    '';

    installPhase = ''
      mkdir -p $out/bin
```

```
    cp advanced-tool $out/bin/
  '';

  meta = {
    description = "An advanced tool with custom build phases.";
    homepage = "https://github.com/example/advanced-tool";
    license = pkgs.lib.licenses.gpl2;
  };
}
```

This example customizes the build process by defining 'preBuild', 'buildPhase', 'preInstall', and 'installPhase'. This approach allows for fine-grained control over individual build steps, ultimately resulting in packages that fulfill specific operational criteria and integrate seamlessly within their anticipated deployment contexts.

Custom Nix expressions can take advantage of external libraries, additional build utilities, and the rich repository of existing Nix expressions. The 'import' function plays a critical role in establishing and manipulating dependencies, improving the compositional ease and modularity of custom Nix expressions. The ability to imperatively amend and extend, or functionally compose, ensures substantial flexibility:

```
{ lib, stdenv, fetchFromGitHub }:

stdenv.mkDerivation rec {
  pname = "composable-tool";
  version = "3.0.0";

  inherit (lib) encodeBase64;

  src = fetchFromGitHub {
    owner = "example";
    repo = "composable-tool";
    rev = "v3.0.0";
    sha256 = encodeBase64 "
        f3eed690cea327dcd1ba81c796b25ec6b86b723269ddcd1419e0f33b1e3dcec6";
  };

  buildInputs = [ ];

  installPhase = ''
    mkdir -p $out/bin
    cp run-tool $out/bin/composable-tool
  '';

  meta = {
    description = "A tool highlighting extensibility and composition.";
    homepage = "https://github.com/example/composable-tool";
    license = lib.licenses.mit;
  };
}
```

Here, ‘fetchFromGitHub‘ is imported and it simplifies fetching repositories from GitHub. Furthermore, by inheriting functions from ‘lib‘, such as ‘encodeBase64‘, expressions can directly utilize pre-existing functionalities for tasks like managing checksums or encoding data, minimizing repetitive tasks.

Beyond single-package management, custom Nix expressions often encapsulate entire environments or configurations, dealing with everything from libraries to services, to systemd configurations. As configurations become more complex, the nested use of attribute sets allows for sophisticated definitions of states and desired system layouts:

```
{ config, pkgs, ... }:

{
  imports = [ ./hardware-configuration.nix ];

  config = {
    boot.loader.grub.device = "/dev/sdX";

    networking.hostName = "customnix";

    services = {
      sshd.enable = true;
      httpd.enable = true;
    };

    environment.systemPackages = with pkgs; [
      vim
      git
      curl
      wget
    ];

    users = {
      users = {
        admin = {
          isNormalUser = true;
          shell = pkgs.zsh;
          extraGroups = [ "wheel" "network" "docker" ];
        };
      };
    };
  };
}
```

This complex NixOS configuration file specifies an entire system’s setup, demonstrating the power of Nix expressions to manage comprehensive state and configurations for system environments. Through this definition, services, user profiles, package installations, and boot settings are consolidated into a single, reproducible declarative file capable of managing a complete deployment.

Moreover, Nix's lazy evaluation model enables writing expressions that adapt their behavior dynamically at runtime while maintaining consistency and transparency across the board. Through effective use of this model, developers avoid unnecessary computations until needed, often yielding performance efficiencies in appropriately complex scenarios.

The process of creating custom Nix expressions requires both an understanding of the basic building blocks and the ability to integrate more advanced features such as environments, services, and compositions. As with any skill, proficiency comes through practice, where users increasingly become adept at leveraging the balance of simplicity and extensive capacity that Nix offers.

In summary, writing custom Nix expressions involves combining elements of the Nix language to address specific requirements, constructing finely-tuned derivations, enriching complex configurations, and harnessing the deterministic nature of Nix to ensure reliable and reproducible environments that align perfectly with modern software development and deployment methodologies.

4.5 Importing and Using Expressions

The ability to import and use expressions is a vital aspect of working with Nix, improving code reuse, modularity, and maintainability across software projects. Nix expressions, due to their functional and declarative nature, support the importing of other expressions, packages, and modules, permitting developers to construct complex systems and environments from smaller, composable units. This section delves into the mechanisms and best practices involved in importing and utilizing Nix expressions effectively, exploring the nuances and showcasing practical examples.

Importing in Nix facilitates the incorporation of external Nix expressions or modules into a current scope, thereby extending the capabilities and enabling reuse of existing configurations. This is achieved using the 'import' function or keyword, which evaluates a referenced Nix expression file and makes its attributes available within the context of the importing expression. Here's an elementary example demonstrating this concept:

```
let
  sharedConfig = import ./shared-config.nix;
in
  {
    package = "app-with-dependencies";
    version = sharedConfig.version;
    dependencies = sharedConfig.baseDependencies;
  }
```

In this example, a file 'shared-config.nix' is imported, potentially containing common configurations or global settings shared across multiple projects. By importing this configuration, values like 'version' and 'baseDependencies' can be accessed as part of the importing expression, avoiding duplication and promoting consistency.

The 'import' function in Nix is flexible and can reference expressions stored locally or fetched remotely using specific fetchers found in the Nix package set such as 'fetchurl' or 'fetchgit' for remote repositories. For instance:

```
let
  remoteExpression = import (fetchurl {
    url = "https://example.com/external-expression.nix";
    sha256 = "abcdefghijklmnopqrstuvwxy1234567890abcdefg321";
  });
in
  remoteExpression.module
```

When importing remote expressions, security best practices dictate verifying the integrity of the fetched file using hash validation, ensuring authenticity and safeguarding against undesired alterations.

Nix's approach to importing supports parameterization, which permits passing arguments to imported expressions, enabling more dynamic and adaptable configurations. This is particularly useful in scenarios where different configurations or build environments need to be instantiated with varying parameters. Consider the example of a parameterized expression:

```
# shared-config.nix
{ pkgs, userConfig }:

{
  version = "2.0";
  baseDependencies = with pkgs; [ python3 nodejs ];
  userEnv = userConfig.buildEnv;
}
```

This file could then be imported with specific parameters:

```
let
  pkgs = import <nixpkgs> {};
  userConfig = { buildEnv = "production"; };

  sharedConfig = import ./shared-config.nix { inherit pkgs userConfig; };
in
  sharedConfig.userEnv
```

The parameterized approach allows the reuse of the same configuration logic with varying inputs, enabling conditionally constructed environments based on different requirements, use cases, and user-defined settings.

Nix encourages modular expression design, advocating the separation of concerns into distinct modules or components that encapsulate discrete functionalities. This ensures that each module is responsible for a specific aspect of the system, encapsulating logic appropriate to its domain. Let's consider the modularization of a full-stack application into distinct server and client components, further divided through importing:

```
# server.nix
{ pkgs, serverSettings }:

pkgs.stdenv.mkDerivation {
  name = "server";
  src = serverSettings.source;
  buildInputs = [ pkgs.nodejs ];
  buildPhase = ''
    npm install
    npm run build
  '';
  installPhase = ''
    mkdir -p $out/bin
    cp -r build/* $out/bin/
  '';
}

# client.nix
{ pkgs, clientSettings }:

pkgs.stdenv.mkDerivation {
  name = "client";
  src = clientSettings.source;
  buildInputs = [ pkgs.nodejs ];
  buildPhase = ''
    npm install
    npm run build
  '';
  installPhase = ''
    mkdir -p $out/bin
```

```
    cp -r dist/* $out/bin/
  ";
}

# top-level.nix
{ pkgs }:

let
  serverSettings = { source = ./server-source; };
  clientSettings = { source = ./client-source; };

  server = import ./server.nix { inherit pkgs serverSettings; };
  client = import ./client.nix { inherit pkgs clientSettings; };
in
  rec {
    serverBuild = server;
    clientBuild = client;
  }
```

Here, the 'server.nix' and 'client.nix' files define separate derivations for building server and client components. Each file potentially focuses on specific tasks like fetching dependencies, building from source, and installing outputs. These components are then imported into a 'top-level.nix' module, orchestrating the builds as a unified application suite. Each import points to the differentiated source and fluently composes into the broader application configuration dictated by the top-level module.

Another powerful aspect of importing and using expressions in Nix is the practice of maintaining a versioned set of configurations, enabling precise control over environments in comparison to a universal non-versioned setup. This aligns with the pillar of reproducibility Nix aims to achieve.

For example, defining different configurations for stable, testing, and development environments can be facilitated through importing:

```
# environment-stable.nix
{ pkgs }:
{
  name = "stable-environment";
  packages = with pkgs; [ nginx ];
}

# environment-testing.nix
{ pkgs }:
{
  name = "testing-environment";
  packages = with pkgs; [ nginx someTestingTool ];
}
```

```
# deploy.nix
{ env ? "stable" }:

let
  pkgs = import <nixpkgs> {};
  environment = import ./environment-${env}.nix { inherit pkgs; };
in
  environment.packages
```

This pattern grants the ability to build and deploy environments using specific designations, and the selection of environment configurations could even be automated based on branch names in a CI/CD system, for example.

Overall, the import capabilities of Nix offer significant flexibility in designing stateful configurations and declarative packages, allowing developers to leverage shared resources and develop modularly-scalable systems without the overhead of redundancy. The clear division between various modules enhances readability, maintainability, and ultimately the resilience of the configurations, while conforming to DRY (Don't Repeat Yourself) principles.

Understanding and employing the Nix import capabilities is pivotal to maximizing Nix's efficiency and extensibility, allowing configurations to be reshaped as compounds of well-defined, limited-functionality modules. This clearly demonstrates how Nix's design philosophy—leveraging functionality focused on immutability, reusability, and modularity—empowers developers to iteratively build software systems that are both stable and adaptable.

4.6 Debugging Nix Expressions

Debugging Nix expressions is a crucial skill for developers and system administrators working within the Nix ecosystem, as it ensures that configurations and package builds behave as intended. Due to the declarative and functional nature of Nix, the strategies for diagnosis and rectifying issues differ from traditional imperative programming environments. This section provides a comprehensive guide to debugging Nix expressions, discussing techniques, tools, and best practices to identify and resolve common pitfalls, with illustrative examples enhancing understanding.

The first step in debugging Nix expressions involves understanding the primary types of errors that can occur: syntax errors, evaluation errors, and runtime errors. Each requires a different approach, from carefully examining the code structure to tracing the execution path and understanding how Nix evaluates expressions. Syntax errors typically arise from incorrect use of language constructs, evaluation errors occur when expressions fail to produce a valid result, and runtime errors are encountered during package build or execution.

A crucial tool in the debugger's toolkit is the Nix command-line utility, particularly the nix-instantiate and nix-build commands, which provide feedback on expression evaluation and build processes. The command nix-instantiate allows users to test whether a Nix expression can be successfully evaluated without attempting a full build:

```
$ nix-instantiate example.nix
```

Errors here indicate issues in evaluation before any actions performed during a build, such as fetch or compile. Syntax errors often become apparent in this phase, letting the developer correct them prior to initiating resource-intensive build processes.

When writing new expressions or extending existing ones, introducing incremental builds is vital. Incremental building avoids recompiling unmodified parts, which not only conserves resources but isolates variables, minimizing potential failure points seen in large systems. Using environment variables like NIX_DEBUG provides a verbose output during builds, yielding insights beneficial for isolating errors:

```
$ NIX_DEBUG=1 nix-build -A example
```

With NIX_DEBUG set to 1, this command provides detailed logs of each phase within the build, including fetching sources, verifying hashes, and linking dependencies.

At times, it may be necessary to inspect the intermediate temporary files produced during the build. This can provide invaluable information, especially when incomprehensible or improper outputs arise. The temporary working directory is removed automatically after a successful build, but can be preserved using the –keep-failed option provided to nix-build, allowing inspection post-failure:

```
$ nix-build --keep-failed -A brokenPackage
```

In unsuccessful build scenarios, this approach allows developers to examine what's transpiring during package preparation, offering clues to potential faults in configuration scripts, dependencies, or other build inputs.

Another essential aspect of debugging in Nix involves effectively using .drv files, known as derivations. These store metadata about packages and their build instructions, serving as a point of traceability where all dependencies and build steps are outlined. By inspecting .drv files, one verifies whether an expression has correctly encapsulated all necessary details for a deterministic outcome.

One can display a derivation's inputs using:

```
$ nix-store --query --requisites /nix/store/path-to-package.drv
```

This command lists each requirement necessary for your build to complete, aiding in determining whether an expression has accurately captured the package dependencies essential for successful construction.

The Nix language provides constructs that aid in debugging individual expressions. The trace function, for example, allows you to output a custom message and/or print intermediate values as debugging steps throughout expression evaluation. Here's how it can be implemented:

```
let
  x = 2;
  y = 3;
  sum = x + y;
in
  builtins.trace "Current sum value: ${sum}" sum
```

When evaluated, the expression outputs the traced values, offering opportunities to verify whether intermediate computations align with expectations or if there's logic misalignment—a frequent source of error.

For debugging purposes, specifically when creation or modification of packages is required, overlays can be incredibly useful. Overlays allow for modifying the behavior of packages or introducing custom logic without changing original expression trees directly. Here's an example that utilizes overlays to inject debug code into the Nixpkgs package set:

```
self: super: {
  hello = super.hello.overrideAttrs (old: {
    buildInputs = old.buildInputs or [ ] ++ [ self.gdb ];
    preConfigure = "echo 'Debugging overlay applied'";
  });
}
```

By declaring this overlay, the hello package now includes a debugging echo statement during pre-configuration, as well as GDB as a build input. This technique illustrates a powerful mechanism for injecting changes or facilitating troubleshooting while maintaining clean separations in Nix expressions.

Effective debugging in Nix also entails managing and understanding builds' levels of reproducibility, where upstream changes can affect outcomes. It is vital for discrepancies to be accounted for, traceable, and resolvable. Here's where the Nix language's immutability comes into play. Pure and deterministic, Nix expressions warrant a disciplined approach where input changes or deviations are straightforwardly identifiable, contributing to a controlled debugging environment.

Visualizing dependency graphs using nix-build options like –dry-run helps anticipate actions a build takes before runtime execution, flagging unavailable or misplaced dependencies preemptively:

```
$ nix-build --dry-run -A target
```

Once flagged, developers can address constraints or wrong references without incurring the cost of a failed build, refining input paths or expressions as needed.

Lastly, contributing to broader codebases or multi-user platforms with Nix requires awareness of cache usages and store paths to avoid local anomalies adversely impacting shared environments. Cleaning build caches with nix-collect-garbage ensures successful outcomes. Here's a basic example of cleaning unused store paths:

```
$ nix-collect-garbage -d
```

By doing this periodically, accumulations are managed, alleviating environmental drift and memory lapse scenarios that could otherwise confound debugging efforts.

Debugging Nix expressions becomes effective with a rigorous, practiced approach leveraging these techniques. Beyond mere error rectification, they encourage better comprehension of Nix as a system, augmenting developers' capabilities to build robust, reproducible environments systematically. This enables the resolution of issues but also reinforces foundational skills aligned with Nix's virtues: predictability, transparency, and rigour.

Chapter 5

Nix Packages and the Nixpkgs Repository

Understanding Nix packages and the Nixpkgs repository is essential for effectively managing software within the Nix ecosystem. Nix packages are defined through expressions that specify their source, build instructions, and dependencies. The Nixpkgs repository serves as a comprehensive collection of these packages, offering a vast array of software that can be seamlessly integrated into any Nix-managed system. By navigating this repository, users can find, utilize, and customize packages according to their needs. Additionally, contributing to and extending the repository with custom packages is facilitated by Nix's flexible override and overlay mechanisms, fostering an environment of collaboration and innovation.

5.1 Exploring Nix Packages

Nix packages form the foundational element of the Nix system, encapsulating software in a manner that ensures reproducibility, minimal side effects, and flexibility in deployment. The cornerstone of Nix packages lies in the functional approach to package management, allowing users to define packages through immutable expressions. These expressions specify how software is built, along with its dependencies, in a declarative manner.

Nix packages are defined using a specialized functional programming language that expresses build processes as pure functions. This demarcation from traditional package management systems, where installations may directly alter the system state, elevates Nix to a category where package builds are isolated and controlled. Each package expression includes key attributes that define its nature and behavior, such as version, src (source), buildInputs, and more.

```
{ lib, stdenv, fetchurl }:

stdenv.mkDerivation rec {
  pname = "hello";
  version = "2.10";

  src = fetchurl {
    url = "http://ftp.gnu.org/gnu/hello/hello-${version}.tar.gz";
    sha256 = "0ssi1wpaf7plaswqqjwigppsg5fyh99vdlb9kzl7c9lng89ndq1c";
  };

  buildInputs = [ ];

  meta = with lib; {
    description = "A program that produces a familiar, friendly greeting";
    license = licenses.gpl3Plus;
    maintainers = [ maintainers.alice ];
    platforms = platforms.all;
  };
}
```

This example demonstrates the core components of a Nix package. The mkDerivation function constructs a derivation, which is an abstraction that represents the build actions to obtain the package. The pname and version fields specify the package name and version, respectively. The src field uses fetchurl to download the tarball for the hello package from the GNU mirror, secured by a SHA-256 checksum that verifies integrity.

Central to Nix's unique approach is the concept of the Nix store. Packages are stored in /nix/store, a directory that maintains a hash of the entire build input as part of the file path. This hash-based approach ensures that packages are immutable and reproducible, as only the exact combination of build inputs leads to a particular store path. This mechanism negates the possibility of dependency conflicts, as each package's dependencies are encapsulated and isolated within their specific paths.

The functional nature of Nix packages provides several benefits over traditional configuration approaches. Primarily, it facilitates a model where the output of each package build is deterministic, provided the inputs remain unchanged. This determinism enables several powerful features, including precise rollbacks, reproducible builds, and parallel installations of different versions of the same package.

While highlighting these concepts, consider the build dependencies in Nix expressed via lists such as buildInputs. These lists determine the other packages needed during the build process. In traditional systems, these would be akin to build-dependencies, but with Nix, these dependencies do not affect the global system state or interfere with other builds.

Beyond the basics of package specification, Nix accommodates other attributes that further define how packages behave within the system. These include:

- configureFlags: To customize the configuration phase of package builds.
- patches: To apply local or community patches to source code.
- nativeBuildInputs: For dependencies required during the build process but not at runtime, essential for cross-compilation.
- meta: Contains metadata such as the license, description, and maintainers.

The additional fine-grained control provided by these attributes allows users to adapt package builds to nearly any scenario, simplifying integration with different environments and toolchains.

Another critical component of Nix packaging is the absence of global state changes during package builds and installations. This is significant because it allows multiple versions of a package to coexist without conflict. Consider a scenario where different applications require different versions of a library. In traditional systems, this leads to "dependency hell," but Nix obviates this by ensuring each package version remains isolated.

```
{ lib, stdenv, fetchurl, cmake }:

stdenv.mkDerivation rec {
  pname = "mysoftware";
  version = "1.0";

  src = fetchurl {
    url = "https://example.com/mysoftware-${version}.tar.gz";
    sha256 = "19qivz3nlbq03a52ar4i8ybn5r4i8mcc28cg0lr0p3n9z2z9kyaq";
  };

  nativeBuildInputs = [ cmake ];

  meta = with lib; {
    description = "A custom software package";
    license = licenses.mit;
    maintainers = [ maintainers.bob ];
    platforms = platforms.linux;
  };
}
```

In this example, cmake is specified as a nativeBuildInput, providing an essential tool for configuring the build process without impacting the resulting runtime environment.

Nix packages are powerful due to their extendibility and the robust ecosystem of existing packages within the Nixpkgs repository. This repository serves as a database for Nix expressions, providing a vast array of software packages that can be built and customized through the flexible Nix language. Users can override and extend existing packages, tailoring software to fit specific needs without altering the original package definitions thanks to Nix's inheritance and overlay capabilities.

The declarative model of Nix not only minimizes the surface area for errors but also promotes a culture of collaboration: expressions written by one contributor can be utilized and further refined by others. This collaborative environment thrives on the automation and predictability introduced by the functional model, which are augmented by comprehensive testing and community best practices.

To further explore the efficacy of Nix packages, consider the aspect of runtime closure. A runtime closure is the minimal set of files required for a package to run, defined by its transitive runtime dependencies.

One of the significant advantages of Nix's approach is the consciousness of package closure size, which aids in ensuring lightweight deployments, especially crucial in constrained environments such as containers or embedded systems.

A comprehensive understanding of the declarative syntax and the operational semantics of Nix expressions not only helps in constructing efficient package expressions but also plays a critical role in debugging and optimizing package builds. The deterministic nature of these builds helps surface discrepancies stemming from environmental differences, which are common pitfalls in traditional package management.

Understanding and utilizing Nix packages extend beyond development into production, enabling smoother CI/CD pipeline integrations. With mechanisms such as channel-based updates and substitution from binary caches, building and deploying packages efficiently in a controlled and predictable manner is possible, aligning well with modern continuous integration (CI) environments.

Nix channels contain pre-built binaries of Nix packages, continuously updated and maintained, allowing for binary substitution that saves time and computational resources. This makes it possible to use binaries instead of building packages from scratch, thus significantly accelerating deployments. Moreover, the substitution is both secure and reliable, as it utilizes the hash-based path and cryptographic verification of package content integrity.

The paradigm shift introduced by Nix packages, rooted in functional programming principles and reproducibility, offers an evolution in how software is managed, built, and deployed. With a detailed conceptual understanding and practical aptitude in manipulating Nix expressions, users can master the advantages conferred by the Nix system, crafting software solutions that are more robust, controllable, and maintainable. The consistency provided by Nix shapes a landscape where both developers and systems administrators can rely on automation to handle the nuances of software deployment, ensuring systems are both predictable and verifiable.

5.2 Navigating the Nixpkgs Repository

The Nixpkgs repository stands as a central pillar within the Nix ecosystem, serving as a comprehensive collection of Nix package expressions. This repository hosts an extensive array of software packages, providing users with access to a diverse set of tools that can seamlessly integrate into any Nix-managed system. Mastering navigation of the Nixpkgs repository is essential for leveraging its full potential, allowing users to discover, utilize, and extend packages efficiently.

The Nixpkgs repository is organized hierarchically, with a directory structure that categorizes packages based on functionality, language, and platform, among other criteria. Understanding this organization enables effective searching and browsing within the repository, ensuring swift access to the desired package configurations.

A typical Nixpkgs repository directory tree includes multiple subdirectories, each corresponding to different package categories and functions. These contain package expression files that define software builds. The essential directories and files include:

- pkgs/: Contains the bulk of package definitions. Subdirectories within pkgs/ group related software packages based on language or functionality.
- lib/: Houses library functions used by multiple packages, offering reusable code snippets and standard library functionalities.
- maintainers/: Includes a list of package maintainers, documenting the individuals responsible for different packages within the repository.
- default.nix: A critical file that serves as the entry point of Nixpkgs, facilitating importing and building of multiple packages.

Effectively navigating these directories requires understanding the underlying organizational principles and conventions adopted by the Nixpkgs community. By exploring the pkgs/ directory, one can notice packages grouped by utility, such as development, languages, servers, applications, and more, simplifying the process of locating specific software based on its purpose.

Using the Nix command line tools, such as nix-env, nix search, and nix run, provides powerful methods for searching and managing packages within Nixpkgs. The nix-env -qaP command, for example, lists all available packages along with their respective paths, offering a global view of accessible software.

```
$ nix-env -qaP
```

This command fetches and displays a comprehensive directory of package expressions organized by attribute paths, helping users quickly locate and explore the definitions of specific packages.

The nix search command empowers users to search for packages using keywords, which can be invaluable when the exact package name is not known. Utilizing this function requires an understanding of simple search patterns and keyword combinations to filter results effectively.

```
$ nix search nixpkgs hello
```

This command searches the Nixpkgs repository for packages related to the keyword "hello," illustrating how full-text search mechanisms expedite package discovery.

Each package within Nixpkgs is defined by an expression written in the Nix language. These expressions specify package dependencies, source location, build instructions, and metadata. Understanding the specific syntax and conventions used within package expressions is vital for both using and modifying packages. For example, the buildInputs, nativeBuildInputs, and passthru attributes articulate the functional connections between the packages. Reviewing examples of package expressions in Nixpkgs reveals typical patterns and best practices employed by the Nix community.

```
{ lib, stdenv, fetchurl }:

stdenv.mkDerivation rec {
  pname = "example-package";
  version = "1.0";

  src = fetchurl {
    url = "https://example.com/example-package-${version}.tar.gz";
    sha256 = "...";
  };

  buildInputs = [ libexample1 ];
  nativeBuildInputs = [ cmake ];
```

```
  meta = with lib; {
    description = "An example package within the Nixpkgs repository";
    homepage = "https://example.com";
    license = licenses.mit;
    maintainers = [ maintainers.johndoe ];
  };
}
```

The architecture of package expressions captures the declarative essence of Nix, with the mkDerivation function creating derivations that are then realized into store paths, ensuring consistent reproducibility and isolation across different environments.

To enhance workflow efficiency, developers and users often rely on tools like nixos-rebuild and nix-shell. These tools facilitate the building, testing, and modifying of packages directly from Nixpkgs, without requiring installation onto the system.

```
$ nix-build '<nixpkgs>' -A example-package
```

The above command builds the example-package from Nixpkgs. Such commands showcase the functional model that Nix employs, keeping system states pristine and making isolated package tests an operational norm rather than an exception.

Furthermore, the Nixpkgs repository often interacts with various overlays and overrides mechanisms, providing a method for users to extend packages without modifying the original Nixpkgs. This capacity for extensibility is a cornerstone of Nix's resilience to change and evolution. With overlays, users can introduce or modify packages by defining their expressions atop the existing repository, preserving original states and facilitating concurrent independent development.

```
self: super:

{
  example-package = super.example-package.overrideAttrs (oldAttrs: {
    version = "1.1";
  });
}
```

This snippet demonstrates modifying an existing package within Nixpkgs using an overlay, changing the version attribute without altering the original package definition.

Understanding the components, tools, and methodologies employed in searching and leveraging the Nixpkgs repository empowers users to adopt and adapt Nix packages efficiently. The breadth and depth of packages available in the Nixpkgs repository are testament to the collaborative power inherent in the Nix philosophy — an open, transparent, and reproducible approach to software packaging that continues to guide developers toward sustainable software management practices.

For more advanced usage, developers can delve into the intricacies of package management by interacting directly with the Nix build and evaluation codes. Navigating the repository on systems running Nix-based distributions, such as NixOS, provides the added advantage of system and environment integration — a recurring benefit of the homogeneity between the configuration language of individual packages and the system itself.

Through understanding the structure and navigation techniques of Nixpkgs, users can capitalize on the collective knowledge embedded across many thousands of package expressions. This repository serves not merely as a collection of software but a blueprint for deploying, using, and maintaining a coherent ecosystem that is robust, flexible, and capable of accommodating the needs of diverse computing environments and workflows. As with any open-source endeavor, contributing to the ongoing enrichment of Nixpkgs ensures that this repository remains a vital resource for software professionals dedicated to making computational resources more predictable and manageable for the future.

5.3 Package Expressions in Nix

The heart of software management in the Nix ecosystem lies within Nix package expressions. These expressions form the building blocks of package definitions in Nix, offering a declarative and functional syntax that describes the construction, composition, and dependencies of software packages. Understanding package expressions in Nix is essential not only for creating new packages but also for customizing and adapting existing ones through overlays and modifications.

At its core, a package expression in Nix captures the essence of software package management through a set of attributes defined in a purely functional programming language. This section explores the various components and syntax elements that constitute a robust package expression, highlighting the significant differences from traditional package managers, as well as providing practical coding examples.

Nix package expressions are normally written in files with a .nix extension and are evaluated in the context of a Nixpkgs environment to produce derivations, which later result in build outputs. These expressions effectively eliminate common issues like dependency conflicts and environment contamination by enforcing immutability and reproducibility across software components.

A typical package expression begins with attribute bindings, followed by a call to mkDerivation, which prepares a build environment based on the inputs specified. Consider the following simple example of a Nix package expression:

```
{ stdenv, fetchurl }:

stdenv.mkDerivation {
  pname = "sample";
  version = "1.0";

  src = fetchurl {
    url = "https://example.com/sample-${version}.tar.gz";
    sha256 = "0ssi1wpaf7plaswqqjwigppsg5fyh99vdlb9kzl7c9lng89ndq1c";
  };

  buildInputs = [ ];

  meta = {
    description = "A sample software package";
    license = stdenv.lib.licenses.mit;
  };
}
```

Attributes and their Significance:

- pname and version specify the package name and version respectively, crucial for generating unique and descriptive store paths.
- src defines the source of the package, typically obtained using the fetchurl function, which downloads source code and verifies its integrity with a checksum.
- buildInputs lists the dependencies required at build time. These

dependencies do not affect the runtime unless explicitly included in runtime dependencies.

- meta contains package metadata, such as the description, license information, and maintainers. This section aids package discovery and proper attribution.

Custom Build Phases: Nix allows the specification of custom build phases using override mechanisms, which offer flexibility in altering default build behaviors. Custom build phases can be declared using buildPhase, installPhase, etc. Here is an example illustrating the use of a custom build phase:

```
{ stdenv, fetchurl }:

stdenv.mkDerivation {
  pname = "custombuilder";
  version = "0.1";

  src = fetchurl {
    url = "https://example.com/custombuilder-${version}.tar.gz";
    sha256 = "1a2b3c4d5e6f7g8h9i0j1k2l3m4n5o6p7q8r9stuvwxyz";
  };

  buildInputs = [ ];

  buildPhase = ''
    echo "Building custombuilder..."
    make all
  '';

  installPhase = ''
    echo "Installing custombuilder..."
    mkdir -p $out/bin
    cp custombuilder $out/bin/
  '';

  meta = {
    description = "A package using custom build and install phases";
    license = stdenv.lib.licenses.mit;
  };
}
```

In this example, the buildPhase and installPhase attributes override the default phases with custom shell commands. This flexibility allows developers to tailor package builds to specific requirements without globally modifying the build system.

Nix Language Constructs: The Nix language provides rich constructs for composing expressions, including let bindings, conditionals, and function abstractions. These constructs increase expression modularity and reusability.

```
{ stdenv, fetchurl }:

let
  commonVersion = "2.0";
in

stdenv.mkDerivation {
  pname = "let-example";
  version = commonVersion;

  src = fetchurl {
    url = "https://example.com/let-example-${version}.tar.gz";
    sha256 = "abc123...456def";
  };

  meta = {
    description = "A package demonstrating let bindings";
    license = stdenv.lib.licenses.mit;
  };
}
```

In this expression, the let construct binds commonVersion, showcasing the capacity to define reusable components within package expressions. This feature not only reduces duplication but also streamlines updates and maintenance.

Function Abstractions: Nix package expressions can be defined as functions, where the inputs are explicitly passed as parameters. This abstraction allows packages to be flexible and reusable across different contexts. Below is an illustration of how one might define a package as a function:

```
{ stdenv, fetchurl }:

let
  makePackage = { name, version, sha256 }: stdenv.mkDerivation {
    pname = name;
    version = version;

    src = fetchurl {
      url = "https://example.com/${name}-${version}.tar.gz";
      sha256 = sha256;
    };

    meta = {
      description = "Function-based package for ${name}";
      license = stdenv.lib.licenses.mit;
    };
  };
in {
```

```
  sample1 = makePackage { name = "sample1"; version = "1.0"; sha256 = "111aaa
      ...333ccc"; };
  sample2 = makePackage { name = "sample2"; version = "2.0"; sha256 = "222bbb
      ...444ddd"; };
}
```

This function-based approach facilitates constructing customized derivations without replicating entire build instructions, which enhances both flexibility and clarity, especially when managing multiple similar packages. It also demonstrates the scalability of using Nix expressions in larger repositories.

Extensions and Overrides: The extensibility of Nix expressions is significantly enhanced by the use of overrides. Users can customize existing packages by changing or extending attributes without altering the original expression, which is crucial in maintaining software versions aligned with user-specific requirements.

```
let
  overrideExample = old: old.overrideAttrs (oldAttrs: {
    version = "2.1";
    meta = oldAttrs.meta // {
      description = "An overridden version of the package with a new description";
    };
  });
in

{ stdenv, fetchurl, examplePackage }:

overrideExample examplePackage
```

This snippet illustrates how the overrideAttrs function tailors an examplePackage, demonstrating the malleability of expressions in Nix for creating custom builds and adaptations without disrupting existing infrastructures.

Complex Dependencies and Conditional Builds: Nix supports complex dependency management, where conditional logic can adapt packages based on system configurations or environmental factors, ensuring compatibility and alignment with specific platforms or use cases.

```
{ stdenv, fetchurl, optionalDependencies ? null }:

stdenv.mkDerivation {
  pname = "conditional-package";
  version = "1.2";
```

```
  src = fetchurl {
    url = "https://example.com/conditional-package-${version}.tar.gz";
    sha256 = "...";
  };

  buildInputs = optionalDependencies != null then optionalDependencies else [ ];

  meta = {
    description = "A package with optional, conditionally included dependencies";
    license = stdenv.lib.licenses.mit;
  };
}
```

This method of leveraging optional parameters in Nix expressions extends a package's adaptability to different environments, emphasizing Nix's functional approach to reconciling platform-specific requirements.

Through this detailed exploration of package expressions in Nix, one gains insight into the versatile methodology underpinning the creation and management of software packages. Nix's functional paradigm offers precise control for developers while maintaining high levels of system consistency and reproducibility. The combination of declarative syntax with powerful functional constructs positions Nix as a leading solution for effective package management, enhancing the agility and sustainability of software systems. Understanding these principles paves the way for mastering Nix expressions, essential for maximizing Nix's potential in automation, scalability, and complexity management.

5.4 Building and Modifying Packages

Building software packages from source and making modifications to existing package expressions are foundational practices within the Nix ecosystem. The ability to compile software from its source code creates a highly customizable environment, allowing users to tailor software to specific needs while maintaining the reproducibility and isolation that Nix provides. This section explores the detailed processes involved in building and modifying packages using Nix, from configuring derivation attributes to best practices in testing and contributing changes.

In the Nix system, packages are defined as derivations. A derivation is a build plan that specifies how software is to be compiled, including input files, build instructions, and dependencies. The beauty of Nix's approach to building packages lies in its completely declarative nature, which eliminates build-time side effects and ensures consistency across different systems.

Building from Source:

Building packages from source in Nix involves several steps:

1. **Defining the Derivation:** To initiate a build, a package expression must first be crafted, specifying the components needed such as source code and dependencies.

```
{ stdenv, fetchurl }:

stdenv.mkDerivation {
  pname = "simple-package";
  version = "1.0";

  src = fetchurl {
    url = "https://example.com/simple-package-${version}.tar.gz";
    sha256 = "0badcafe1234567890deadbeefcafebabe1122334455667788990ffee";
  };

  buildInputs = [ dep1 dep2 ];

  meta = {
    description = "A simplified package build example";
    license = stdenv.lib.licenses.mit;
  };
}
```

2. **Executing the Build:** The build process is executed using the nix-build command, which evaluates the derivation and produces the package in the Nix store.

```
$ nix-build -A simple-package
```

3. **Verifying Outputs:** After the build, verify the outputs in the Nix store to confirm the package has been constructed successfully.

```
Output path '/nix/store/xyz-simple-package-1.0' should contain the built package artifacts.
```

Building packages from source is often required when pre-built binaries are not available or when custom configuration options are needed. Nix's reproducible build process ensures that the package's behavior will be identical whenever it is built, given consistent inputs.

Modifying Existing Packages:

Modifying existing packages involves changing attributes or build instructions in their derivation. Nix facilitates this through various mechanisms allowing end-users to adapt packages without disrupting the original definition.

1. **Overriding Package Attributes:** The overrideAttrs function allows developers to specify changes to package attributes without duplicating the entire expression.

```
let
  modifiedPackage = origPackage.overrideAttrs (old: rec {
    version = "1.1";
    src = fetchurl {
      url = "https://example.com/simple-package-1.1.tar.gz";
      sha256 = "1234567890deadbeef1234567890deadbeef1234567890deadbeef1234567";
    };
  });
in

{ stdenv, fetchurl, origPackage }:

modifiedPackage
```

2. **Adding Additional Patches or Build Inputs:** Including patches or additional build inputs can be executed using similar override operations or modifications directly in the derivation.

```
{ stdenv, fetchurl, origPackage, patchfile }:

origPackage.overrideAttrs (old: rec {
  patches = old.patches or [] ++ [ ./path/to/patchfile ];
})
```

3. **Customization with Configuration Flags:** Customizing the build configuration is often necessary to enable or disable features in the software build process. This is achieved through the configureFlags attribute.

```
{ stdenv, fetchurl, origPackage }:

origPackage.overrideAttrs (oldAttrs: {
  configureFlags = oldAttrs.configureFlags or [] ++ [ "--enable-featureX" ] ++ [ "--
        disable-featureY" ];
})
```

Best Practices in Building and Modifying:

To ensure consistency and maintainability while building and modifying packages, several best practices are recommended:

- **Use Variables for Common Values:** Use Nix's let bindings or functions to define commonly reused values like versions or source URLs. This reduces repetition and errors when updating expressions.

```
let
  commonVersion = "2.1";
in

{ stdenv, fetchurl }:

stdenv.mkDerivation {
  pname = "example-package";
  version = commonVersion;

  src = fetchurl {
    url = "https://example.com/example-package-${version}.tar.gz";
    sha256 = "...";
  };

  meta = {
    description = "Example package with common version variable";
    license = stdenv.lib.licenses.mit;
  };
}
```

- **Minimize Side Effects:** Ensure side-effect-free builds by using Nix's sandboxing capabilities, ensuring builds occur in a controlled environment.

- **Test Changes Thoroughly:** Use Nix's testing and sandbox environments to verify changes comprehensively, reducing the risk of inconsistencies in production systems.

- **Document Extensively:** Maintain clear and detailed comments within the package expressions to explain rationale behind build configurations and modifications. This aids maintainability and collaboration.

Nixpkgs Testing and Contribution:

When introducing changes or new packages to the Nixpkgs repository, the contribution process involves additional steps of verification and adherence to community guidelines. This facilitates high-quality and reproducible contributions in line with Nixpkgs standards.

1. **Create a Feature Branch:** Begin by developing modifications in a feature branch, ensuring the main branch remains stable.

```
$ git checkout -b feature/new-package
```

2. **Use Nixpkgs Review Tools:** Utilize tools such as nixpkgs-review to automate the testing of changes against existing packages and configurations.

3. **Collaborate with Community:** Engage with the Nix community through pull requests and discussions to refine contributions and gain feedback.

```
# Commit your changes
$ git commit -m "Add new package example-package"

# Push to the remote repository
$ git push origin feature/new-package
```

Nix's structured build and modification processes enable system administrators, developers, and enthusiast users alike to manage and test software with unparalleled efficacy. The alignment of Nix's functional philosophy with rigorous build practices helps modulate the challenges associated with modern software deployments, making it an essential tool in the DevOps toolkit.

By adhering to best practices in building and modifying packages, users not only enhance their control over software configurations but also contribute to an ecosystem where software environments are more predictable, repeatable, and collaborative. This alignment not only drives individual productivity but also fosters collective enhancement of shared systems, abiding by Nix's principle of reproducible builds as a universally shared goal.

The knowledge gained in building and modifying packages embodies a core aspect of mastering the Nix ecosystem, empowering users to harness Nix's full potential in creating sophisticated software environments that meet the nuanced demands of diverse applications. Through these practices, one truly appreciates the transformative effect of Nix's declarative and functional approach in the realm of package management.

5.5 Contributing to Nixpkgs

The Nixpkgs repository represents a dynamic, collaborative effort and a central hub for Nix packages. It is a living repository that thrives on contributions from a vibrant community of developers, maintainers, and users. Contributing to Nixpkgs not only enhances the repository but also drives the open-source ecosystem forward, ensuring that a rich variety of software is available to Nix users. This section delves into the nuances of contributing to Nixpkgs, covering the workflow, guidelines, and tools necessary for effective engagement and collaboration.

Understanding the Contribution Process:

Engaging with Nixpkgs requires a structured approach to ensure contributions are productive and align with community standards. Here is a high-level overview of the typical contribution process, which involves discussing ideas, implementing changes, and submitting them for review.

- **Identify and Discuss Issues:** Begin the contribution process by identifying packages or improvements that align with your skills and interests. Utilize community platforms such as GitHub Issues, the NixOS Discourse, and IRC to discuss your ideas, ensuring they align with repository goals.
- **Fork and Clone the Repository:** Create a personal fork of the Nixpkgs repository on GitHub to serve as a basis for making changes.

```
# On GitHub, click "Fork" on the Nixpkgs repository page
$ git clone https://github.com/yourusername/nixpkgs.git
$ cd nixpkgs
```

- **Create a Branch:** Work within a dedicated branch for your changes, isolating development from the main branch.

```
$ git checkout -b add-new-package
```

- **Make and Test Changes:** Implement changes to the package expressions or other areas of interest. Thoroughly test modifications locally using Nix's comprehensive build and test tools to ensure the changes do not introduce issues.

```
{ lib, stdenv, fetchurl }:

stdenv.mkDerivation {
  pname = "new-package";
  version = "0.1";

  src = fetchurl {
    url = "https://example.com/new-package-${version}.tar.gz";
    sha256 = "
        abcdef1234567890fedcba0987654321abcdef1234567890fedcba0987654321
        ";
  };

  meta = with lib; {
    description = "A new package for contributing to Nixpkgs";
    license = licenses.mit;
    maintainers = with maintainers; [yourGitHubHandle];
  };
}
```

- **Run Linting and Review Tools:** Use tools like nixpkgs-review to verify conformity with the repository's coding standards and ensure quality and consistency of changes.

```
$ nixpkgs-review pr
```

- **Submit a Pull Request:** Push changes to your fork and create a pull request on the official Nixpkgs repository. Clearly state the purpose and significance of changes, including any issue references, in the pull request description.

```
# Push changes to the branch on GitHub
$ git push origin add-new-package
```

Upon creating a pull request (PR), engage with reviewers and the community for discussions, feedback, and iterations.

Adhering to Nixpkgs Guidelines:

Contributions to Nixpkgs must adhere to well-established guidelines paramount for maintaining the quality and stability of the repository. Key guidelines include the following:

- **Ensure Reproducibility:** Packages should build reproducibly on supported platforms, ensuring consistency across different systems.

- **Provide Extensive Documentation:** Accurate metadata along with clear comments and descriptions in package expressions enhance comprehension and usage. Updating relevant documentation, release notes, or changelogs is often necessary when changes impact end users.

- **Conform to Repository Standards:** Code must adhere to formatting and organizational standards within Nixpkgs. Running formatters and linters, such as nixpkgs-fmt, is recommended.

```
$ nixpkgs-fmt path/to/package.nix
```

- **Integrate Tests where Applicable:** Ensure packages include tests for build and runtime verification when feasible. Use passthru.tests for defining NixOS tests as part of package attributes.

```
{ lib, stdenv, fetchurl }:

stdenv.mkDerivation {
  pname = "test-package";
  version = "0.1";

  src = fetchurl {
    url = "https://example.com/test-package-${version}.tar.gz";
    sha256 = "...";
  };

  passthru.tests = {
    testPhase = ''
      run-test-suite
    '';
  };

  meta = with lib; {
    description = "A package with an integrated test suite";
    license = licenses.mit;
  };
}
```

- **Maintain Backward Compatibility:** Ensure modifications do not break existing workflows or dependents. Provide migration paths or aliasing for deprecated features or versions.

Engaging with the Community:

The vibrant Nix community offers an inclusive environment for collaboration, learning, and knowledge sharing. Actively participating in discussions and reviews not only strengthens one's skills but also contributes to a culture of mutual growth.

- **Participate in Discussions:** Leverage forums and mailing lists to engage with other contributors, seek advice, and stay informed on community happenings.
- **Review Existing Pull Requests:** Providing reviews and feedback on others' pull requests enhances quality control and fosters reciprocal contributions, enriching the development ecosystem.
- **Attend or Host Meetups:** Taking part in, or hosting, community events such as NixCon or local meetups aids in networking, facilitating knowledge exchange, and driving enthusiasm.

Overcoming Challenges and Impediments:

Contributing to open-source repositories like Nixpkgs, although rewarding, presents challenges such as understanding existing systems, ensuring cross-compatibility, and navigating evolving specifications. Strategies to overcome these include:

- **Continuous Learning:** Stay updated on changes in the Nix ecosystem through official documentation, emerging tools, and peer discussions to adapt to evolving paradigms.
- **Seek Mentorship:** Collaborate with more experienced community members or mentors to gain insights and practical experience in advanced package management.
- **Iterate and Improve:** Utilize a feedback-driven approach to iterate rapidly on changes, refining solutions in response to user and peer input.

Through diligent adherence to best practices and proactive engagement with the Nix community, contributors to Nixpkgs play a pivotal role in reinforcing the integrity, diversity, and functionality of the repository. This participatory model underpins the growth and sustenance of an open-source model, leveraging collective expertise to tackle the complexities of modern software distribution and management.

Engaging in this collaborative practice not only enriches the Nixpkgs repository but also nurtures an ecosystem conducive to innovation and excellence. The open-source landscape of Nix serves as a testament to the power of community-driven development, where every contribution adds to the shared value and utility, enhancing the collective capability to forge resilient, future-ready systems.

5.6 Customizing Packages with Overrides

Customizing software packages in Nix through overrides is a powerful feature that enables users to adapt existing package expressions to meet specific requirements without altering the underlying package definitions. This capability provides immense flexibility within the Nix ecosystem, allowing changes to be applied on a per-instance basis while maintaining the integrity of the original package set. This section explores the mechanisms for customizing packages using Nix's override capabilities, detailing the syntax, methodologies, and best practices that facilitate comprehensive package customization.

Introduction to Overrides:

Overrides in Nix allow users to redefine or extend the attributes of existing package expressions. By employing overrides, developers can introduce modifications such as changing build inputs, applying patches, or updating versions without modifying the original Nix expressions stored within the Nixpkgs repository. This practice ensures that local customizations do not interfere with global package definitions, maintaining clean and universal configurations.

The primary mechanism for implementing overrides in Nix involves the functions override and overrideAttrs. These functions provide a way to selectively alter the package's attributes or customize how they are used in the derivation process.

Using overrideAttrs**:**

The overrideAttrs function offers the capability to alter specific fields within a package's attribute set. It accepts a function that returns a set of attributes to replace or extend the existing ones.

```
{ stdenv, fetchurl, originalPackage }:

originalPackage.overrideAttrs (oldAttrs: rec {
  version = "2.0";
  src = fetchurl {
    url = "https://example.com/new-version-2.0.tar.gz";
    sha256 = "ab12cd34ef56gh78ij90kl12mn34op56qr78st90uvwx12yz3456a789bcdef123
        ";
  };
  buildInputs = oldAttrs.buildInputs ++ [ newDependency ];
})
```

In this example, the overrideAttrs function is used to update the version and src fields of the original package while adding an additional build input. By accessing the oldAttrs, users can build upon the existing expression, maintaining desired properties and adapting others.

Advanced Attribute Overrides:

Beyond simple field replacements, overrideAttrs supports deeper customizations involving build phases, patches, and other derivation behaviors.

- **Customizing Build Phases:** Developers can specify custom building operations by overriding phases such as buildPhase or installPhase.

```
{ stdenv, fetchurl, originalPackage }:

originalPackage.overrideAttrs (oldAttrs: rec {
  buildPhase = ''
    echo "Running custom build phase..."
    make all
  '';
})
```

- **Applying Patches:** Overrides allow patches to be introduced to source code before building, facilitating bug fixes or feature enhancements.

```
{ stdenv, fetchurl, originalPackage, patchFile }:

originalPackage.overrideAttrs (oldAttrs: rec {
  patches = oldAttrs.patches or [] ++ [ ./path/to/patchFile ];
})
```

Using override**:**

The override function modifies packages by altering the arguments passed to them. It operates on a slightly higher level than overrideAttrs, allowing changes in the inputs provided to the package function itself.

```
(originalPackage {
  inherit arg1 arg2;
}).override (args: {
  arg1 = "newValueForArg1";
  arg2 = "alteredConfigurationValue";
})
```

This approach is beneficial when the customization requires adjusting underlying dependencies or the initial configuration of the package derivation function.

Combining Overrides with Overlays:

In scenarios where extensive customizations are necessary, combining overrides with overlays offers a powerful strategy. Overlays allow layers of customization to be stacked upon existing expressions, composed of custom attributes or even fully new package expressions.

```
self: super:

{
  customPackage = super.originalPackage.overrideAttrs (oldAttrs: {
    version = "3.0";
    buildInputs = oldAttrs.buildInputs ++ [ self.additionalTool ];
  });
  additionalTool = super.someTool.overrideAttrs (oldAttrs: {
    meta = oldAttrs.meta // {
      description = "Customized version with additional functionality";
    };
  });
}
```

Through overlays, users have a flexible mechanism to define and apply batch customizations, reducing duplication and enhancing the manageability of changes across multiple packages.

Best Practices for Package Customization:

To effectively leverage Nix's override system, certain best practices should be followed to ensure maintainability, clarity, and compatibility:

- **Encapsulation with Function Abstractions:** Utilize functions to encapsulate complex or repetitive customization patterns, promoting modularity and reusability.

```
let
  customizePkg = pkg: attrs: pkg.overrideAttrs (oldAttrs: attrs);
in

{ stdenv, fetchurl, originalPackage }:

customizePkg originalPackage {
  version = "3.1";
  patches = [ ./patchFile1 ./patchFile2 ];
}
```

- **Separation of Concerns:** Isolate overrides from core package definitions to prevent unintentional alterations of default behaviors. This separation helps maintain clean delineations between system-global defaults and local customizations.

- **Documentation and Clarity:** Provide thorough commentary and documentation in override expressions to make clear why certain changes are applied. This practice assists future maintainers and collaborators in understanding the effects and intent behind customizations.

- **Robust Testing:** Ensure customizations are thoroughly tested using isolated environments or devshells, relying on Nix's inherent sandboxing to verify compatibility and functionality.

- **Integration with Continuous Integration (CI) Pipelines:** When deploying custom packages in production environments, integrating override expressions with CI pipelines is crucial for validating changes across development iterations.

Use Cases Highlighting Customization Needs:

Customizing Nix packages using overrides is driven by various real-world needs:

- **Environment-Specific Builds:** Adjust builds for different deployment targets, such as enabling optimizations for specific architectures or enabling features constrained to enterprise-level deployments.

- **Experimental Feature Testing:** Easily toggle experimental features or patches on a per-environment basis, facilitating rapid testing cycles without impacting stable environments.
- **Dependency Upgrades or Downgrades:** Swiftly adapt to upstream changes in dependencies, either by upgrading to leverage new improvements or downgrading to maintain compatibility with other systems.
- **Collaborative Development:** Collaborate on ephemeral versions of packages for development projects, sharing overrides without impacting master sources in communal repositories.

By mastering the use of overrides, Nix users can harness the full range of customization possibilities within the Nix ecosystem, tailoring software experiences to precise requirements. This adaptability not only empowers individual developers but also ensures that system deployments can be aligned with dynamic operational needs, supporting a proactive software management philosophy fostered by Nix's declarative and functional paradigms.

Through sophisticated customization strategies, an enterprise or personal environment can leverage Nix's reproducibility and consistency to cultivate sustainable, versatile, and continuously evolving software infrastructures. This flexibility contributes to maximizing the potential of Nix package management in crafting solutions that resonate with the demands of modern, complex computing landscapes.

Chapter 6

Building and Installing Software with Nix

Building and installing software with Nix revolves around its ability to create deterministic and isolated builds. Using Nix build expressions, users can specify precise instructions for compiling and packaging software, ensuring that outputs are consistent regardless of the underlying system. The build process leverages the Nix store to manage inputs and outputs securely, facilitating the installation and retrieval of packages without conflict. Nix's approach eliminates common issues related to dependency management and version mismatches, providing a streamlined and reliable method for software deployment across multiple environments while maintaining reproducibility and integrity.

6.1 Understanding the Build Process

The Nix build process operates as a sophisticated system designed to compile software in a unique deterministic manner. By meticulously tracking dependencies and the environment, Nix ensures that each build is an exact reconstruction, regardless of where or when it is conducted. This section delves into the intricacies of the Nix build process, highlighting how it achieves precision and consistency.

At the core of Nix's ability to ensure a consistent build environment is its use of *pure functions*. A Nix build expression acts as a pure function where the outputs solely depend on the specified inputs, without any hidden or hidden states. This dichotomy between input and output is fundamental in understanding how Nix achieves reproducibility in software builds.

One of the critical components of the build process is the Nix *derivation*. A derivation is a low-level representation of a package build, encapsulating various attributes such as build dependencies, build scripts, and any necessary metadata. The derivation dictates how Nix derives outputs from the specified inputs.

Nix employs a *lazy evaluation* strategy in managing derivations. It evaluates expressions only when their outputs are required, which optimizes efficiency by avoiding unnecessary computations.

```
{ stdenv, fetchurl }:
stdenv.mkDerivation {
  name = "hello-2.10";
  src = fetchurl {
    url = "http://ftpmirror.gnu.org/hello/hello-2.10.tar.gz";
    sha256 = "sha256:0ssi1wpaf7plaswqqjwigppsg5fyh99vdlb9kzl7c9lng89nd21i";
  };
  buildInputs = [ ];
}
```

This simple derivation defines a build for the "hello" software version 2.10. It leverages the stdenv.mkDerivation function to encapsulate the build details. The src attribute specifies the source, downloaded via the fetchurl function, complete with the corresponding SHA-256 checksum to ensure integrity.

Within the build process, the Nix runtime environment is meticulously constructed to reflect a closed world. This principle implies that all dependencies are declared explicitly, leaving no room for untracked or unpredictable influences from the local environment. During the build, Nix generates an isolated filesystem hierarchy under the Nix store, with paths like /nix/store/$<hash>-$<name>-<version> representing different derivation components.

A pertinent example of Nix's controlled environment can be demonstrated through hermetic builds. Hermetic or sandboxed builds run in a chroot environment isolated from the host system, ensuring complete dependency traceability.

```
$ nix-build --option build-use-sandbox true hello.nix
```

The use of the –option build-use-sandbox true flag in this example enforces the sandbox environment, enhancing discipline in defining dependencies.

One noteworthy feature of Nix is its ability to manage multiple versions of a package concurrently without interference. This is a direct outcome of the Nix store's structure, allowing hashed paths rather than traditional global names. Consequently, different builds and versions reside independently, avoiding "dependency hell."

Nix's dependency model emphasizes exactness and predictability. Dependencies are pinned by specific versions, checksums, or hashes, meaning that once a build is stabilized on certain dependencies, it can be reliably reproduced. This rigour during the specification phase makes Nix powerful for different development stages, from development to production deployment.

Consider a scenario wherein a project uses an external library with a specific version demand. A standard system would require manually ensuring compatibility, while Nix's model natively incorporates version locking within its expression.

Another distinctive feature of Nix's build process is the comprehensive garbage collection mechanism. While the Nix store accumulates packages over time, users can safely execute garbage collection to reclaim disk space without risking breaking dependencies associated with still-referenced packages.

```
$ nix-collect-garbage
```

This command only removes packages not referenced by any current derivations, demonstrating Nix's robust dependency tracker.

Furthermore, the Nix build process recognizes when a specific build is already present in the Nix store, bypassing redundant builds. This 'build once, run anywhere' philosophy boosts efficiency on repeated or shared builds.

```
$ nix-build hello.nix
building path(s) '/nix/store/<hash>-hello-2.10'
...
$ nix-build hello.nix
these derivations will be built:
  /nix/store/<hash>-hello-2.10.drv
building '/nix/store/<hash>-hello-2.10.drv'...
no change
```

As illustrated, once the build is completed, subsequent attempts reflect the presence of existing outputs in the Nix store, obviating the need for redundant compiling.

Nix's approach reduces integration issues prevalent in conventional systems by ensuring precise management of dependencies and environments. Beyond creating deterministic builds, this model seamlessly aligns with concepts like continuous integration (CI) and continuous delivery (CD), where consistent environments across build stages are imperative.

Furthermore, advanced use cases extend to cross-compilation scenarios, wherein Nix leverages the defined system-specific attributes to produce binaries tailored to different architectures without modification to the core expression.

In this comprehensive examination, we have analyzed the foundational methodologies of the Nix build process, revealing how it orchestrates the transformation of build inputs into reliable, repeatable outputs unaltered by external conditions. In progressing through the subsequent sections, these principles form a vital basis for deeper exploration into sophisticated Nix functionalities.

6.2 Writing a Simple Build Expression

A build expression in Nix defines the series of steps and dependencies required to transform source code into a binary package. By writing a build expression, users communicate the necessary instructions to compile and configure software environments in a reproducible manner. This section explores the essentials of crafting a Nix expression that encapsulates these processes, providing a clear understanding of its components and their purposes.

The fundamental structure of a Nix expression lies in the *attribute set*, which allows for an organized specification of essential parameters such as the source, dependencies, and resulting outputs. Each attribute within the set has a specific role, fostering clarity and readability in the definition.

An essential fragment of a typical build expression is the mkDerivation function. It abstracts the process of creating a derivation, the computational step resulting in a software build ready for evaluation.

```
{ pkgs ? import <nixpkgs> {} }:
let
  stdenv = pkgs.stdenv;
in
stdenv.mkDerivation {
  name = "myProgram";
  src = pkgs.fetchurl {
    url = "http://example.com/myProgram-1.0.tar.gz";
    sha256 = "sha256-hash";
  };
  buildInputs = with pkgs; [ gcc openssl ];
  buildPhase = ''
    ./configure --prefix=$out
    make
  '';
  installPhase = ''
    make install
  '';
}
```

This example outlines a straightforward Nix expression. The expression starts with importing the nixpkgs repository, facilitated indirectly through the pkgs attribute, to gain access to a comprehensive set of predefined packages.

In this context, stdenv acts as a standard environment providing default functionalities used throughout the build process, including basic compiler infrastructure like gcc.

The name attribute designates the resultant package's identifier, crucial for distinguishing outputs within the vast Nix store. The src attribute invokes the fetchurl function, occasionally providing network route information to obtain the required source files and ensuring they align with an expected SHA-256 checksum for authenticity verification.

Dependencies vital for compilation or runtime as delineated in the buildInputs attribute are crucial in identifying libraries or tools the package depends on. The with statement streamlines namespace access, allowing intuitive referencing within the expression.

The buildPhase and installPhase scripts embody the operational core, where actual build and installation commands are executed. These attribute phases can encapsulate standard language constructs such as bash scripting, enabling versatile and comprehensive procedural definitions.

Understanding these components enables the authoring of a build expression that succinctly describes the transformation sequence and dependencies from source to binary. Each attribute is customizable, fostering adaptability and optimizing for specific requirements or contexts.

The syntax of the Nix language underpins the expression creation process, characterized by its functional nature and immutability principles. A *let-in* construct enables fine-grained control over variable scoping, offering a robust mechanism for simplifying expressions and ensuring referential transparency.

Further refinement can occur through the use of *overlays* or the *overrideAttrs* function, which enhance modularity and encourage more extensive reuse of existing expressions by altering or extending attributes of derivations.

```
let
  original = import ./default.nix;
in
original.overrideAttrs (oldAttrs: rec {
  buildInputs = oldAttrs.buildInputs ++ [ additionalLibrary ];
})
```

In this example, attributes from a pre-existing derivation are overridden, demonstrating modularity by incorporating additional libraries with the assistance of functional programming paradigms inherent in Nix.

The *meta* attribute provides informative metadata about the package, such as its license type, home page, or maintainers, promoting greater transparency, compliance, and manual curation.

```
meta = {
  description = "An example program";
  license = lib.licenses.gpl3Plus;
  maintainers = with lib.maintainers; [ yourName ];
```

```
  platforms = lib.platforms.linux;
};
```

This enhances integration with other Nix tooling and facilitates automated processes, such as dependency resolution and license tracking.

Parsing through nix-env outputs or the structure of extended repositories like nixpkgs, developers gain insights into the multi-layered architecture and dependency interactions, effectively learning from community-defined patterns.

In crafting a Nix expression, validation and iterative improvements are crucial. Users are encouraged to leverage tools such as nix-instantiate for testing build expressions and nix-env for environment manipulation, ensuring output consistency throughout extended lifecycles.

```
$ nix-instantiate --eval myProgram.nix
```

This preview activity enables an ahead-of-time evaluation approach, flagging errors or misconfigurations in complex expressions before final build execution.

The delineated principles in writing a Nix build expression establish a foundation for more practical applications in constructing verbose, adaptable expressions efficiently and accurately aligning with the Nix paradigms of reproducibility and isolation.

6.3 Managing Build Inputs and Outputs

One of the central tenets of the Nix package manager is its capability to precisely manage build inputs and outputs, ensuring complete reproducibility and dependency tracking throughout the build lifecycle. In this section, we explore the mechanisms by which Nix maintains control over these critical aspects, facilitating further understanding and mastery of its potent ecosystem.

At its core, managing build inputs involves explicitly declaring all dependencies required to transform source code into a functional output. These inputs can be classified into two primary categories: *build-time dependencies* and *runtime dependencies*. Build-time dependencies constitute tools and libraries necessary during the compilation phase, whereas runtime dependencies are libraries or services required by the software during its execution.

Nix requires an explicit statement of these dependencies to create a *closed world*, a paradigm wherein only specified, derivation-bound elements influence the build process. This principle underlies Nix's deterministic guarantee, providing assurance that all dependencies are tracked and controllable.

```
buildInputs = [ gcc make ];
propagatedBuildInputs = [ openssl zlib ];
```

In this sample snippet, buildInputs acts as an attribute listing direct build dependencies—tools like gcc and make, integral for compiling the program in question. On the other hand, propagatedBuildInputs delineates dependencies that must persist beyond the build process, effectively becoming part of the runtime environment seen by dependent packages.

Nix utilizes hashes to ensure that inputs remain unspoiled. It calculates the SHA-256 hash for all inputs in the /nix/store path, automatically coupling the inputs to the outputs through these computational fingerprints.

Creating a derivation, the build expression undergoes evaluation through the nix-instantiate command or similar, generating a *store path*—a unique directory within the /nix/store associated with the output of the build.

```
$ nix-instantiate myProgram.nix
/nix/store/<hash>-myProgram.drv
```

Outputs stem from the *name, version*, and content of input derivations, representing the conclusive artifacts, typically binaries in the form of executables or libraries, resulting from the build process.

Managing multiple outputs in a highly granular manner is feasible in Nix.

```
{
  outputs = [ "out" "dev" ];
  ...
  installPhase = ''
    mkdir -p $out/bin
    cp myProgram $out/bin
    mkdir -p $dev/include
```

```
    cp myProgram.h $dev/include
  '';
}
```

Here, multiple output paths are defined within a single derivation via the outputs attribute, splitting the primary output (out) from a secondary development output (dev), where header files or auxiliary information might reside.

Beyond merely identifying the fundamental constituents of inputs and outputs, effective management extends to version control and dependency graphing—ensuring that all target environments operate from an identical set of libraries and tools.

```
nix-store --query --graph
```

provides a powerful mechanism to visualize the dependency tree associated with a specific derivation, aiding developers in identifying and resolving potential conflicts or redundancy within dependencies.

```
$ nix-store --query --graph /nix/store/<hash>-myProgram | dot -Tpdf -o myProgram-
      deps.pdf
```

This command uses Graphviz to produce a visual representation of the interlinked dependencies contained within the nix store path, granting insight into the often-complex hierarchical dependencies in an accessible format.

The advantages of Nix's dependency model are further exemplified during dependency update or rollback scenarios. Through the integration of nix-pull and nix-rollback, systems can flexibly transition between states or environments:

```
$ nix-env --rollback
```

This command allows a smooth regression to prior environments within the nix profile, serving as a corrective measure against unintended consequences from newly introduced dependencies.

Fundamentally, no tool like Nix exists in isolation. Managing inputs and outputs also encompasses networking aspects, like caching. Using Nix's-in-built *binary cache*, package builds are stored for rapid retrieval, mitigating redundant compilation and conserving computational resources.

```
$ nix copy --to cache.somerepo.org /nix/store/<hash>
```

This example command replicates store paths to a remote binary cache, enabling downstream consumers to reap the benefits of cached builds—fundamental for CI/CD pipelines or organizations deploying at scale.

As projects grow in complexity, the orchestration sculpts a need for nested dependencies or developmental environments encapsulated through *overlays* and *overrides*. These constructs manipulate build inputs more dynamically, promoting extensibility while maintaining control over compositional components. They become pivotal when collating various dependencies beyond the capabilities of individual nix expressions.

Ultimately, the principles unfolding from effective management of build inputs and outputs embody the broader ethos of functional package management via Nix. Expanding usage borders, translating methodologies to broader built ecosystems, and perpetuating development agility are transcendent goals enabled by the robust, deterministic control over dependencies and environments within Nix's frameworks.

6.4 Using Nix-build for Software Compilation

The nix-build command forms a cornerstone of the Nix package management system, providing a robust mechanism for software compilation. This section concentrates on detailing the functionalities, options, and refined usage of the nix-build command, demonstrating its pivotal role in transforming Nix expressions into functional software outputs.

At its essence, nix-build evaluates a build expression and triggers the derivation process, orchestrating the creation of all necessary dependencies as described in corresponding .nix files. This evaluation ensures all paths leading to the desired output are traversed and calculated, fostering integrity and completeness in generating the final output.

Consider a basic command invocation:

```
$ nix-build myProgram.nix
```

This command initiates the process of interpreting the Nix expression in myProgram.nix, overseeing the transformation from source to executable binary, depositing results in the ./result symlink within the current directory. The simplicity conceals a significant degree of under-the-hood sophistication, primarily driven by the Nix expression's defined derivation and dependencies.

To facilitate more detailed examinations, options like –show-trace enable users to observe execution paths more granularly, exposing any irregularities or errors encountered during processing:

```
$ nix-build myProgram.nix --show-trace
```

This diagnostic utility provides comprehensive feedback, crucial for debugging complex derivations or significant dependency graphs.

One of nix-build's strengths is its ability to accommodate project-specific configurations through the use of attributes and variables, tapping into greater flexibility. It can be argued that real-world projects often necessitate individualized settings, tailored via command-line arguments or environment variables during the build process.

```
$ nix-build myProgram.nix --argstr version "1.2.3"
```

Here, the –argstr option specifies a particular version to be incorporated into the build process, as dynamically determined from within the expression. Expressions use these parameters for configurations anticipated to benefit from runtime modifications, offering adaptability without explicit changes to the original file.

The output directory of nix-build is customizable via the –out-link flag, dictating an alternative symlink destination for build products, aiding organization of multiple builds.

```
$ nix-build myProgram.nix --out-link=./build-results
```

As with many modern compilation systems, nix-build supports parallelization to expedite build processes across multicore architectures. Factors such as system configuration and available hardware govern resource allocation, controlled using the –max-jobs parameter:

```
$ nix-build myProgram.nix --max-jobs 4
```

In systems with robust hardware capabilities, the option to split workloads is invaluable, enhancing throughput and accelerating resource-intensive compilation processes.

For projects encapsulating multiple build targets, the –attr flag provides a mechanism to pinpoint specific derivations:

```
$ nix-build release.nix --attr myProgram
```

Employing this option enables selective builds from among projects with compound derivations, enhancing modular development workflows and promoting efficient allocation of build resources.

Furthermore, Nix-build incorporates extensive logging facilities to monitor real-time build progress, employing verbosity flags to calibrate output levels according to stage requirements, such as –verbose or –quiet for detailed or minimalism-focused output control, respectively.

However, what distinguishes nix-build within the ecosystem is its interplay with the Nix store and binary caches. Each build evaluation naturally contours to create and reference specific /nix/store paths, alongside functionality accommodating secure, facile sharing of build outputs through caching mechanisms.

The synergy between nix-build artifacts and binary caches circumvents redundant recompilation and aligns perfectly with systems configured for continuous build and test cycles, typical to DevOps strategies. By caching output hashes, subsequent builds can rely upon previously-completed derivations, enhancing process efficiency:

```
$ nix-build myProgram.nix --fallback
```

The integration of caches means pre-existing outputs are utilized, immediately reverting to locally compiling only when no valid external derivations exist, preserving time and resources.

In illustrative terms, consider invoking nix-build across distributed systems or CI platforms—where nix-build executes freshly within sandboxed environments:

```
$ nix-build --option sandbox true myProgram.nix
```

This inert build environment—sandboxed by nature—ensures that each build session remains insulated from any host system variabilities or detrimental configurations, safeguarding consistency throughout the application's final deployment.

The principles governing nix-build's behavior also foster extensive reproducibility in derived artifacts, ensuring uniformity across diversified infrastructures—whether an independent workstation build or enterprise-scale deployment. This consistency, coupled with the functionality of comprehensive diagnostics, flexibility through argument passing, caching utilities, and support for parallelized workloads, underscores nix-build as invaluable to handling complex software compilation scenarios reconcilable within Nix-based ecosystems.

6.5 Installation of Software via Nix-store

The Nix store, structured under /nix/store, is a sophisticated repository designed to manage and store software packages within the Nix ecosystem. Within this section, we explore the nuances of software installation, retrieval, and management facilitated by the Nix store, elucidating the key principles and mechanics that underpin this process to ensure reproducibility and integrity.

Fundamentally, the Nix store operates as an immutable, content-addressed storage for all packages and their dependencies. Each package stored in the Nix store is represented as a symlink uniquely identified by a hash, derived from a combination of the package's build inputs and parameters—the very cornerstone of Nix's guarantee of immutability and reproducibility. This content-addressable nature ensures that the same derivation will always result in the identical store path, thus manifesting one of Nix's highly determinative aspects.

```
/nix/store/<hash>-<name>-<version>
```

Here, <hash> is an SHA-256 hash generated from all inputs and build instructions, demonstrating the closed-world principle—the foundation of Nix's capabilities to avoid conflicts like dependency hell by isolating all components within these paths.

The installation process within the Nix store begins with the evaluation of a Nix expression. Upon evaluation, the output is a derivation encapsulating the necessary build parameters, dependencies, and outputs. The Nix store only includes packages once the build process concludes successfully, guaranteeing consistency in its entries.

Building upon these properties, the nix-env command plays a crucial role in facilitating user interaction to install, uninstall, or update packages. Consider the following command, which realizes an installation task:

```
$ nix-env -iA nixpkgs.hello
```

This command installs the package hello from the nixpkgs channel directly into the user environment. -iA signifies an attribute path, providing an intuitive and precise method for specifying package sources from expanding store repositories.

Similar in importance is the update mechanism, vital to maintaining environments coherent with the latest available versions, which can be executed using:

```
$ nix-channel --update
$ nix-env -u '*'
```

Updating nixpkgs channels synchronizes local expressions with remote repositories, subsequently allowing nix-env to upgrade each package within the profile to its latest form. This feature is instrumental for developers accessing ever-evolving libraries and tools, ensuring their applications are aligned with current improvements and security patches.

Further detailing, nix-store –realise culminates the transformation from a derivation file into an executable, retrieving a measurable output within the Nix store:

```
$ nix-store --realise /nix/store/<hash>-myProgram.drv
```

This command reifies the derivation into a physical binary, elapsing through any embedded reference pointers to compose a cohesive software artifact.

In cases where one might remove or clean up unused software, the Nix store proposal applies precise, non-destructive garbage collection through:

```
$ nix-collect-garbage
```

Garbage collection evaluates the reference graph concerning current live paths, expunging unreferenced packages while preserving file integrity across extended installations. This nuanced arrangement of obliterating unused builds without disrupting dependent software underlines Nix's intelligent garbage management.

Multi-user environments leverage nix-daemon, drastically expanding nix-store's versatility in shared ecosystem applications. The daemon permits users to leverage shared Nix stores across different user accounts, negating redundant installations while ensuring environment isolation. This is achieved through user-level profiles located beneath the /nix/var/nix/profiles/per-user/$USER path:

```
$ sudo systemctl start nix-daemon
```

Starting the nix-daemon heralds efficiency improvements, especially across collaborative or academic environments where package uniformity augments workflow consistency.

Moreover, transactions between local and remote infrastructures align seamlessly with advanced features, including binary caches. Employing binary caches allows systems to leverage pre-built packages, facilitating swift deployments and aligning versioning across distributed environments. The binary cache effectively acts as an extension of the Nix store, enabling teams to share verified builds:

```
$ nix-build --option binary-caches http://cache.domain.org myPackage.nix
```

By preferring a cache, this command relieves substantial dependency-checking workloads, redeeming computational resources for future builds or installations.

Another cornerstone in Nix-store's utility is its support for transactionality—the atomic nature in which operations occur ensures that in-progress changes do not affect the stability of existing installations. Any partial builds revert cleanly, without influencing prior store conditions, upholding system integrity.

Nix's origin in minimal interventions spurs usage scenarios where reproducibility and reliability outweigh typical software management concerns. Encapsulating both desired properties, the Nix Store and its suite of commands bring forward a mentioned, reproducible, conflict-free package installation process free from the common ailments plaguing conventional package managers.

Efficient use of the Nix Store necessitates understanding and leveraging its full capabilities, from managing large-scale deployments to maintaining clean local environments. The principles, commands, and attributes explored here illustrate the processes and advantages underlying Nix's proficient service in software management solutions, emphasising its democratic approach to package isolation and multi-user harmony.

6.6 Creating Reproducible Builds

The concept of reproducible builds is a powerful paradigm within software development, fundamentally ensuring that builds are consistent and identical across varied systems and environments. In the context of the Nix package manager, reproducible builds are an innate feature maintained through rigorous control over dependencies and environments. This section delves into the methodologies and implications of employing Nix to create deterministic and reproducible build processes.

Reproducibility begins with the well-defined and declarative nature of Nix expressions. By specifying exact versions and environments, these expressions create a predictable scaffolding that ensures consistent outcomes. The Nix approach isolates builds from local environmental variations such as locale or path differences by generating an entirely closed ecosystem around each package build.

At the foundation of reproducible builds is the elimination of side effects. Nix builds execute within clean chroot environments, devoid of external interference, guaranteeing that the only variables impacting the build process are the ones explicitly defined within the Nix expression.

Consider an example build expression:

```
{ stdenv, fetchurl }:
stdenv.mkDerivation {
```

```
  name = "demoApp";
  src = fetchurl {
    url = "http://example.com/demoApp-1.0.tar.gz";
    sha256 = "sha256-hash";
  };
  buildInputs = [ ];
  buildPhase = ''
    ./configure --prefix=$out
    make
  '';
  installPhase = ''
    make install
  '';
}
```

This expression encapsulates the entirety of the build requirements and processes, ensuring that every step taken towards obtaining the final artifact is reproducibly contained within the declared dependencies and script phases.

Central to supporting reproducible results within Nix is the computational storage of inputs and outputs, primarily through the Nix store. Each build's identity is tied to its derivation hash, encoding not just the source or commands, but also the compiler and library versions engaged. This approach ensures that the same derivation remains invariant over repeated builds on any machine with access to the Nix store.

Nix offers powerful tooling and strategies to further reinforce reproducibility:

- Fixed Output Derivations: By specifying outputs with fixed hashes for derivations where outputs can be independently verified, Nix ensures byte-for-byte equivalency. This constructs a self-reinforcing loop wherein only correct derivations can successfully conclude with matched outputs.

```
src = fetchurl {
  url = "http://example.com/data";
  sha256 = "predefined-hash";
};
```

- Build environments: Sandbox-enabled builds render the host system configuration irrelevant, encapsulating each build with strict resource, path, and environment isolation.

```
$ nix-build --option sandbox true myPackage.nix
```

- Content Addressed Builds (CABs): With newer Nix implementations, CABs extend reproducibility guarantees by associating Nix store paths directly with their outputs' content hashes, further negating potential derivation discrepancies due to input changes alone.

The rigorous application of these techniques allows developers to manage complex projects with contextual transparency. Manifold underlying dependencies become manageable; encapsulated components converge into a reproducible build pipeline, facilitating developments such as verifiable binaries.

Reproducibility inherently mitigates several common concerns:

- Security Compliance: Reproducible builds thwart attempts at introducing hidden vulnerabilities or backdoors, as the public can independently re-create and verify binaries from shared source expressions.
- Cross-platform Uniformity: Given identical expressions and dependencies, Nix facilitates uniform build outputs independently of platform variations, simplifying deployments across diverse environments.
- Historical Consistency: Reproducibility allows historical build recreation, validating past versions, or sustaining previous application states—even when forward growth within the codebase might preclude retroactively aligning dependencies.

Addressing variability additionally requires monitoring dynamic content and dynamic build sequence aspects. Tools like `nix-prefetch-url` can assist in creating pinned fetcher hashes, while Nix Flakes provide a framework for locking dependencies' content, aligning package checks to commit hashes.

Potential challenges to maintaining reproducibility typically arise from areas such as:

- Non-deterministic Outputs: Certain operations, including timestamp embeddings or parallel build sequences, can introduce irreducibility. Solutions might entail neutralizing timestamps through SOURCE_DATE_EPOCH setting or serialized build flags.

```
$ export SOURCE_DATE_EPOCH=$(date +%s)
```

- External Resources: Ensuring certificates, downloads, or data sources are version-locked, or applying strategies such as local mirroring for ephemeral resources.
- Third-party Build Scripts: Adapting scripts to conventional Nix paradigms may require intervention for full replicability, ensuring CentOS or similar scripts adhere to deterministic practices.

Conceiving reproducible builds through Nix broadens potential development opportunities while reducing forensic debugging complexity. By maximizing these powerful builds underpinnings, development teams gain predictability and confidence, fueling software of higher integrity and interoperability across the industry's demands.

Chapter 7

Managing Package Dependencies

Managing package dependencies in Nix is a process of utilizing its functional characteristics to ensure precise and conflict-free software environments. Nix expressions explicitly declare dependencies, enabling exact version control and isolation from other packages. This approach prevents the commonly encountered "dependency hell" by allowing multiple versions of dependencies to coexist without interference. Through overlays, users can customize dependency resolutions, and by pinning versions, they can ensure consistency over time. These features combine to offer a robust system where dependencies are managed transparently and accurately, aligning with the broader goals of reproducibility and reliability in software management.

7.1 Defining Package Dependencies

In software development, managing package dependencies accurately and systematically is paramount to ensuring reliable software builds and executions. The Nix package manager presents a unique and innovative approach to package dependency management. Dependencies in Nix are explicitly declared within Nix expressions, allowing software builds to be entirely functional and deterministic.

Nix expressions are written in the Nix expression language, a domain-specific language designed for infrastructure management and package configuration. Central to managing dependencies is understanding how to define them within Nix expressions. This section explores the mechanisms for specifying dependencies, focusing on ensuring that all requisite packages are correctly included for both building and running software.

```
{ mkDerivation, stdenv, fetchurl, pkgconfig, libxml2 }:

mkDerivation {
  pname = "my-package";
  version = "1.0.0";

  src = fetchurl {
    url = "http://example.com/my-package-1.0.0.tar.gz";
    sha256 = "0rw1f930h2mqlr3jx3ch8sjbrxmrrf3vfgxad8mkqlx95zrn7x5d";
  };

  buildInputs = [ pkgconfig libxml2 ];
}
```

This example demonstrates a simple Nix expression defining a package named ‘my-package‘. One of the distinctive characteristics of this system is the specification of ‘buildInputs‘, which denotes the list of packages required during the build phase of the package. In this instance, the build inputs are ‘pkgconfig‘ and ‘libxml2‘. These inputs are often other Nix expressions themselves, thereby creating a graph-like dependency structure that Nix can resolve.

In Nix, ‘buildInputs‘ include dependencies necessary for building the package, but it is crucial to differentiate them from ‘propagatedBuildInputs‘. The latter refers to dependencies that must also exist in the build environment of any packages depending on ‘my-package‘.

Understanding and defining these kinds of inputs accurately is essential for maintaining the functional purity of Nix builds. In Nix, each package and its dependencies live in separate directories, allowing multiple versions of the same package to coexist without conflict. This capability effectively eliminates "dependency hell" scenarios commonly encountered in traditional package management systems.

```
{ mkDerivation, stdenv, fetchurl, python3Packages }:

mkDerivation {
  pname = "example-with-python";
  version = "2.0.0";

  src = fetchurl {
    url = "http://example.com/example-with-python-2.0.0.tar.gz";
    sha256 = "14fc6zxzg8yj7c5rx0r7k29f9aalcnq3bbslzf1v0j6y9kld4s3g";
  };

  nativeBuildInputs = [ python3Packages.python ];
}
```

In the latter example, a dependency on Python 3 is specified through 'python3Packages.python'. Nix's ability to have multiple versions of the same software package installed concurrently without interference is particularly advantageous when different parts of a software project require different versions of Python, for instance.

There is inherent flexibility in Nix's handling of external libraries. In traditional systems, differing versions often lead to conflicts. However, Nix employs a symlink forest for packages under its management, isolating each version. This system not only supports multiple versions but also permits extensive custom configurations without altering upstream packages.

The language semantics further allow the fine-tuning of dependencies, as specific attributes of dependencies themselves can be manipulated. The capability to parameterize the package derivations ensures that dependencies can be dynamically resolved based on external inputs, environment variables, or user configurations.

Consider a scenario requiring specific compiler options based on the environment:

```
{ mkDerivation, stdenv, fetchurl, gcc, autoconf }:

mkDerivation {
  pname = "configurable-package";
  version = "3.5.2";

  src = fetchurl {
    url = "http://example.com/configurable-package-3.5.2.tar.gz";
    sha256 = "3c21f7y0xlzky8np10rw2rdu5nl0y4f98lbx1cqd7xy6vx5rfd3r";
  };

  buildInputs = [ gcc ];
```

```
  configureFlags = stdenv.lib.optionalString stdenv.isDarwin "--enable-mac-specific-
       feature";

  nativeBuildInputs = if stdenv.isDarwin then [ autoconf ] else [];
}
```

In this instance, we use the 'stdenv' to conditionally modify the 'configureFlags' depending on whether the build environment is Darwin (macOS). Similarly, the 'nativeBuildInputs' selectively includes 'autoconf' if the environment is Darwin. Leveraging 'optionalString' and conditional logic greatly enhances the portability and versatility of Nix expressions, particularly when supporting various environments.

Moreover, this approach illustrates how Nix expressions streamline cross-platform compatibility. By adopting a functional paradigm, expressions are uninfluenced by their historical state and rely solely on their input specifications and the function's inherent logic.

Another key functionality of Nix in managing package dependencies is through the 'with' statement, which imports a set of packages into the scope. This can be particularly beneficial when working with large projects involving numerous dependencies.

```
with import <nixpkgs> { };

stdenv.mkDerivation {
  pname = "scoped-project";
  version = "0.8.1";

  src = fetchurl {
    url = "http://example.com/scoped-project-0.8.1.tar.gz";
    sha256 = "4fcd3z8w0r6n7xqlm5s70xn3vlk9n8y3jqfl29nvqb9vcdtk8jfl";
  };

  buildInputs = [ python37 python37Packages.numpy ];
}
```

In this example, the 'with' statement allows for bringing the entire 'nixpkgs' set into the current namespace, simplifying the referencing of dependency expressions. This can lead to cleaner and more readable Nix expressions, particularly in large projects with extensive dependencies.

The inclusion of dependencies is securely managed by Nix's hash-based system, allowing for the deterministic rebuilding of package environments. Each combination of versions, flags, inputs, and configurations uniquely determines the hash of the derivation, thus ensuring that a given computation always produces the same result. This characteristic elegantly addresses issues of reproducibility and ensures confidence in the built outputs across different environments and over time.

Nonetheless, one must remain vigilant about the recursive nature of dependency resolution in complex projects. When defining packages, it is essential to ensure all potential paths through the dependency graph converge satisfactorily to avoid infinite loops or other deductions that may compromise the deterministic nature of builds in Nix.

Furthermore, Nix projects may employ the concept of environment variables to further enhance dependency management. These variables can influence the build process, configuring dependencies dynamically and flexibly.

A typical pattern involves defining environment variables in Nix script, which are accessible during the build phase. This method complements dependency management by introducing environmental flexibility on top of deterministic builds:

```
{ mkDerivation, stdenv, fetchurl, libmysqlclient }:

let
  verbose = stdenv.lib.optionalString (builtins.getEnv "BUILD_VERBOSE" == "true
      ") "--enable-verbose";
in

mkDerivation {
  pname = "adaptive-package";
  version = "2.9.4";

  src = fetchurl {
    url = "http://example.com/adaptive-package-2.9.4.tar.gz";
    sha256 = "8bq33n72jwb71fx6zkcdq5jqx5vzhff29fmsgkhwk2pxb6rlcnlk";
  };

  buildInputs = [ libmysqlclient ];

  configureFlags = [ verbose ];
}
```

Incorporating the use of 'builtins.getEnv', it is possible to conditionally modify build flags based on environment settings. This introduces a dynamic aspect to Nix builds, which should be exercised with caution to maintain dependency resolution correctness and build safety.

Defining package dependencies with Nix lays the foundational bedrock for reliable and reproducible software builds. By employing its functional characteristics, explicit version control, and innovative input expressions, Nix ensures sophisticated dependency management, eliminating traditional obstacles and paving the way for multi-faceted software development endeavours that are robust and modular.

7.2 Handling Dependency Conflicts

The management of package dependencies in complex software systems often encounters a significant challenge known as "dependency conflicts." These arise when different packages require incompatible versions of the same dependency. Traditional package management systems frequently struggle with such conflicts, leading to what is commonly referred to as "dependency hell." Nix offers a unique paradigm to address this issue, leveraging its ability to handle multiple versions of dependencies in a coherent manner. This section delves deeply into the mechanisms and strategies employed by Nix to resolve dependency conflicts effectively.

At its core, Nix utilizes a purely functional approach to store build artifacts in a manner that isolates dependencies by their specifications rather than by system-wide states. This method encompasses a filesystem structure where each package resides in its uniquely hashed directory, based on its build inputs and environment. Consequently, different versions or configurations of the same dependency can coexist harmonically within the Nix store without interference.

In traditional systems, conflicts typically manifest when two packages want different versions of a library, but Nix completely side-steps this issue by creating separate derivations. To illustrate, consider a scenario where two applications require different major versions of the sqlite library. With Nix, both versions can reside separately:

```
{ mkDerivation, sqlite, sqliteOlderVersion }:

let
  app1 = mkDerivation {
    pname = "app-one";
    version = "1.0.0";

    buildInputs = [ sqlite ];
  };

  app2 = mkDerivation {
```

```
    pname = "app-two";
    version = "2.0.0";

    buildInputs = [ sqliteOlderVersion ];
  };
in
  [ app1 app2 ]
```

In this example, both app-one and app-two can use their required versions of the sqlite library without any conflict. Nix achieves this by isolating each derivation's dependencies, providing a robust solution that circumvents dependency hell.

One of the novel techniques employed by Nix to manage such conflicts is through the use of **overlays**. Overlays in Nix allow users to modify or extend the existing package set, adjusting dependencies and configuration details without the need to change the upstream Nixpkgs repository. This modular approach permits seamless integration of custom package versions to resolve conflicts or enrich the environment with additional functionalities.

```
self: super: {
  sqliteCustom = super.sqlite.overrideAttrs (oldAttrs: rec {
    version = "3.30.1";
    src = fetchurl {
      url = "http://example.com/sqlite-3.30.1.tar.gz";
      sha256 = "some-hash-value-here";
    };
  });

  myApp = super.myApp.override {
    buildInputs = [ self.sqliteCustom ];
  };
}
```

In this overlay, a customized version of the sqlite library is introduced and then used to build myApp. Overlays offer a flexible mechanism to manage versions and dependencies, allowing for precise control over package configurations within development workflows.

Moreover, Nix also introduces the concept of **conditional dependencies**, allowing the build configuration to adapt based on specified conditions, which further assists in resolving conflicts. This capability ensures that the requisite dependencies are selected according to the build platform or other environmental criteria.

```
{ stdenv, mkDerivation, fetchurl, pythonPackages, pythonOlderPackages }:
```

```
mkDerivation {
  pname = "cross-platform-app";
  version = "4.4.2";

  src = fetchurl {
    url = "http://example.com/cross-platform-app-4.4.2.tar.gz";
    sha256 = "another-hash-value-here";
  };

  buildInputs = if stdenv.isLinux then [ pythonPackages.someLibrary ]
               else [ pythonOlderPackages.someLibrary ];
}
```

In this example, the dependency someLibrary is selected conditionally based on the platform being Linux or not. Such a facility ensures that only compatible library versions are used, effectively mitigating potential conflicts across varied environments.

Navigation of unresolved dependencies often requires careful analysis of the conflict graph. Nix supports this with tools like nix-store –query –references to trace dependencies, revealing how packages are interconnected. This analytical approach empowers developers to comprehend and rectify conflicts by understanding their origin accurately.

Another valuable feature in managing dependency conflicts is Nix's **allowsCollisions** setting, which explicitly permits package collisions in certain controlled scenarios. This is particularly evoked when legacy systems or applications necessitate specific dependency overrides irrespective of the existing packages.

```
{ stdenv, writeTextFile }:

stdenv.mkDerivation {
  pname = "legacy-support-lib";
  version = "1.5";

  buildInputs = [ /* Some conflicting libraries here */ ];

  meta = {
    allowsCollisions = true;
    description = "A legacy library requiring controlled collisions";
  };
}
```

Using allowsCollisions should be approached judiciously as it overrides Nix's default avoidance of dependency overlap, potentially leading to unpredictable behavior if not managed correctly.

When addressing dependency conflicts, Nix further supports **test en-**

vironments via nix-shell, providing an isolated context for experimentation. This allows developers to iteratively test dependency graphs until a satisfactory resolution is achieved. By launching a shell with specific dependencies, one can experiment and derive compatible versions before committing to an exact dependency configuration for builds.

```
nix-shell -p myApp -I nixpkgs=channel:nixpkgs-unstable
```

The command initializes a testing environment with the specified package and a chosen Nixpkgs channel, augmenting the capability to narrow down conflicting dependencies experimentally.

In certain complex systems where conventional resolution techniques do not suffice, employing **NixOS modules** can serve as a higher-order solution. Modules abstract away complexity and encapsulate dependency configurations, providing a way to structure projects with interdependent configurations systematically.

The adoption of these apparatuses in Nix not only resolves immediate dependency conflicts but also establishes a robust infrastructure for prevention in future iterations. Through functional declarativity and version agility, Nix guides the development communities out of dependency complexities and toward stable and reproducing software systems.

Therefore, Nix offers extensive strategies for handling dependency conflicts, building upon a solid foundational philosophy of functional purity and referential transparency. By enabling multiple versions, overlays, conditional resolutions, and modular configurations, Nix not only addresses present-day issues but proposes a steadfast system for sustaining software dependencies well beyond contemporary development boundaries. With these features, conflicts transition from being formidable challenges to solvable components within the architectural design.

7.3 Using Overlays for Customization

The Nix package manager introduces a sophisticated system for building and managing software dependencies, with overlays serving as a potent feature for customization. Overlays provide a mechanism to supersede or augment the existing Nixpkgs repository without directly altering the source. This capability is particularly valuable in scenarios requiring custom package versions, experimental features, or site-specific modifications, enabling developers to adapt package sets fluidly while maintaining the integrity of the upstream repository.

At its core, an overlay is a function that receives two arguments: *self* and *super*. The *super* argument references the original package set before applying the overlay, while *self* refers to the package set including all preceding overlays. This structure allows for seamless combination and extension of packages, crucial for evolving software projects.

An overlay can redefine or extend the attributes of existing packages. This is typically achieved by overriding specific attributes of a package derivation to alter its behavior. Consider the need to customize a package with additional build inputs or a modified build procedure:

```
self: super: {
  examplePackage = super.examplePackage.overrideAttrs (oldAttrs: rec {
    buildInputs = oldAttrs.buildInputs ++ [ self.customDependency ];
    version = "2.1.0-custom";
  });
}
```

In this instance, the *overrideAttrs* function is employed to modify the build inputs and version of *examplePackage*, introducing a new dependency and designating a specific version. Utilizing overlays provides the flexibility needed to adapt the package ecosystem without deviating from the central repository's trajectory.

Overlays also facilitate the introduction of entirely new packages into the package set. This is advantageous when integrating proprietary, experimental, or local software into the Nix ecosystem:

```
self: super: {
  myCustomApp = super.callPackage ./path/to/myCustomApp.nix { };
}
```

This example displays the definition of a *myCustomApp* package using *callPackage* to draw in its respective Nix expression. By incorporating such packages directly into the Nixpkgs scope via overlays, one can harmonize custom software developments and maintain them alongside conventional packages with minimal friction.

A principal advantage associated with overlays in Nix is the preservation of upstream compatibility, which ensures that the core package collection remains pristine and updateable. This is critical in collaborative environments, where multiple team members might share a common base set of packages and selectively apply their own overlays for personalized configurations.

Further, overlays offer an elegant solution to circumvent potential restrictions in package availability, whereby a newer version or feature of a package is needed before it is accessible in the upstream repository directly. In such cases, overlays are utilized to locally integrate adaptations or backports:

```
self: super: {
  recentPackage = super.oldPackage.overrideAttrs (oldAttrs: rec {
    src = fetchFromGitHub {
      owner = "author";
      repo = "recentPackage";
      rev = "abcd123";
      sha256 = "1q2w3e4r5t6y7u8i9o0p";
    };
  });
}
```

This overlay exemplifies introducing a newer version of a package by fetching it directly from the repository's source, potentially containing features not yet released in the stable branch of Nixpkgs. Such accommodation empowers rapid innovation cycles without forgoing the advantages of Nix's deterministic build processes.

However, the effectiveness of utilizing overlays in Nix extends beyond singular package customizations. Developers can institute comprehensive transformations across a package set, tailoring entire environments by adding functional capabilities or addressing architectural constraints.

Consider an overlay setup where dependencies for multiple packages are aligned with specific architectural goals, such as optimizing for a particular processor or enabling debugging symbols for development environments. Such a strategy leverages Nix's reproducibility feature to foster consistency across diverse machines and contexts:

```
self: super: {
  gdbWithDebugSymbols = super.gdb.overrideAttrs (oldAttrs: rec {
    buildInputs = oldAttrs.buildInputs ++ [ self.libdw ];
    configureFlags = oldAttrs.configureFlags ++ ["--with-debug"];
  });
```

```
  gccForOptimization = super.gcc.overrideAttrs (oldAttrs: rec {
    configureFlags = oldAttrs.configureFlags ++ ["--enable-targets=all"];
  });

  customEnv = {
    gcc = self.gccForOptimization;
    gdb = self.gdbWithDebugSymbols;
  };
}
```

In the aforementioned overlay, two key packages, *gdb* and *gcc*, are redefined to include debugging symbols and target all architectures, respectively, thereby standardizing environment attributes beneficial to development and testing phases.

Moreover, overlays can be composed hierarchically, employing them not just singularly, but in a cascading series, where one overlay serves as the base for subsequent customizations. This modular approach allows for the decomposition of overlay functionalities into coherent components that can be composed strategically depending on the project needs.

Integration and application of overlays are typically managed through a user's configuration file or channel specification when using Nix tools or NixOS, the Linux distribution built atop Nix. It involves referencing overlay paths or constructing overlay functions directly in configuration files:

```
{ pkgs, ... }:

{
  nixpkgs.overlays = [ (import ./path/to/overlayOne.nix)
                       (import ./path/to/overlayTwo.nix)
                     ];
}
```

By listing overlays within a configuration context, users instruct the Nix package manager or operating system to interpret these customization files alongside the standard Nixpkgs repository, enabling the live application of chosen adjustments without necessitating direct modification of the package definitions themselves.

Furthermore, variable scoping and dependency encapsulation manage potential conflicts when multiple overlays interact, permitting safe coexistence and predictable outcomes even when broad changes are administered.

In practical software engineering and system administration environments, overlays serve as a cornerstone for achieving agile workflows with the Nix ecosystem, empowering teams to balance dependability with adaptability. Organizations increasingly adopt these methodologies to align software deployments with specific business objectives, facilitate innovation across diverse technological domains, and enhance collaborative development frameworks.

Ultimately, overlays offer a tailored approach to package management in Nix, embracing configuration fluidly, promoting strategic flexibility, and adhering to the functional programming principles that underpin the Nix ethos. By robustly managing packages while ensuring compatibility and reproducibility, overlays advance the development paradigm within the modern Nix framework, contributing profound value to both individual contributors and organizational infrastructures in software deployment.

7.4 Pinning and Ensuring Reproducibility

In the dynamically evolving landscape of software development, reproducibility emerges as a critical necessity, enabling consistent builds across environments and time periods. Nix excels in ensuring reproducibility, primarily through its ability to "pin" dependencies. Pinning denotes the action of specifying exact versions of packages or sets of packages, ensuring that any subsequent build or deployment process repeats precisely as intended, unaffected by updates or changes in the broader package ecosystem.

The principal mechanism for pinning in Nix is the use of *nixpkgs*, which represents the collection of Nix packages available from the Nixpkgs repository. By pinning *nixpkgs* to a particular state or version, developers can lock in the dependencies of a project to their exact versions at that state, ensuring that the builds remain stable and reproducible.

```
{
  pkgs ? import (fetchTarball {
    url = "https://github.com/NixOS/nixpkgs/archive/
          abcdef1234567890abcdef1234567890abcdef12.tar.gz";
    sha256 = "sha256-hash-value-of-tarball";
```

```
  }) {}
};
```

In this example, a specific Git revision of the Nixpkgs repository is used to fetch a tarball. The 'fetchTarball' function ensures that the specified version is retrieved and the integrity of the download is verified via a SHA-256 hash. By employing this method, developers can pin their projects to this particular manifestation of Nixpkgs, securing all dependencies at the known state.

Nix offers several methods beyond pinning the entire package set to ensure that builds remain consistent and reproducible. One prevalent strategy is adopting *nix-shell* with shell.nix or default.nix files that define the fixed environments associated with projects. These files encapsulate all necessary dependencies, providing a reliable and straightforward route to instantiate replicas of the development setup on any machine.

Consider the use of shell.nix for environment pinning:

```
{ pkgs ? import <nixpkgs> {} }:

pkgs.mkShell {
  buildInputs = with pkgs; [
    python39
    numpy
    myPinnedPackage
  ];
}
```

This configuration ensures that any collaborator using the nix-shell command in the repository directory initializes a shell environment with precisely the specified dependencies, fostering consistency across developer setups.

Moreover, Nix's ability to deterministically track and replicate dependencies is strongly supported via the Nix language's expression syntax. The entire dependency graph associated with a build follows a functional paradigm where each derivation depends solely on its inputs. Given identical inputs and Nix expressions, the outputs are guaranteed to remain the same.

In practice, pinning methodologies are indispensable when transitioning from development to production environments. By aligning development builds with the versions pinned for deployment, the potential for introducing discrepancies or errors in live environments is drastically reduced. Within complex stack environments, pinning ensures each layer—be it application, service, or library—operates in tandem as verified in non-production testing phases.

Beyond individual projects, organizations implementing continuous integration/continuous deployment (CI/CD) pipelines profoundly benefit from reproducible builds. The assurance that code tested locally by developers performs congruously during integration tests or production deployment fosters seamless pipeline execution.

```
nix-shell shell.nix --run "ci-test-suite"
```

In this bash script snippet, a CI pipeline step is invoked within a reproducible environment derived from a shell.nix specification, underscoring consistent execution through rigorous pinning practices.

Another topic inherent in ensuring reproducibility is the concept of purity. Purity in Nix ensures that builds are insulated from the global state. One can utilize nix-build to execute a derivation defined in a default.nix file, prominently showcasing purity-bound reproducibility:

```
{ pkgs ? import <nixpkgs> {} }:

pkgs.stdenv.mkDerivation {
  name = "example-app";
  src = ./src;

  buildInputs = with pkgs; [
    gcc
    openssl
  ];

  buildPhase = ''
    gcc -o myapp myapp.c -lssl -lcrypto
  '';
}
```

Here, nix-build executes the build within a pure environment, adhering strictly to specified dependencies, thus elevating the prospects for reproducible outcomes.

Additionally, employing niv, a Nix package manager tool, provides enhanced pinning capability. It effectively captures the ecosystem's state at a defined version trail, including all dependencies via locked dependencies files, and can be integrated into Nix configurations for meticulous reproducibility:

```
niv add nixpkgs -v release-20.09
niv init
niv update
```

With `niv`, dependency management and lockfile generation extend Nix's capabilities, empowering teams to lock complex stack setups effectively.

Reproducibility enables developers and systems architects to reclaim control over ever-changing software landscapes. Pinning serves not only as a foundational strategy central to the Nix ecosystem but as a broader philosophy in stable software construction. By conscientiously coupling exact variants of necessary inputs, combined with Nix's functional attributes, stakeholders accomplish a unified avenue for developing, testing, and deploying software substantively.

From individual packages to encompassing projects, Nix's pinning underwrites long-term sustainability in both small-scale and enterprise-level software endeavors. Teams relying on reproducibility underscore the mantra of ensuring that the software being nurtured adheres to the principles of integrity, reliability, and cohesion, transcending ephemeral states and standing resilient against the winds of technological transience.

7.5 Advanced Dependency Management with Nix

The Nix package manager introduces a paradigm shift in handling software dependencies through its unique functional approach. Beyond basic dependency management, Nix offers advanced features that cater to managing complex dependency graphs, addressing conditional dependencies, and incorporating optional build inputs, thus enhancing developers' control over software environments. This section delves into these sophisticated mechanisms, providing detailed insights and practical examples to illuminate the capabilities of Nix in advanced scenarios.

At the heart of Nix's advanced dependency management is its ability to handle multiple dependency graphs and resolve them in a coherent and conflict-free manner. The referential transparency of Nix derivations, along with its precise dependency tracking mechanism, ensures that the build outcomes are deterministic and reproducible. By managing package derivations in a purely functional context, Nix empowers developers to define complex configurations and dependency trees without encountering the traditional woes of dependency hell.

```
{ mkDerivation, lib, fetchurl, pkgconfig, zlib, openssl }:

mkDerivation {
  name = "complex-package";
  version = "1.4.5";
  src = fetchurl {
    url = "https://example.com/complex-package-1.4.5.tar.gz";
    sha256 = "19abd245acea402f3b2d59441234c329aba7133951d45ad1bcda8b95b8c1";
  };
  buildInputs = [ pkgconfig zlib openssl ];
  nativeBuildInputs = [ lib ];

  configureFlags = [ "--enable-featureX" ];
}
```

In this example, the package complex-package depends on several libraries, utilizing Nix's functional language to precisely specify the graph. Each dependency here is clearly articulated, ensuring that any changes in the dependencies are reflected transparently in the build process.

Nix further accommodates sophisticated dependency handling through its support for **conditional dependencies**. Conditional dependencies allow developers to define alternate paths in the build configuration depending on external factors such as the platform or build options. This capability is crucial in creating cross-platform applications or adding features that might only be available on certain systems.

```
{ stdenv, fetchurl, someSpecialLib }:

stdenv.mkDerivation {
  name = "platform-specific-package";
  version = "2.0";

  src = fetchurl {
    url = "https://example.com/platform-specific-package-2.0.tar.gz";
    sha256 = "abcdef1234567890abcdef1234567890abcdef1234567890abcdef1234567890";

  };

  buildInputs = if stdenv.isDarwin then [ someSpecialLib ]
               else [];
```

```
  configurePhase = ''
    ./configure --prefix=$out
  '';

  buildPhase = ''
    make
  '';

  installPhase = ''
    make install
  '';
}
```

Here, the build expression utilizes the stdenv.isDarwin flag to check if the build environment is macOS and includes someSpecialLib only in that case. This adaptability simplifies the handling of environment-specific dependencies, reducing complexity in managing builds across different systems.

The provision for **optional dependencies** also augments Nix's strength in advanced dependency management. Optional dependencies allow derivations to declare non-mandatory build inputs that can be toggled based on configuration parameters, yet ensure reproducibility by clearly stating these potential inputs.

Leveraging the lib attributes, optional dependencies can be defined and controlled conditionally as required by the build logic:

```
{ mkDerivation, fetchurl, optionalDependency ? null }:

mkDerivation {
  pname = "optional-dependent-package";
  version = "0.9.3";

  src = fetchurl {
    url = "https://example.com/optional-dependent-package-0.9.3.tar.gz";
    sha256 = "09876abcdef1234567abcdef09876abcdef12345678909876abcdef12345";
  };

  buildInputs = lib.optionals (optionalDependency != null) [ optionalDependency ];
}
```

The use of lib.optionals provides a convenient method to include the optionalDependency only if it is explicitly specified. Such a method harnesses Nix's functional language to articulate conditionality crisply and concisely.

Another powerful concept within Nix is the use of **imported deriva-**

tions. Imported derivations permit a higher level of dynamism by allowing the build steps, including fetching sources, to occur at runtime, thereby enabling complex dependencies setup on demand. This technique, although requiring careful handling, expands the possibilities of what can be expressed and accomplished within a Nix derivation:

```
{ pkgs, dynamicDependencyFetcher }:

let
  dynamicDependency = dynamicDependencyFetcher "dependency-name-version";
in pkgs.stdenv.mkDerivation {
  pname = "dynamic-package";
  version = "1.0";

  src = fetchurl {
    url = dynamicDependency.url;
    sha256 = dynamicDependency.sha256;
  };

  buildInputs = [ dynamicDependency ];
}
```

This example showcases an environment where dependencies might be determined dynamically and incorporated into the static build logic—resulting in flexible build configurations while retaining the reproducibility tenet.

Complex software environments further benefit from **cross-compilation** facilities in Nix, where building software for varied architectures becomes streamlined. Developers can specify separate build and host platforms, accommodating cross-compiled dependencies without altering the derivation's fundamental structure. This capability addresses scenarios where development environments differ from target runtime environments.

```
{ stdenv, pkgs, fetchurl, gcc-cross }:

stdenv.mkDerivation {
  pname = "cross-compiled-software";
  version = "1.2.3";

  src = fetchurl {
    url = "https://example.com/cross-compiled-software-1.2.3.tar.gz";
    sha256 = "789abcdef123456789abcdef123456789abcdef123456789abcdef";
  };

  nativeBuildInputs = [ pkgs.pkg-config ];
  crossDrv = {
    build = stdenv.buildPlatform;
    host = stdenv.targetPlatform;
    target = "armv7l-unknown-linux-gnueabihf";
```

```
  };
  buildInputs = [ gcc-cross ];
}
```

Here, cross-compilation provides the capability to develop for the armv7l-unknown-linux-gnueabihf architecture while executing builds on, say, an x86 machine. Such facilitation heightens the versatility and potency of Nix in managing complex, diverse builds.

Finally, the ability to incorporate **user-defined functions** and abstractions into Nix derivations translates to a more programmable and modular dependency declaration approach. By encapsulating common build logic into reusable constructs, developers enhance their capability to manage dependencies concisely and repeatedly across different projects.

In summary, Nix's advanced dependency management capabilities provide a comprehensive toolkit for software developers tasked with handling multifaceted build requirements. By effectively leveraging conditional dependencies, optional inputs, imported derivations, and cross-compilation, Nix empowers developers to tailor dependency configurations around their unique project needs while maintaining the deterministic, reproducible core that defines the Nix approach. This ensures consistent and reliable software environments that scale robustly across development phases and environments, reflecting Nix's unmatched adaptability in managing the intricacies of modern software lifecycle demands.

7.6 Leveraging Built-in Package Sets

Nix distinguishes itself not just through its functional approach, but also by its extensive collection of built-in package sets that provide structured ecosystems tailored to ease software management. These pre-defined sets encapsulate related sets of software, offering immense opportunities for simplifying dependencies and enhancing integration across a vast array of software platforms. By effectively leveraging these package sets, developers can tap into optimized configurations and streamlined dependency management pathways that suit both generic and specific use cases, enhancing both the speed and reliability of software development processes.

Package sets in Nix, including nixpkgs, haskellPackages, pythonPackages, among others, align curated software collections with programming language ecosystems and application domains. Each package set offers a consistency-enabling foundation for developing and maintaining software, affording components needed for holistic environments with minimal effort and configuration overhead.

```
{ pkgs ? import <nixpkgs> {} }:

let
  haskellPackages = pkgs.haskell.packages.ghc8104;
in
haskellPackages.mkDerivation {
  pname = "my-haskell-app";
  version = "0.1.0.0";

  src = ./.;
  buildDepends = with haskellPackages; [ base containers ];
}
```

In this example, haskellPackages signifies a built-in package set and is used to compile a simple Haskell application. By encapsulating dependencies such as base and containers, the package set guarantees the compatibility and consistency of dependencies across different projects.

These curated package sets extend substantial efficiencies to developers in various domains:

- **Ecosystem Compatibility**: Built-in package sets ensure that libraries and dependencies are vetted for compatibility, reducing the likelihood of conflicts or integrations stumbling due to mismatched dependencies.
- **Version Cohesion**: By providing pre-selected library versions, package sets guarantee a stable environment for development, testing, and deployment, alleviating the developer's burden to manually resolve and test singular library versions.
- **Streamlined Updates**: Package sets present a unified target for ecosystem updates. As they are updated as a whole, developers can apply upgrade paths systematically, retaining compatibility across dependencies in a more structured manner than linear or ad-hoc updates.

Beyond language-specific package sets, Nix supports domain-specific package collections that aid in boosting productivity. An illustrative scenario is utilizing nodePackages for Node.js applications, creating a comprehensive framework around web development or scripting.

```
{ pkgs ? import <nixpkgs> {} }:

let
  nodePackages = pkgs.nodePackages;
in
nodePackages.node2nix {
  src = ./web-app/;
}
```

Utilizing this approach, developers leverage the nodePackages set to ensure that JavaScript dependencies are properly managed and consistent with the rest of the ecosystem, facilitating package installations and removals in a resolute manner.

Moreover, considering scientific computation environments, pythonPackages plays a significant role, hosting an extensive array of scientific and data analysis libraries, creating an ecosystem conducive to robust numerical and analytical computing.

```
{ pkgs ? import <nixpkgs> {} }:

let
  pythonEnv = pkgs.python38.withPackages (pythonPackages: with pythonPackages; [
    numpy
    scipy
  ]);
in
pkgs.mkShell {
  buildInputs = [ pythonEnv ];
}
```

This configuration initializes a Python shell equipped with numpy and scipy, illustrating how seamlessly package sets can form a cohesive development environment for data science tasks. By invoking pkgs.python38.withPackages, Nix streamlines the inclusion of desired libraries, setting up a highly consistent and predictable computation space.

The power of built-in package sets in Nix extends further with tools like overlays and custom package configurations, affording greater flexibility within these predefined ecosystems. For instance, developers can modify and extend package sets to accommodate specific needs or project constraints while maintaining the base setup's overall coherence and compatibility.

Another significant advantage of leveraging built-in package sets lies in **cross-compilation scenarios**. Nix facilitates developing applications for different hardware architectures using appropriate package sets, ensuring that dependencies and libraries are correctly aligned for target environments:

```
{ pkgs ? import <nixpkgs> {} }:

let
  stdenv = pkgs.stdenv;
  crossPkgs = import <nixpkgs> { crossSystem = pkgs.lib.systems.examples.musl; };
  crossGcc = crossPkgs.gcc;
in
pkgs.stdenv.mkDerivation {
  pname = "cross-compiled-app";
  version = "0.1";

  NIX_CFLAGS_COMPILE = "-march=armv7-a";

  buildInputs = [ crossGcc ];
  unpackPhase = "tar xvfz ${src}";
  buildPhase = "make";
}
```

Cross-compiling applications with this setup maintains adherence to architecture-specific needs while utilizing package sets to manage dependencies effectively.

Furthermore, package sets can serve educational roles, providing a curated introduction for students and newcomers to programming ecosystems or specific application domains. Leveraging built-in package sets allows for structured exploration and learning without encountering the often intricate initial setup hurdles.

Finally, in production environments, package sets underpin reliability by ensuring all dependencies are consistent and validated against upstream standards, minimizing runtime anomalies caused by unforeseen package interactions. Organizations thus leverage them to maintain a high standard of operational assurance across their software stacks.

By consolidating dependencies, promoting ecosystem integrity, and facilitating cross-platform interoperability, Nix's built-in package sets empower developers to engage in informed and strategic software management practices. This foresight assures that the workflows employing these sets retain agility, adaptability, and robustness in the face of evolving technological landscapes, aligning with broader organizational goals for innovation and efficiency. As such, Nix's approach to package sets not only serves immediate development needs but also contributes significantly to sustainable software lifecycle management.

Chapter 8

NixOS: A Linux Distribution Built on Nix

NixOS is a unique Linux distribution that leverages the Nix package manager to deliver a fully declarative operating system configuration. By defining the entire system in a single configuration file, NixOS offers unparalleled consistency and ease of management, allowing users to reproduce entire system states effortlessly. This approach supports atomic upgrades and rollbacks, enhancing stability and flexibility. Built on the principles of reproducibility and immutability, NixOS provides a reliable platform for deploying complex systems with assurance and simplicity, transforming traditional Linux administration through its innovative use of Nix.

8.1 Overview of NixOS

NixOS stands as an illustrious example of innovation within the realm of Linux distributions. Built atop the Nix package manager, it redefines the conventional methodologies employed in system configuration and package management. To truly understand the distinctive qualities that NixOS offers, it is imperative to delve deeper into its foundational aspects, including its use of the Nix package manager, the benefits of declarative configuration, atomic upgrades, and an advanced rollback capability.

The Nix package manager provides the core infrastructure for NixOS, offering a distinct approach that ensures consistency and reproducibility. Unlike traditional package managers that modify the system state incrementally, Nix operates by creating isolated environments and builds packages declaratively. Each package in NixOS is stored in its own unique directory, typically under /nix/store, identified by a hash that includes the dependencies and source used to build it. This storage paradigm ensures that installing or upgrading a package does not interfere with existing software, permitting multiple versions of packages to coexist.

Here's a basic example illustrating the fundamental difference in package management with Nix:

```
# Installing a package with Nix
nix-env -iA nixos.hello
```

In contrast to other package managers, this command ensures that the installed package, "hello" in this case, does not alter other existing packages or system libraries, due to the isolated nature of the Nix package store.

Declarative configuration, a hallmark of NixOS, enables the definition of entire system environments via a single, comprehensive configuration file. This concept not only simplifies system management but also allows version control of system configurations, making it feasible to revert to previous system states. The configuration file, /etc/nixos/configuration.nix, serves as the nucleus of system setup information. Within this file, everything from user specifications, package installations, to service configurations is defined declaratively. Here's an excerpt from a potential configuration.nix:

```
{ config, pkgs, ... }:

{
  environment.systemPackages = with pkgs; [
    vim
    git
  ];

  services.sshd.enable = true;

  users.users.jdoe = {
    isNormalUser = true;
    home = "/home/jdoe";
    shell = pkgs.zsh;
  };
}
```

In the above configuration snippet, the definition involves installing fundamental packages such as vim and git, enabling the SSH service, and configuring a user account with specific characteristics. This declarative approach eliminates discrepancies often introduced by manual configuration, thereby enforcing a predictable system state.

Furthermore, NixOS features atomic upgrades, which execute system updates as indivisible operations, effectively eliminating the old issues with configuration drifts and partial updates leading to inconsistent states in a system. At any given time, the entire set of installed packages and configurations can be rolled back or moved forward seamlessly, offering unparalleled system reliability. When an upgrade is initiated, NixOS utilizes the nixos-rebuild command:

```
# Upgrading the system atomically
nixos-rebuild switch --upgrade
```

This command reconstructs the system as defined in configuration.nix, by potentially altering only the relevant data within the Nix store, and switches seamlessly to the new configuration. If needed, rollback is inherently supported due to generation tracking.

Rollback capabilities in NixOS are tightly coupled with its generational management system. Each changeset applied to the system through the nixos-rebuild command leads to a new generation. This feature stands in stark contrast to traditional systems where rollback might necessitate re-installations or involve complex reverse-engineering of upgrades. The rollback operation is straightforward:

```
# Rolling back to the previous generation
sudo nix-env --rollback
```

This powerful yet simple mechanism, rooted in the isolation and immutability principles, highlights the robustness that NixOS introduces. The rollback operation does not tamper with the current generation directly but rather reinvokes the previous system state by reconfiguring the system to a prior generation.

NixOS facilitates a paradigm where the software dependencies' management is entirely automated and does not impact global library directories, preventing the typical 'dependency hell' scenario. The emphasis on isolated environments means that dependencies required by a particular package do not affect other packages or applications. Moreover, this environment can easily be realized for projects, fitting perfectly within containers or sandboxed environments, showcasing the flexibility NixOS offers for reproducibility.

The Nix language, utilized for the configuration and package definitions, is a functional programming language, emphasizing purity and the lack of side effects, which reinforces the deterministic nature of the builds. It enables highly customizable and tailored configuration because it allows users to essentially "program" their configurations:

```
{ pkgs ? import <nixpkgs> {} }:

pkgs.mkShell {
  buildInputs = [ pkgs.hello ];
  shellHook = ''
    echo "Customized development shell"
  '';
}
```

In this snippet, a shell environment tailored for development initializes with predefined package inputs and custom initialization commands. Such programmability enables the creation of complex configurations and environments using simple, declarative statements framed within the Nix language.

The generational nature of NixOS is supported further by the integrally connected boot loader, GRUB2, which maintains a list of system generations. When a system encounters issues during the boot process or operational instability, users can select a previous configuration generation directly during the boot process, thus circumventing immediate problems and restoring system access quickly.

As an operating system built on principles of reproducibility and immutability, NixOS represents a watershed moment in Linux distributions, fundamentally challenging traditional paradigms with its unique approach. This distribution orchestrates an environment where system setups can be precisely replicated, thus offering unparalleled opportunities for systems' maintainability and collaboration especially beneficial for teams developing complex systems.

Reproducibility extends beyond individual workstation settings into full-scale deployments, where application environments for development and deployment must remain consistent. This capability enhances CI/CD pipelines, bridging the gap between development and production systems, thus streamlining software delivery. Software projects' dependencies encapsulated as reproducible builds ensure identical environments are crafted effortlessly, reducing deployment time and nurturing collaboration.

The immutability of system configurations ensures finite control over changes, as required modifications are always applied to a new system state rather than altering the current configuration thereby mitigating risks associated with mutable states. This architecture inherently minimizes the attack surface potentially exploited due to unintentional modifications, rendering NixOS not only a flexible but secure operational environment.

As the discourse around NixOS continues to evolve, it acts as a potent vehicle transforming traditional Linux administration by leveraging its association with Nix. This self-contained world stands on the cutting edge of operating system technology, heralding a new era of precision, certainty, and a future-proof approach to system management. Its methodology has already borne significant impacts within educational institutions, research environments, and enterprises, continually driving the inquisitive Linux community towards innovation with its robust design principles.

8.2 Installing NixOS

The installation process of NixOS underscores its robust and flexible architecture, enabling users to customize installations tailored to specific needs and environments. This section elucidates the step-by-step process of installing NixOS, detailing various installation options, partitioning strategies, and configurations necessary for diverse system environments.

Installation of NixOS begins with obtaining its ISO image, which can be found on the official NixOS website. NixOS offers different ISO images optimized for different architectures; choose the appropriate one depending on whether you are using x86_64, aarch64, or another architecture. Once the image is downloaded, it will need to be written to a USB drive.

To write the ISO to a USB drive from a Unix-like system, utilize a command such as:

```
sudo dd if=nixos-minimal-<release>.iso of=/dev/sdX bs=4M status=progress
```

Ensure /dev/sdX correctly represents your USB device, as a mistake here can overwrite critical data on another drive. With the USB drive prepared, boot the target system from the device. This action should load a NixOS environment where the installation process can begin.

Upon booting into the NixOS live environment, you are greeted with a minimalist command-line interface. From this point, it's essential to plan the partitioning strategy. NixOS installations usually require at least two partitions: one for the root filesystem and another for swap. Additional partitions, such as for home directories, can be included based upon personal preference or organizational policy.

Partitioning can be accomplished using tools such as fdisk or gdisk for MBR and GPT partition tables, respectively. Below is a succinct example using gdisk:

```
# Start 'gdisk' on /dev/sda
sudo gdisk /dev/sda

# Create new partition, select partition type
n # New partition
1 # Partition number
  # Default first sector
```

```
+512M # Last sector for EFI partition
t # Change partition type
1 # EFI System

# Repeat for other partitions, e.g., root and swap

# Write changes to the disk and exit
w
```

During this interactive session, you ensure to create required partitions like EFI system partition for UEFI-enabled systems. Traditional BIOS setups do not require this and will proceed with simply boot partitions.

Once partitioning is complete, it is imperative to create filesystems on these partitions. For the root filesystem, a recommendation is to use ext4 or btrfs due to their reliability and features, while swap should be initialized using mkswap.

```
# Create ext4 filesystem for root partition
sudo mkfs.ext4 /dev/sda1

# Process any other partitions, such as /home

# Initialize swap
sudo mkswap /dev/sda2
```

After devising the filesystem, mount these partitions. NixOS requires only the root filesystem to be mounted initially, although configuration files may refer to mounting additional partitions:

```
# Mount the root partition
sudo mount /dev/sda1 /mnt

# Optionally create and mount other directories
sudo mkdir /mnt/boot
sudo mount /dev/sdaX /mnt/boot
```

Once the filesystems are properly mounted, NixOS installation can commence by generating a configuration based on your partitions and preferences. The command `nixos-generate-config` generates initial configuration files for NixOS.

```
# Generate configuration files
sudo nixos-generate-config --root /mnt
```

This command creates a directory /mnt/etc/nixos/, containing hardware-configuration.nix and configuration.nix. The hardware-configuration.nix file includes hardware-specific details imperative for a successful system boot.

The configuration.nix file defines the entire system setup. At this point, aspects such as bootloader configurations, network settings, and most importantly, user definitions, should be reviewed and edited appropriately. A minimal example is illustrated below, although adjustments will depend on system-specific needs:

```
{ config, pkgs, ... }:

{
  boot.loader.grub.device = "/dev/sda"; # or "nodev" to use efi only
  networking.hostName = "nixos";

  fileSystems."/" = {
    device = "/dev/disk/by-label/nixos";
    fsType = "ext4";
  };

  swapDevices = [ { device = "/dev/disk/by-label/swap"; } ];

  users.users.username = {
    isNormalUser = true;
    home = "/home/username";
    shell = pkgs.bash;
  };

  services.sshd.enable = true;
}
```

Beyond this base level, configuration.nix permits extensive customization, from setting up the networking interfaces and enabling SSHD to specifying system packages and services. Users should pay careful attention to entries concerning the boot loader. For systems using UEFI, GRUB entities might involve specifications for the EFI partition:

```
boot.loader.grub.efiSupport = true;
boot.loader.efi.canTouchEfiVariables = true;
```

When you're confident the configuration resonates with your desired setup, execute the installation procedure from the live environment. This may take some time due to the installation deriving packages and performing initial setups defined by the configuration file:

```
# Install NixOS
sudo nixos-install
```

This command completes without errors, signaling a successful installation. You are prompted to set a root password during the process, essential for gaining root access to the installed system.

Post-installation procedures are pivotal. You must restore the boot sequence to prioritize the installed system, detaching any installation media. Before rebooting, inspect generated files, making amendments if necessary to fine-tune specific settings. Once booted, the installed system mirrors the setup encapsulated in configuration.nix, ensuring reproducibility across installations.

NixOS accommodates various partitioning schemes and configurations, nurturing a broad canvas for system architects. Non-trivial installations, such as those intended for production-grade servers and specific deployment environments, can opt for RAID, encrypted filesystems using LUKS, or leveraging ZFS for its advanced features including snapshot management.

Rejuvenating older systems or combining newer hardware components can involve arcane drivers or unusual configurations. hardware-configuration.nix might require tweaking to accommodate unorthodox setups. Integrating custom drivers can sometimes necessitate adjusting kernel parameters or adding custom packages.

Special deployments, including those on virtualized environments like VirtualBox, require modifications to settings involving virtual interfaces and might benefit from cloud-init configurations.

To visualize a modernization approach towards installing NixOS on cloud platforms or containers, you would consider automated installations using NixOps or Terraform with Nix integration, emphasizing Infrastructure as Code (IaC) principles. These platforms allow scaling configurations to multi-node setups, exemplifying NixOS's adaptability towards contemporary DevOps practices.

The variety of installation configurations and environments that NixOS supports truly blurs the line between flexibility and control. Mastery of configuration.nix and hardware-configuration.nix nurtures an agile administration landscape, solidifying NixOS as an effective operational system across personal, development, and enterprise solutions. The profound detailing in its configuration stems an elaborate framework crucial for tailored, repeatable, and resilient deployments, reflecting the ingenuity intrinsic to NixOS.

8.3 System Configuration with NixOS

The architecture of NixOS is deeply rooted in its singular, declarative configuration model, a standout feature that distinguishes it from traditional Linux distributions. By expressing system configurations via a single, comprehensive configuration file, NixOS empowers users to define the full state of an operating system—from packages to services, users, and networks—ensuring consistent and reproducible environments. This section delves into the intricacies of system configuration with NixOS, examining the syntax, structure, and various elements that make it a robust tool for managing and maintaining Linux systems.

Central to NixOS's configuration is the /etc/nixos/configuration.nix file. This file embodies the entire system's desired state declaratively. The syntax is structured, yet flexible, owing to its foundation—a bespoke, functional programming language known as Nix. This language introduces constructs that enable systems to be described in an expressive format, eliminating ambiguity prevalent in script-based traditional configuration formats.

At a fundamental level, the configuration.nix file uses curly braces to encapsulate configuration attributes. Each attribute corresponds to a specific configuration aspect of the system, ranging from enabling services to installing software packages or setting system-wide parameters:

```
{ config, pkgs, ... }:

{
  boot.loader.grub.device = "/dev/sda";
  networking.hostName = "my-host";

  environment.systemPackages = with pkgs; [
    vim
    wget
  ];

  users.extraUsers.jdoe = {
    isNormalUser = true;
    home = "/home/jdoe";
    description = "John Doe";
    extraGroups = ["wheel" "networkmanager"];
  };

  services.sshd.enable = true;
}
```

This example introduces several key configuration features. The environment.systemPackages section specifies user-installed packages, automatically generating and updating the package derivations each time the system is built. The users.extraUsers attribute graphs user accounts, each defined as an attribute set containing specific properties. In this instance, the definition includes the assignment of supplementary groups.

Next, the nixos-rebuild command is utilized to apply modifications defined within the configuration file. Rebuilding the system achieves synchronization between the current and target states by re-deriving packages and ensuring services reflect newly declared states:

```
# Apply configuration changes
nixos-rebuild switch
```

Executing this command results in NixOS implementing the configured environment without jeopardizing existing system stability. This prompt shifting achieves a consistency that becomes fundamental for systems demanding high reliability.

Another notable aspect of system configuration in NixOS is service management. Services are expressed as modules within the configuration.nix file. Enabling or configuring them simply entails defining a service's attributes, often set within the broader configuration scope. Let's explore the potential configuration of commonly used services:

```
{
  services.httpd = {
    enable = true;
    adminAddr = "admin@mydomain.com";
    extraModules = [ "rewrite" ];
  };

  services.mysql = {
    enable = true;
    package = pkgs.mariadb;
    ensureDatabases = [ "exampleDB" ];
    ensureUsers = [
      { name = "user"; password = "secret"; }
    ];
  };
}
```

The configuration above starts the HTTP and MySQL services whilst tuning specific parameters. Declaring services declaratively imbues predictability as each instantiation occurs securely upon system rebuild. Users can trust services are neither left running outdated versions nor bogged by misuse, common in manually managed environments.

Network configurations, too, artfully embrace this declarative mindset. NixOS allows network interfaces to be described precisely using attributes that pinpoint device states and acquire necessary settings consistently:

```
{
  networking.interfaces.ens33.useDHCP = true;

  # Static IP configuration
  networking.interfaces.eth0 = {
    ipv4.addresses = [
      {
        address = "192.168.1.100";
        prefixLength = 24;
      }
    ];
    gateway4 = "192.168.1.1";
  };
}
```

The above configuration toggles DHCP for one interface while assigning a static IP to another, enabling adaptable and swift network provisioning. In multi-interface systems, these definitions quickly converge into operational readiness reflective of dynamic customer workloads and locale policies.

Within NixOS, application isolation is synonymous with configurational scope. This granularity is achievable through an innovative employment of the Nix language, defining multiple environment constituents. NixOS makes use of profiles and overlays, enhancing and overriding dependencies as needed without interference:

```
# Overlay example introduced in configuration.nix
{
  nixpkgs.overlays = [
    (self: super: {
      myCustomVim = super.vim.overrideAttrs (oldAttrs: {
        version = "8.2";
        source = super.fetchurl {
          url = "http://my.cdn.url/vim-8.2.tar.gz";
          sha256 = "0hash";
        };
      });
    })
  ];
```

```
  environment.systemPackages = with pkgs; [ myCustomVim ];
}
```

Overlays manipulate package attributes, yielding innovative custom-variant definitions producing tailor-made distributions inherently capable of version control. At the same time, profiles facilitate distinct configuration baselines transferable across machines, further disentangling dependency chains.

The rapid adoption trajectory of NixOS attributes much to its penchant for automation and infrastructure consistency, a sentiment exemplified in deploying configurations on remote servers via tools such as NixOps. Infrastructure as code (IaC) emerges seamlessly, enabling declarative deployments to cloud providers, KVMs, or cross-network architectures efficiently:

```
{
  deployment.targetHost = "192.168.1.10";
  deployment.targetUser = "admin";
  deployment.keys = "/home/admin/.ssh/id_rsa";
  deployment.options.hostname = "prod-server";
}
```

Configuring nixops complements the earlier discussed configuration.nix, transitioning NixOS from a single-host environment towards orchestrating expansive node clusters.

NixOS stands apart not only through its declarative nature but also due to immutable directories, including /nix/store. This crate operates through hash-locking dependencies, providing a failsafe boundary circumventing traditional pitfalls surrounding updates or regular package cycles—a fundamental revolutionizing package management itself.

Rewriting entire sets of scripts and conventional package installations into reusable NixOS modules brings advanced repeatability options. Each chance includes stargazing into new ways to enhance configurations as dynamically as user-centric needs evolve, namely including version upgrades for entire groups by meticulously re-declaring their dependencies as modules.

In exploring NixOS's overarching architecture, every update accruing to configurations subsequently achieves synchronized precision, underpinned by explicit specification reduction toward immutable yet entirely flexible abstractions evolving modern systems. Synchronizing once-untraceable, complex transitions fortifies reliability and upgrade commitments concurrently.

As technologists explore, forage, and adhere to swift computational shifts, the ideological bedrock staffing NixOS's system configuration enables unprecedented systematic expressions. Engineers leverage flexibility into fortifying comprehensive, holistic visions cultivating environments for cancer research, cloud-scale computing, modular educational deployments, and beyond.

NixOS's declarative format is rigorously crafted, transforming monolithic architectures into reliable, portable paradigms fostering interconnected thought leaders solving interdependent confounders flexibly across daily operational systematics. From abstraction configuration methodologies and tooling flexibility to exact management of constraints and integrations ahead, NixOS remains a herald of agile systematized control, imperative to expansive change constituents.

8.4 Services and Modules in NixOS

NixOS leverages a modular architecture that profoundly affects how services are configured and managed, enabling remarkably flexible and scalable system setups. In this section, we delve into the intricacies of services and modules in NixOS, exploring their definition, customization, and the underlying mechanism that supports their dynamic configurability. This methodological approach allows services to be managed more comprehensively compared to conventional means, blending fine-grained control with seamless declarative statements that enhance system consistency and facilitate advanced integrations.

Modules in NixOS define services through a declarative language that abstracts individual service responsibilities into reusable and customizable components. Each module corresponds to a particular service or group of related services and is included in the NixOS configuration model via the /etc/nixos/configuration.nix file, where specific services are enabled or configured.

An introductory example illustrates service configuration, where an SSH daemon is enabled within the declarative scope of NixOS:

```
{
  services.openssh.enable = true;
  services.openssh.forwardX11 = true;
  services.openssh.permitRootLogin = "no";
}
```

The core NixOS repository provides a vast number of pre-defined modules, encapsulating common service configurations for daemons like Apache, PostgreSQL, or more extensive setups like Kubernetes. By abstracting traditionally explicit configuration logic, these service modules ensure that inconsistencies arising from manual configurations are minimized.

Each service definition typically includes a set of options that map directly to appropriate configuration settings applicable to that service. These options may vary between services, highlighting the flexibility and specificity with which each module is crafted. Modules can be found under the directory /nixpkgs/nixos/modules/services, encompassing an extensive selection geared towards ready-made deployment.

A more complex instance demonstrates how MySQL is configured:

```
{
  services.mysql.enable = true;
  services.mysql.package = pkgs.mysql;
  services.mysql.ensureDatabases = ["nixosDB"];
  services.mysql.ensureUsers = [{ name = "nixosUser"; password = "securePass"; }];
}
```

The NixOS module system relies on a tree of modules where configuration data flows from leaf to root, amalgamating specific service stages into a cohesive whole through the module declaration process. In this system, each module can claim various assignments or overwrite default settings as dictated by the enclosing scope.

A principal advantage of this modularity is facilitating compound services, enabling complex behaviours to arise from seemingly fundamental definitions. For example, the configuration of a web server can seamlessly integrate additional components like reverse proxies, cache mechanisms, or SSL termination by declaring these in configuration:

```
{
  services.nginx = {
    enable = true;
    virtualHosts.server1 = {
```

```
      root = "/var/www/my-site";
      serverName = "example.com";
      enableACME = true;
      forceSSL = true;
    };
    extraConfig = ''
      gzip on;
      gzip_types text/plain application/xml;
    '';
  };

  security.acme.certs = {
    example-cert = {
      email = "admin@example.com";
      domains = [ "example.com" "www.example.com" ];
    };
  };
}
```

In this context, the nginx configuration integrates the ACME client to retrieve SSL certificates through its declarative expressions. The structure augments the potential for a holistic web service encapsulation within a few succinct lines, greatly reducing operational overhead.

Custom service creation in NixOS extends the modular pattern further. A custom module must define its Nix attributes and delineate the specific behaviour or configurations required for the encapsulated service. The creation process utilizes Nix language constructs and typically involves defining the module's config, options, and configurations attributes.

A minimal custom service module could look like this:

```
{ config, pkgs, lib, ... }:

{
  options.myService = {
    enable = lib.mkOption {
      default = false;
      description = "Whether to enable my custom service.";
    };
  };

  config = lib.mkIf (config.myService.enable) {
    systemd.services.myService = {
      enable = true;
      description = "My Custom Service";
      script = ''
        echo "Running my custom service"
      '';
      wantedBy = [ "multi-user.target" ];
    };
  };
```

```
}
```

Within this example, lib.mkOption establishes an attribute switch, enabling the construction of systemd services only when the enable property is true. This paradigmatic use of functional programming constructs leads to significant flexibility and extension potential within NixOS.

The dynamic nature of NixOS modules not only allows experts to implement their solutions but also grafts into existing setups alternative workflows or innovations. As real-world scenarios increase in complexity, modularity mitigates concerns about emergent configurations or structure since every state explicitly declares its intent and target scope.

Moreover, the inclusion of NixOS modules within version control (such as Git) provides profound benefits when managing systems at scale. Infrastructure changes rendered as code push boundaries grounded in DevOps and agile practices, creating provable deployments that synchronize continuously as new configurations or tools develop. This inherent bit of modular design strengthens the reliability of independent yet interdependent services, substantially simplifying rollback or update procedures.

NixOS modules extend beyond configuring individual services. They grant an orchestration layer catering to complex infra setups like multi-consumer environments found in data centers or cloud deployments. Services become composable entities aligned strategically for horizontal scaling where failovers, redundancy tactics, and load distributions manifest through interconnected modules driving edge-to-core solutions.

Given their nourished versatility and fine-grained control scope, NixOS modules succinctly express the myriad strategic directions. As digital transformation accelerates, incorporating modules into automation tools and CI/CD workflows promotes collaboration, audit trails, and organizational transparency.

The seamless integrative opportunity NixOS services and modules deliver roots itself into fundamental administration principles, where automation, declarative infrastructure, composability, and consistency intertwine. Whether for educational settings, intricate DevSecOps environments or edge computing, these capabilities ensure every specification manifests into predictable, repeatable, and robust systems—a testament to the ideological achievements inherent within NixOS.

Earlier operating systems often treated services as first-class administrative functions, seated in obscure settings juxtaposed by explicit file manipulations. NixOS evolved the approach with modules reflecting cohesive methodology, enhancing scalability, and driving innovation ecosystems. Each system may bear modules deploying rejuvenated configurations effectively without partially executed stages or stressed migration cycles opposed to legacy operations.

With NixOS, traversing services and modules hallmarks a progression towards concise operational adaptive constructs, operating in an environment enriched by an internal language mechanism and agile abstraction unfixated by contrivance.

It simplifies complexity while harboring reproducible declarations; a dialect ennobling comprehensiveness within personalized adaptable landscapes. In this manner, NixOS converges traditional service paradigms toward revolutionary modularity, fostering predictable deployments, sustainability, and cutting-edge transpositions well-poised for rapid technological migrations. This ingenuity represents a pronounced departure from any uniform prior methodology, underpinning flexibility and coherence within foreseen infrastructures contoured towards the age of digital flux where services dynamically harmonize.

8.5 Upgrading and Rolling Back NixOS

NixOS embodies distinct capabilities that differentiate it profoundly from other operating systems, especially in its approach to upgrading and rolling back system states. A pivotal attribute of NixOS is its ability to manage changes atomically, ensuring system upgrades are both secure and reversible. This section elucidates the procedures, benefits, and intricacies involved in upgrading and rolling back NixOS configurations, with detailed examples and insightful analysis.

At the heart of NixOS's reliability in upgrades and rollbacks is the Nix package manager. This system manages software and configurations in a purely functional manner, wherein every change results in a new generation. A generation is effectively an immutable system snapshot, created each time the system configuration is modified and built using the nixos-rebuild command.

```
# Standard system upgrade
nixos-rebuild switch --upgrade
```

This fundamental command performs two crucial tasks: synchronizing the Nix package repository, nixpkgs, to the latest upstream state, and rebuilding the system configuration as outlined in /etc/nixos/configuration.nix. Consequently, the switch flag makes it active. During this process, NixOS ensures that the current system can continue running as is, without being disrupted until it's explicitly instructed to switch over to the new version.

The atomic nature of NixOS upgrades is akin to transactional systems in databases. Each configuration rebuild occurs in a manner where the system transitions fully from one coherent state to another. This contrasts with package-by-package upgrade processes seen in traditional distributions, decreasing the risk of partial upgrade failures that might leave systems in unsupported or inconsistent states.

As new generations develop over time, users are equipped with an unprecedented capability to rollback seamlessly:

```
# Rollback to previous generation
sudo nix-env --rollback
```

This command reverts the operating system to a prior generation, effectively undoing any changes introduced by the most recent upgrade or configuration modification. Rolling back is typically instantaneous, as Nix merely reactivates the previous store path without physically reinstalling components.

NixOS's library of generations allows users to view and manipulate specific system states over time:

```
# List system profiles
sudo nix-env --list-generations

# Activate a specific generation
sudo nix-env -G "target_generation_number"
```

The –list-generations flag enumerates all recorded generations, labeling each with an associated generation number and timestamp. System administrators can use this listing to identify the desired rollback point by referring to the known stable configuration they wish to restore.

This rigorous versioning contributes notably to NixOS's standing as a secure and navigable platform. Generations align with immutable principles, ensuring that once a system state is captured, it remains visible and utilisable irrespective of any subsequent updates. Such an approach reduces potential security exposure, as each rollback reinstates a guaranteed, previously secure configuration without the risk of untracked state drift.

The relationship between rollbacks, upgrades, and system profiles also ensures that system downgrades are just as viable as upgrades, which can be paramount in troubleshooting scenarios. If an upgrade introduces unexpected behavior or functional disruptions, reverting promptly mitigates risk.

An important consideration during upgrades is managing dependencies. For compatibility, ensure that the /etc/nixos/configuration.nix file accurately reflects elements required by the new version. Users might also wish to adapt the configuration to match repository changes or newly available feature sets.

Sometimes, transitioning to newer releases of NixOS might entail shifting configurations to accommodate deprecations and new practices. For instance, changes in configuration syntax or improvements to services might necessitate the review of configuration.nix. Architects designing systems reliant on certain baselines will need to take advantage of consultations with updated documentation or tools like nix-diff, which facilitates the evaluation of proposed changes prior to the switch.

Rollback capabilities extend beyond kernel space alone, encompassing user space files added or updated by services or applications. When rolling back, ensure user-managed data aligns with prior configurations to retain consistency.

Through a process known as Garbage Collection, administrators have the flexibility to eventually prune unused generations, liberating disk space once they have transcended their usefulness:

```
# Run garbage collection to clean up unused paths
sudo nix-collect-garbage
```

This task helps maintain system efficiency, albeit with the consideration that once collected, a generation is permanently removed, invalidating its linkage from rollback lists.

An exemplary demonstration is continuous integration or deployment pipelines extending rollbacks to manage system snapshots across numerous machines. Enterprises manipulating NixOS nodes can tightly integrate backups with rollback strategies, coupling them with unit tests ensuring system integrity per generation.

Overlay techniques enhance operational flexibility, offering provisional changes to configurations in a safe, previewing environment before cementing into production generations. This construct not only nurtures experimental innovation but augments trust for stakeholders in both development and release cycles.

For enhanced auditing, use auxiliary tools tracking generation changes over time with services like Prometheus or Grafana, supporting ongoing maintenance with pipelines monitoring version states. Layers interacting beneficially with state tracking and rollback procedures encourages thorough visual feedback of infrastructure journeys.

Encompassing the NixOS upgrade and rollback architecture is a guiding usurpation of systemic fail-safes, underpinning practices inherent in high-trust environments. As evolutionary improvements become the norm, practitioners gain assurance from extensible, immutable infrastructures epitomizing the practical and systematic utility of generation-based systems over traditional paradigms.

The harmonized approach to upgrading and rolling back states marks a fundamental shift empowering administrators to diligently control Unix-like systems without compromise — a pivot reflecting resilient operational motives coinciding with tightly coupled administrative foresight inherent within modern computing implementations. This capability yields far-reaching, reliable operational landscapes, fostered by NixOS's innovative architecture resting amidst adaptable methodologies unrestrained by historical limitations.

8.6 Community and Development in NixOS

The development and continuous enhancement of NixOS are driven by a vibrant, collaborative community that fuels its momentum both as a cutting-edge Linux distribution and a pioneering approach to system configuration. This section delves into the essential roles played by the NixOS community, the processes involved in contribution, and the tools and resources that enable its collaborative ecosystem.

NixOS thrives in an open-source environment where developers, users, and enthusiasts converge to build and extend its capabilities. This collective effort forms the backbone of NixOS's dynamic development process, exemplifying the power of community-driven innovation. At the core of this community are individuals and organizations who leverage Nix's unique properties to drive reproducibility, stability, and configurability in their digital operations.

Participation in the NixOS community unfolds through several channels. The nix-dev, nixos-users, and nixpkgs mailing lists serve as primary venues for in-depth discussions, where members engage in conversations about development practices, troubleshooting, and new feature proposals. These mailing lists create an interactive platform that facilitates knowledge sharing, enabling both new and experienced users to contribute significantly.

GitHub is an essential artery for community contributions within NixOS, where the primary repository, nixpkgs—hosting all package definitions—is maintained. Contributions are encouraged through pull requests, which are reviewed by one or more maintainers before being integrated. This rigorous review process ensures that all code meets NixOS's stringent quality standards and adheres to consistency and compatibility regulations.

An illustrative example demonstrates how developers can contribute a package to nixpkgs:

```
# Create a new branch for your changes
git checkout -b my-package-branch

# Navigate to the nixpkgs repository and add your package
cd nixpkgs/pkgs/applications/my-package
```

```
# Create a default.nix file with package details
cat << EOF > default.nix
{ stdenv, fetchurl }:

stdenv.mkDerivation rec {
  pname = "my-package";
  version = "1.0";

  src = fetchurl {
    url = "https://example.com/my-package-1.0.tar.gz";
    sha256 = "0sha256hash";
  };

  buildInputs = [ ];

  meta = with stdenv.lib; {
    description = "My sample package.";
    homepage = "https://example.com/my-package";
    license = licenses.mit;
    maintainers = with maintainers; [ yourGitHubUserName ];
  };
}
EOF
```

Within this default.nix file, essential metadata for packaging the application is included, demonstrating how simplicity in definitions aligns with NixOS's functional paradigms. After testing locally and ensuring compliance, this code is submitted as a pull request for eventual review and integration.

Documentation plays a critical role within the NixOS community, ensuring that knowledge is readily available and disseminated through official means. Comprehensive guides, beginner tutorials, and extensive references are provided, outlining clear steps for installation, configuration, advanced customizations, and debugging. The official NixOS manual and its associated wiki serve as cornerstone educational resources, while community forums such as Reddit and Discourse engage wider participation, fostering user interaction and community spirit.

NixOS Conferences and meetups, like NixCon, bring together Nix community members annually, providing them with an opportunity to present, learn, and exchange ideas. These gatherings spark collaborations, project initiatives, and prospective innovations that breathe life into the community's developmental prospects.

The modular nature of NixOS extends significant advantages to developers and contributors. Developers crafting new modules or services can rely on a consistent framework provided by Nix expressions. Custom packages can overlay existing setups floating optionally during prototyping while maintaining compatibility with established baselines. Modules offer contributors the flexibility to augment the operating system without violating structural integrity.

NixOS facilitates research and academic engagement by encouraging scenarios exploring cutting-edge computational ideas, leading to an infusion of unique perspectives. Such engagement manifests in the form of specialized modules, experimental sandbox environments, or contributing uniquely to computational science or reproducibility studies.

One exploratory avenue is the nixpkgs-fmt, which encourages consistent Nix expression code formatting across repositories, ensuring collaborative uniformity. Automation tools, including nix-diff and nix-linter, empower developers to inspect and refine contributions, aligning submissions closely with ongoing project futures.

Social media channels, including Twitter and Mastodon, further amplify community interaction by disseminating updates, discussions, and informative articles to a broader audience. They function as interactive means of opposition to static content, catering to timely updates about releases, security advisories, or newly introduced projects.

Governance within the NixOS community is democratic, relying on tiered maintainership and decentralized leadership structures. Core teams emerge organically from interests and proven expertise, delineating contributory responsibilities across key areas such as project management and package administration. Monthly and annual reviews consolidate achievements highlighting outstanding contributors, underpinning team coordination and communal aspirations.

NixOS's community brilliantly exemplifies reciprocal development, representing diverse domains and international backgrounds where inclusivity reigns paramount, thus ensuring an interoperable, versatile ecosystem continuously refines every emerging facet. The ethos of shared contribution lies at NixOS's heart preserving community unity.

Deep-rooted in collaborative engagement, NixOS extends manifold opportunities to transcend beyond traditional technical confines, where seamless integration into varied landscapes cultivates adaptation fluency and onto other operating system distributions.

Altogether, the community instills a foundation draped in open-source excellence, realized through transparent cordialities granting all participants an avenue to proclaim their creative liberties and computational dreams across NixOS's boundless and evolving environments. This vividly encapsulates the spirit of freedom, tenacity, and innovation manifesting assuredly as NixOS prevails dynamically amid collective digital transformation.

Chapter 9

Declarative System Configuration with NixOS

Declarative system configuration with NixOS empowers users to manage their entire system setup through a single, comprehensive configuration file. This approach centralizes all aspects of system configuration, including installed packages, services, user settings, and network configurations, allowing for precise control and easy replication across systems. By treating configurations as code, NixOS facilitates versioning, rollback, and sharing of system states, streamlining both setup and maintenance processes. This model ensures that changes are consistent and reversible, enhancing reliability and simplifying the complexities inherent in traditional system administration tasks.

9.1 Principles of Declarative Configuration

Declarative configuration in NixOS represents a paradigm shift from traditional imperative system configuration. It emphasizes describing the 'what' - the desired state of a system - rather than the 'how' - the steps to achieve this state - which is common in imperative approaches. This section explores the core principles underpinning declarative configuration in NixOS, differentiates it from imperative methods, and highlights its inherent advantages.

A declarative system configuration file in NixOS, typically '/etc/nixos/-configuration.nix', employs a high-level abstraction to define system attributes such as packages, services, user accounts, and various configurations. This method offers a significant distinction compared to imperative approaches, where configurations are implicitly altered through a sequence of commands executed in a shell environment.

Consider the following example of a NixOS configuration snippet declaring SSH service activation and defining a user:

```
{ config, pkgs, ... }:

{
  services.openssh.enable = true;

  users.users.jdoe = {
    isNormalUser = true;
    home = "/home/jdoe";
    shell = pkgs.bash;
  };
}
```

This configuration segment demonstrates specifying system roles holistically rather than managing each component individually. In traditional systems, enabling SSH typically involves installing necessary packages, modifying service files, and manually starting services—a task prone to human error and system drift. The declarative model eliminates this complexity.

- The declarative model in NixOS shines due to its idempotency—reapplying a configuration results in the same system state.
- This property is vital for ensuring consistency across develop-

ment, testing, and production environments.

- Imperative commands, on the other hand, are inherently non-idempotent; repeating commands can lead to different system states, causing unpredictability and potential inconsistencies.

Imperative configurations often use scripting languages like bash:

```
# Imperative example to install and start SSH
apt-get update
apt-get install -y openssh-server
systemctl enable ssh
systemctl start ssh

# Adding user 'jdoe'
useradd -m -s /bin/bash jdoe
```

This imperative approach demands knowledge of procedural steps and sequence, leading to errors if script execution diverges from expected order or state. Additionally, rollback procedures are cumbersome as they require manual intervention to undo each step—contrasting sharply with NixOS's simplified rollback capabilities inherent in its configuration-as-code model.

The declarative configuration aligns well with version control systems like Git, allowing configuration files to be versioned and tracked effectively. This integration means changes can be audited, and previous states can be easily restored. Such capabilities are cumbersome in imperative settings where changes are scattered across various files and scripts.

Atomic updates in NixOS are facilitated by the declarative model, as transitions between configurations are complete and instantaneous. In practice, each configuration build results in an atomic update at the system level.

Consider the following scenario:

```
# At a broader scale, the NixOS rebuild switch can be conceptualized as:
nixos-rebuild switch
```

This command simultaneously updates all system components defined in the NixOS configuration, producing a new state without partial transitions. Imperatively managing similar updates entails stopping services, upgrading components, and cautiously restarting to minimize downtime—a resource-intensive and error-prone process.

NixOS ensures reproducibility through its package management system based on a unique hashing mechanism. Each package derivation results in a distinct hash code, enabling precise package versioning:

```
/nix/store/dd3gf7apw6f5k5n5mgyj1r8w9si9fv2k-openssh-8.4p1
```

This guarantees that identical Nix expressions always yield the same binaries, crucial for mitigating the “it works on my machine“ problem prevalent in non-declarative systems.

Rollbacks are streamlined in NixOS by allowing selection among previous configurations within the boot menu. These rollback features are integral, contrasting sharply with cumbersome and manual backups or restoration methods typical in imperative systems.

Declaratively managing configurations mitigates complexity by reducing dependencies on human operations and procedural knowledge. Complex configurations composed verbosely in scripts are distilled into succinct, human-readable form:

```
{
  security = {
    kernelModules = ["nftables"];
    firewall = {
      enable = true;
      allowedTCPPorts = [ 80 443 ];
    };
  };
}
```

This snippet exemplifies the clarity and ease of managing comprehensive security configurations using NixOS, condensing potential lines of error-prone script into a single declaration block.

NixOS embraces modularity through declarative configurations. Modules, often subdivided for logical clarity and reusability, permit organizing configurations into discrete, manageable pieces. By leveraging overlay mechanisms or import statements, system administrators extend or customize configurations elegantly:

```
# Importing additional configuration
imports = [ ./hardware-configuration.nix ];
```

The capacity to compose configurations from multiple sources enhances maintainability and reusability, significantly lowering the cognitive load associated with managing complex systems.

In essence, the principles of declarative system configuration underpin NixOS's resilience, consistency, and efficiency in managing operating systems. By abstracting configurations into a high-level language, these principles facilitate automation, auditability, and control that exemplify the modern paradigm shift in systems administration.

9.2 Writing a NixOS Configuration File

Creating and understanding a NixOS configuration file is a pivotal aspect of administrating a NixOS system. This configuration embodies the entire system setup, offering a unified approach to manage packages, services, hardware settings, and user environment. This section provides a comprehensive guide to writing NixOS configuration files, exploring its structure, key sections, and the syntax used for defining system settings.

At the core of this file is the Nix expression language, which allows users to define system settings declaratively. A standard NixOS configuration file is located at /etc/nixos/configuration.nix. Through this configuration file, administrators specify desired system states in a clean, predictable manner.

The configuration file is framed around several main components:

- **Import Declarations**: At the beginning of the configuration file, prior configurations or modules can be imported using the `imports` attribute. This enables segmentation and modularity, facilitating easier maintenance.
- **Packages and Environment**: This section outlines the packages to be installed and configured on the system, leveraging Nix's powerful package management capabilities.
- **Services**: Service management is decluttered through declarative statements that specify which services should be enabled or disabled.

- **System Settings**: The various hardware and kernel configurations are defined here, including file systems, network settings, and security policies.
- **User Accounts**: User management is incorporated whereby accounts, groups, and permissions are specified in a decluttered manner.

Initially, consider a basic skeleton of a configuration file:

```
{ config, pkgs, ... }:

{
  # Import custom modules:
  imports = [ ./hardware-configuration.nix ];

  # Declare a list of packages
  environment.systemPackages = with pkgs; [
    vim
    wget
  ];

  # Enable SSH service
  services.openssh.enable = true;

  # Define user
  users.users.jdoe = {
    isNormalUser = true;
    shell = pkgs.bash;
  };
}
```

Within the configuration file, the environment.systemPackages attribute defines the packages to be installed. This attribute accepts a list generated by the with pkgs; construct, providing access to all packages available in the Nixpkgs repository. This model contrasts with imperative package management by ensuring package installations are consistent across installs and inherently reversible.

Packages are referred to by their attributes from the Nixpkgs library. For example:

```
environment.systemPackages = with pkgs; [
  firefox
  git
  tmux
];
```

This snippet would ensure the installation of firefox, git, and tmux packages persistently.

Service configuration benefits significantly from the declarative approach. Enabling or disabling system services involves setting logical flags under the services attribute. For instance, to manage the SSH daemon, the following directive is used:

```
services.openssh.enable = true;
```

This automatically handles the startup of the sshd service upon system boot; it abstracts the complexity surrounding service files, start levels, and run commands.

Certain services may require further configuration specifications or module declarations. Consider enabling a web server like nginx:

```
services.nginx = {
  enable = true;
  virtualHosts = {
    localhost = {
      root = "/var/www";
      listen = [ { addr = "127.0.0.1"; port = 80; } ];
    };
  };
}
```

This configuration snippet presents a practical way to define server settings directly within the NixOS configuration file, ensuring server setup is replicable and directly tied to system state.

The NixOS configuration file permits comprehensive system control, extending to hardware configurations, kernel settings, and network parameters. Specific sections within the configuration file manage these aspects gracefully:

```
networking.hostName = "myHost";
networking.useDHCP = false;

networking.interfaces.enol = {
  ipv4.addresses = [ {
    address = "192.168.1.50";
    prefixLength = 24;
  }];
  ipv4.gateway = "192.168.1.1";
};
```

Here, network interfaces and static addresses are prescribed, supplanting manual configuration steps with declarative assurances.

File system configurations are also embodied in the configuration file, articulating mount points and file system types:

```
fileSystems."/data" = {
  device = "/dev/sdb1";
  fsType = "ext4";
};
```

This consistency proffers the certainty that file systems will be established as specified, negating discrepancies common in manual setups.

User and group configuration in NixOS is embedded declaratively, circumventing traditional user management tools. This specification is valuable for automated system setups or in environments necessitating conformity:

```
users.users.janedoe = {
  isNormalUser = true;
  home = "/home/janedoe";
  description = "Jane Doe's account";
  extraGroups = [ "wheel" "networkmanager" ];
  openssh.authorizedKeys.keys = [ "(your-public-ssh-key)" ];
};
```

The inclusion of user home directories, group membership, and SSH keys is seamlessly integrated within the configuration file, underscoring the declarative configuration's power and clarity.

As configurations grow complex, modularizing is indispensable. NixOS encourages such structures by importing configuration fragments:

```
imports = [
  ./servers-config.nix
  ./network-config.nix
];
```

This strategy not only imposes organization but promotes reuse and encapsulation of configurations. By breaking configurations into logical units, administrators can maintain a clean and organized structure:

- servers-config.nix might encapsulate all server-specific configurations.
- network-config.nix could solely define network interface settings.

Future additions or refinements in specific areas require only edits within respective modules, enhancing scalability and maintainability.

Crafting configuration files in NixOS deviates from conventional methods, offering a compelling declarative alternative. By integrating packages, services, system, and user specifications into a singular, coherent document, NixOS provides unmatched versatility in system configuration management. This paradigm is foundational for achieving determinism, efficiency, and robustness in system administration and orchestration.

9.3 Managing Packages and Services Declaratively

Managing packages and services declaratively with NixOS is a groundbreaking shift from traditional operational paradigms. By articulating system configuration as a single source of truth, NixOS empowers users to define the exact specifications for packages and services, ensuring consistency, reproducibility, and ease of management. This section elucidates the methodologies for declaratively managing both operating system packages and services within the NixOS configuration file, highlighting the advantages and applications of this approach.

- **Declarative Package Management**

In NixOS, package management is a declarative construct where packages are defined in the 'environment.systemPackages' attribute. This enables users to specify the exact set of packages needed for a particular system configuration, which NixOS then ensures are installed and maintained in the desired state.

The 'environment.systemPackages' section of the configuration file encapsulates the packages necessary for your system:

```
environment.systemPackages = with pkgs; [
  vim
  git
  firefox
  thunderbird
];
```

This expression designates that the listed packages ('vim', 'git', 'firefox', 'thunderbird') should be installed on the system. The simplicity and clarity of this construct are noteworthy as it handles package installations uniformly across any NixOS system.

The list of packages is determined from Nixpkgs — the package repository of the entire ecosystem:

```
{ config, pkgs, ... }:

{
  environment.systemPackages = [
    pkgs.python39
    pkgs.nodejs
    pkgs.docker
  ];
}
```

This configuration integrates Python 3.9, Node.js, and Docker into the system environment declaratively. Importantly, these configurations ensure that if another system adopts the same configuration, it will end up with the same software installed, free of variants or version discrepancies.

- **Ensuring Consistency and Reproducibility**

Declarative packaging guarantees consistency across environments by maintaining a clear system state. When the configuration file specifies packages and system components, those specifications are deterministically enacted upon every instantiation of the configuration. This model is critical in environments like continuous integration/deployment (CI/CD) setups, where the same configurations need to be reliably recreated across different stages of deployment.

This reproducibility extends naturally across different instances or hardware, making it ideal for spin-up scenarios where virtual machines (VMs), containers, or even new physical servers need replicating precisely configured environments without inconsistency.

- **Service Management in NixOS**

Service management in NixOS enjoys similar declarative syntax and benefits. Services are enabled or configured by altering system descriptions within the configuration file. Let's explore typical service configurations:

```
services.openssh = {
  enable = true;
  permitRootLogin = "no";
};
```

Here, the SSH service is activated, and certain configurations like restricting root login are seamlessly declared. Service configurations are usually aligned with the best practices directly in the configuration file, reducing the need for post-deployment amendments.

For more complex setups, such as web server configurations, it becomes indispensable:

```
services.nginx = {
  enable = true;
  recommendedOptimizations = true;
  virtualHosts = {
    "example.com" = {
      root = "/var/www/example";
      enableACME = true;
    };
  };
};
```

In this nginx setup, domain-specific configurations allow for an easily understandable and directly extensible setup. By including 'enableACME', the configuration further automates obtaining SSL certificates via the Let's Encrypt authority, underscoring the declarative ease by which setups can adapt to differing requirements.

- **Efficiency and Automation Benefits**

A key advantage of declarative management is its automation capacity. Since configurations are predefined, the task of manual intervention or on-the-fly adjustments decreases significantly. This not only architectures within NixOS but conveys seamless integration with broader frameworks for DevOps, Infrastructure as Code (IaC), and configuration management systems.

The declarative model leverages NixOS's unique infrastructure - atomic updates, rollbacks, and garbage collection - to ensure the systems remain functional and minimized from an inefficacy standpoint.

```
# Rebuilding configurations
sudo nixos-rebuild switch

# Active rollback
sudo nixos-rebuild switch --rollback
```

The above commands exemplify the atomic switch to new configurations or reversion to a previous state without disrupting the system's integrity.

- **Customizing and Extending Packages**

Declarative management isn't limited to using existing packages; users can customize configurations or create entirely new packages when specific functionality is required.

Supposing customization to 'vim' is required to include additional plugins, this could be accomplished via overlays:

```
{ config, pkgs, ... }:

{
  nixpkgs.overlays = [
    (self: super: {
      vim = super.vim.override {
        withPlugins = [ pkgs.vimPlugins.fzf ];
      };
    })
  ];
}
```

Overlays permit package extensibility and customization according to user requirements. The overlay mechanism showcases how declarative systems balance out-of-the-box functionality and remarkable extensibility.

- **Integration with User Configurations**

User environment and shell configurations are easily incorporated within the declarative configuration file, extending beyond package and service management to provide tailor-made user experiences.

```
programs.zsh.enable = true;
programs.zsh.ohMyZsh = {
  enable = true;
  plugins = [ "git" "docker" ];
};
```

Such straightforward configurations personalize the command-line environment, evidencing the all-encompassing flexibility prescribed by the declarative management paradigm in NixOS.

- **Service Dependencies and Ordering**

NixOS declarative management accommodates service dependencies, ensuring that all required systems are active and operational in the correct sequence. This alignment is crucial when configuring services that rely on underlying databases or other supporting services.

With a simple declarative setup, necessary dependencies automatically resolve:

```
services.postgresql = {
  enable = true;
  package = pkgs.postgresql_12;
};

services.myapp = {
  enable = true;
  after = [ "postgresql.service" ];
};
```

Here, the application 'myapp' depends on 'postgresql', and NixOS will ensure that all specified dependencies are intact and started accordingly before launching the application service, maintaining service integrity and functionality.

- **Conclusion Without Closure**

The declarative approach to managing packages and services in NixOS underscores an approach grounded in precision, reproducibility, and automation. By consolidating every aspect of software management into concise, maintainable configuration files, this methodology transforms operational complexities into streamlined, transparent procedures. For system administrators, developers, and operators, NixOS provides formidable tools within this declarative framework, leveraging the power of precise configuration to propel system consistency and operational excellence into broader and more demanding contexts.

9.4 Customizing NixOS Configurations

Customizing NixOS configurations offers users the power to shape the operating system to meet specific requirements and preferences, thereby enhancing functionality and user experience. This section delves into various ways NixOS can be tailored to suit individual needs, including setting environment variables, configuring the user interface, and performance tuning. The focus is on understanding the flexibility provided by the Nix expression language and leveraging it to create modular and efficient configurations.

- **Configuring Environment Variables**

Environment variables play a crucial role in configuring the shell environment and applications' behavior. In NixOS, these variables are set within the configuration file, making them consistently reproducible across system rebuilds and simplifications.

To customize environment variables, use the 'programs.bash' or 'environment.variables' options:

```
programs.bash = {
  enable = true;
  shellPrompt = "custom prompt>";
};

environment.variables = {
  "EDITOR" = "vim";
  "LANG" = "en_US.UTF-8";
  "JAVA_HOME" = "/nix/store/path-to-java";
};
```

In this example, the shell prompt is set for the bash shell, while the EDITOR, LANG, and JAVA_HOME variables are established to ensure they are universally available to any shell session or application. This configures a uniform environment suitable for complex workflows or development activities.

- **User Interface Configuration**

Beyond functional modifications, NixOS allows extensive customization of the user interface (UI). The 'services.xserver' attribute facilitates customization options ranging from display managers to window managers and desktop environments.

Consider enabling and configuring 'KDE Plasma':

```
services.xserver = {
  enable = true;
  layout = "us";
  xkbVariant = "intl";

  displayManager.sddm.enable = true;

  desktopManager.plasma5.enable = true;
};
```

This installation facilitates a vast repository of configuration utilities, from theming KDE to installing specific widgets and tweaking in-depth performance notes.

Moreover, users interested in less conventional setups, such as 'i3', can set it in the same manner:

```
services.xserver = {
  enable = true;
  layout = "us";

  windowManager.i3.enable = true;
  windowManager.i3.extraConfig = ''
    bindsym $mod+Return exec i3-sensible-terminal
  '';
};
```

This snippet enables 'i3', a tiling window manager, providing custom keybindings via 'extraConfig', exemplifying highly tailored window management setups with minimal configurations.

- **Hardware Customization and Performance Tuning**

Efficient hardware customization and performance tuning seize the capabilities of the underlying hardware, ensuring optimal performance. NixOS excites with features that permit precise hardware configurations, including kernel parameter tweaks and CPU scheduling policies.

Here's an example involving custom kernel parameters:

```
boot.kernelParams = [ "quiet" "splash" "amd_iommu=on" ];
```

Such custom parameters manage boot verbosity and integrated hardware modules using kernel parameters, suitable for advanced custom setups like GPU passthrough in virtualization environments.

Memory and process management can also be fine-tuned declaratively:

```
nix.settings.memoryPolicy = "swapper";
systemd.services.myservice = {
  serviceConfig.MemoryLimit = "512M";
  serviceConfig.CPUQuota = "50%";
};
```

By incorporating these, the configuration file controls system memory management policies and constrains resource consumption on a per-service basis, elevating overall system stability and performance.

- **Modularizing Configurations for Scalability**

Scaling configurations while keeping them manageable demands a modular approach. In NixOS, separate, logically defined files can encapsulate complex configurations, which subsequently merge through the 'imports' directive.

Modular configuration assists with both maintainability and scalability:

```
# Top-level configuration.nix
imports = [
  ./users.nix
  ./network-security.nix
  ./development-tools.nix
];
```

Each sub-module 'users.nix', 'network-security.nix', and 'development-tools.nix' is designed to encapsulate different system components, preventing the top-level configuration from becoming unwieldy and intricate.

This mechanism permits each module to handle independent contexts, allowing discrete focus areas throughout configuration updates, comprehending deliverables into smaller prevailing units.

- **Security Enhancements and Customizations**

Customization inherently extends to security adjustments. NixOS's declarative model strengthens the ability to set up security measures across services or globally without direct interaction with sensitive system files.

Example configurations include:

```
security.sudo.extraRules = [
  {
    users = [ "admin" ];
    commands = [ { command = "/bin/mkdir"; options = [ "NOPASSWD" ]; } ];
  }
];

services.sshd = {
  enable = true;
  passwordAuthentication = false;
  authorizedKeys.keys = [ "ssh-rsa (public-key-data)" ];
};
```

Here, SSH is configured within defined security guidelines, disabling password authentication in favor of SSH keys. Similarly, 'sudo' configurations allow precise control over user privileges.

Implementing firewalls, an essential security consideration, is direct and modular:

```
networking.firewall.allowedTCPPorts = [ 22 80 443 ];
networking.firewall.enable = true;
```

With these lightweight directives, network defenses are set effortlessly, integrating network exposure protection into configuration management.

- **Developing With Nix: Custom Derivations**

Development ecosystems often rely on unique derivations or environments. NixOS makes it possible to define custom development environments and package derivations efficiently through custom Nix expressions.

For developing in Python with specific dependencies:

```
let
  myPythonEnv = pkgs.python39.withPackages (ps: with ps; [
    requests
    numpy
    flask
  ]);
in {
  environment.systemPackages = [ myPythonEnv ];
```

```
}
```

This block showcases creating environment extensions with Python packages specified. This method defines a highly portable and reproducible development setup beneficial in diversified computational fields.

Furthermore, crafting specific Nix derivations enhances customizability and precise control:

```
{ stdenv, fetchurl }:

stdenv.mkDerivation rec {
  pname = "mysoftware";
  version = "1.0";

  src = fetchurl {
    url = "https://example.com/mysoftware-1.0.tar.gz";
    sha256 = "0lmzm3snziahxjpy0i8gpnrcf55p3jbdcdiy53lhrv3x8lq6hxdp";
  };

  buildInputs = [ ];

  installPhase = ''
    mkdir -p $out/bin
    cp my-binary $out/bin/
  '';
}
```

Here is a custom package derivation scripted within Nix expression language, illustrating a holistic view of source-fetching, building, and installation processes. Each derivation ensures environments tailored in elegance and power.

- **Conclusion Through Furtherance**

Through NixOS, system states are finely detailed and extensible. Customizing NixOS configurations demonstrates this ability from user environments down to kernel sharpness and beyond. In reconceptualizing systems administration through NixOS, operators and developers elevate personalization to a decisive interplay—laying frameworks for innovation underscored with consistency and longevity.

9.5 Deploying and Scaling NixOS Configurations

Effective deployment and scaling of configurations are crucial aspects of any system administration strategy. In NixOS, deployment is streamlined through its fully declarative model, enhancing scalability and consistency across environments. This section delves into strategies for deploying NixOS configurations on multiple systems and scaling setups to accommodate growth and shift in system demands. We explore shared configurations, remote deployment techniques, and the advantages of using NixOps, Nix's tool for deploying NixOS machines.

Shared Configurations

One of the fundamental strengths of NixOS is the ability to use shared configurations, allowing multiple systems to utilize the same configuration file or modules. This reduces redundancy and ensures uniformity across different environments, such as development, testing, and production. Shared configurations can be maintained in a version control system like Git, enabling easy updates and rollbacks.

A shared configuration can be structured into reusable modules:

```
# core.nix
{ config, pkgs, ... }:

{
  environment.systemPackages = with pkgs; [ vim git ];

  services.openssh.enable = true;
}

# deploy.nix
{ config, pkgs, ... }:

{
  imports = [ ./core.nix ];

  networking.hostName = "production-server";
  networking.firewall.allowedTCPPorts = [ 22 80 443 ];
}
```

In this setup, 'core.nix' holds the common packages and service definitions, while 'deploy.nix' extends this base configuration to include environment-specific settings such as hostname and firewall rules, promoting modularity and ease of extension.

Remote Deployment with NixOps

For deploying NixOS machines, NixOps offers an indispensable tool. It simplifies deploying networked systems onto various platforms, be it virtual machines or cloud services, automating tasks like provisioning and configuring VMs.

A sample NixOps deployment configuration might look like this:

```
# configuration.nixops
{ ... }:

{
  network.description = "Web server deployment";

  resources = {
    machine = {
      instances = [
        {
          name = "web-server";
          type = "qemu";
          configuration = ./deploy.nix;
          disks."/var/lib" = { size = 10; device = "/dev/sdb"; };
          memory = 4096;
          cpus = 2;
        }
      ];
    };
  };
}
```

NixOps automates machine lifecycle management, leveraging configuration files to describe resources, automating initialization, and maintaining control over distributed architectures.

Scaling Configurations with Declarative Templates

Scaling configurations involves amplifying them to suit additional resources, such as additional servers or services. This challenge is met with parametric configurations, enabling the creation of templates that adjust according to scaling requirements.

For instance, scaling a database pool can be achieved by parameterizing database instances:

```
let
  mkDatabase = name: {
    services.postgresql.enable = true;
    services.postgresql.dataDir = "/var/lib/postgresql/${name}";
  };
```

```
in
{
  imports = [
    (mkDatabase "db1")
    (mkDatabase "db2")
  ];
}
```

This parameterization approach allows for straightforward instantiation of multiple database servers, adapting configurations consistently without duplicated manual interventions.

Optimizing for Scalability and Performance

Deploying systems at scale demands performance tuning at various layers, from virtualized machines to application-specific tweaks. The declarative nature of NixOS simplifies specifying these optimizations at deployment.

Configure specific system-level optimizations for handling high loads:

```
systemd.services.myapp.serviceConfig.CPUQuota = "75%";
systemd.services.myapp.serviceConfig.MemoryLimit = "2G";

networking.useHostnames = true;
networking.extraHosts = ''
  10.0.0.1 db1
  10.0.0.2 db2
'';
```

Such settings ensure that resource usage aligns with available capacities, weaving resource governance into the fabric of NixOS's repeatable deployment model.

Integrating Continuous Deployment Pipelines

Seamlessly integrating NixOS configurations into continuous deployment (CD) pipelines fortifies modern DevOps practices. The determinism and predictability inherent to NixOS align with CD principles, supporting automated testing and deployment workflows.

Here's a concise pipeline step employing nixos-rebuild as an orchestrator command:

```
# Deployment step example in CD pipeline
steps:
  - checkout
  - name: Deploy
    run: |
      nixos-rebuild switch \
```

```
    --fast \
    --build-host builds.example.com \
    --target-host root@prod-server
```

This pipeline employs 'nixos-rebuild' for efficient deployment, ensuring each change inflicts minimal disruption, thanks to fast-building capabilities and distributed build infrastructures.

Disaster Recovery and Rollbacks

In distributed and scaled environments, swift recovery from inadvertent changes or failures is critical. NixOS's atomic switching and rollback capabilities mitigate such occurrences, enabling seamless transition between system states.

Performing a rollback:

```
# Rollback command on NixOS machine
sudo nixos-rebuild switch --rollback
```

This command swiftly reverts recent configuration changes, proving indispensable when novel changes cause instability—a testament to consistency and safety.

Case Studies of Scaled Deployments

To appreciate NixOS's scalability, consider its application in tech enterprises:

- **Web Hosting Services** utilize NixOS for consistent environment setups across hundreds of servers, each running identical configurations making automation efficient as even clusters scale into the thousands.
- **Data-Centric Applications** embrace NixOS for its precision package control and reproducibility, deploying complex workloads that span multiple cloud providers by abstracting complex needs into modularized configurations.

Several production deployments reflect NixOS's versatility, demonstrating that adoption engenders not only controllability but also inspires confidence in launch security.

Final Insights on Scaling with NixOS

The principles underlying deploying and scaling configurations with NixOS extend the philosophy of reproducibility from singular systems into networked, conglomerated architectures. Successfully managing this entails leveraging declarative descriptions to minimize manual configurations, engage automated deployment tooling like NixOps effectively, and align integrally with CI/CD methodologies for scalable, maintainable environments. Such practices sharpen the tools of system administrators, developers, and engineers to proficiently embrace growth demands, all while retaining the deterministic reliability that NixOS enshrines.

9.6 Using Configuration Modules for Modularity

Modularity in configuration management is a crucial element in maintaining clear, reusable, and scalable setups. In NixOS, configuration modules serve as the foundation for creating modular configurations that can be easily managed and extended. By leveraging configuration modules, system administrators can abstract complex configurations into discrete, manageable components. This section provides an in-depth exploration of using configuration modules in NixOS, emphasizing their benefits and demonstrating practical applications to achieve modularity.

Configuration modules in NixOS are Nix files that contain definitions and configurations for specific aspects of a system. These modules, defined in '.nix' files, can be imported into the main configuration file, effectively creating a structured, layered configuration system. Each module can encapsulate a distinct part of the system configuration, such as network settings, user management, service configurations, and more.

The typical structure of a configuration module includes:

- **Imports**: Specify other modules or configurations that need to be included.
- **Declarations**: Define the settings and services managed by the module.

- **Options**: Specify default configurations and provide options for customization.

A basic module example might look like this:

```
# networking.nix
{ config, pkgs, ... }:

{
  networking.hostName = "myHost";
  networking.useDHCP = false;

  networking.interfaces.eno1 = {
    ipv4.addresses = [ { address = "192.168.1.50"; prefixLength = 24; } ];
    ipv4.gateway = "192.168.1.1";
  };
}
```

In practice, this enables network settings to be contained and managed independently of other system configurations, promoting clarity and reuse.

The adoption of a modular design for NixOS configurations yields multiple benefits:

- **Reusability**: Modules allow configurations to be reused across different systems or environments. This is especially useful in environments where similar setups are required, such as development, testing, and production.
- **Maintainability**: By breaking down complex configurations into smaller modules, the system becomes easier to maintain. Each module can be independently updated, modified, or extended without impacting other parts of the system.
- **Scalability**: Modular configurations allow for easier scaling as the system grows. New functionalities can be added as modules without disturbing the existing configuration.
- **Collaboration**: Developers can work on different modules independently, facilitating parallel development and better collaboration in teams.

When building modules, it is vital to adhere to a structured scheme where each module targets a specific area of the system. Modules can be organized into directories reflecting their purpose, such as '/etc/nixos/modules/users.nix' or '/etc/nixos/modules/services.nix'.

```
# users.nix
{ config, pkgs, ... }:

{
  users.users.jdoe = {
    isNormalUser = true;
    home = "/home/jdoe";
    shell = pkgs.bash;
    extraGroups = [ "wheel" "docker" ];
  };
}
```

The above example represents a user management module that can be imported whenever a specific user configuration is required.

To implement these modules in a main NixOS configuration file:

```
# configuration.nix
{ config, pkgs, ... }:

{
  imports = [
    ./networking.nix
    ./users.nix
  ];

  environment.systemPackages = [ pkgs.git pkgs.htop ];
}
```

Here, 'networking.nix' and 'users.nix' features are easily incorporated alongside other configurations, emphasizing the fluidity alongside system packages.

Modules can be customized or extended to accommodate specific requirements. NixOS supports overriding part of a module without changing its original code, thus preserving the core structure while extending functionalities.

Below is an example of a module that configures a database service with extensibility:

```
# database.nix
{ config, pkgs, ... }:

{
  services.postgresql = {
    enable = true;
    package = pkgs.postgresql_12;
    initialScript = ''
```

```
      CREATE USER admin WITH PASSWORD 'password';
      CREATE DATABASE myapp;
    '';
  };
}
```

To customize additional behavior or settings in this module, overlay mechanisms can be used:

```
{ config, pkgs, lib, ... }:

let
  dbWithExtras = config: {
    services.postgresql.extraConfig = ''
      listen_addresses = '*'
      logging_collector = on
    '';
  };
in
{
  imports = [
    (./database.nix) // dbWithExtras
  ];
}
```

This approach cleanly extends the configuration to meet additional requirements without touching the base module code.

As systems increase in complexity, modularization empowers administrators to focus separately on each aspect, from low-level configurations to high-level abstractions. An effective methodology is to have every aspect configured via modules, such as security policies, access controls, application deployments, and system services.

```
# security.nix
{ config, ... }:

{
  security.sudo.extraRules = [
    {
      users = [ "admin" ];
      commands = [ { command = "/bin/systemctl"; options = [ "NOPASSWD" ]; } ];
    }
  ];

  users.extraGroups = [ "docker" "libvirt" ];
}
```

In complex architectures, modularity translates into a tangible reduction in disentangling intricate parts, preferring direct adjustability and broadened oscillation across similar yet nuanced demands.

Real-world applications and best practices demonstrate the practicality of modular configurations:

- **Infrastructure as Code (IaC)**: Modularized NixOS configurations are integral to IaC paradigms, aligning with tools such as Terraform or Ansible for sophisticated deployment scenarios.
- **Enterprise Environments**: Corporations utilize configurations as templates for OS installations across diverse hardware and geographical locations, preferring a modular approach for universal deployment implications.

Best practice recommendations include:

- Naming conventions that reflect module contents, enhancing readability.
- Using comments judiciously within modules to articulate configurations.
- Decomposing superfluous dependencies to avoid coupling between modules.

NixOS's modular capabilities promote robust deployment automation, refined through adaptive technologies and development efficiencies paraphrased through configuration management philosophies.

Using configuration modules in NixOS engrains modularity into system administration, unifying flexibility with structured accents. Through this narrative, such attributes amplify NixOS's scalability and maintainability, expanding on what began as singular system outlines into colossal, diversified ecosystems fortified with systemic reinforcement and alignment. Integrating modular practices solidifies the foundation from which systems constructs evolve, propelling operational assurance and innovation in system orchestration forward.

Chapter 10

Advanced Nix Usage and Customization

Advanced Nix usage and customization involves leveraging the full capabilities of the Nix programming language and its ecosystem to tailor software environments precisely. Users can exploit advanced features such as overlays, custom derivations, and hooks to modify and extend packages beyond default configurations. Through the NixOS module system and the use of library functions, complex and modular configurations are attainable, enhancing reusability and scalability. This chapter explores these techniques, enabling users to create optimized, performance-tuned setups and maintain proprietary repositories, showcasing the flexibility and depth of Nix amidst diverse computing demands.

10.1 Deep Dive into Nix Language Features

Exploring advanced features of the Nix language allows for precise control and enhanced functionality in software management and deployment. This includes examining higher-order functions, lazy evaluation, and complex attribute sets, which are fundamental in implementing efficient and customizable configurations in Nix environments. These features provide the foundational tools necessary for users to extend and optimize package builds and systems with greater flexibility.

Nix, a purely functional package management system, uses a distinctive language characterized by its emphasis on immutability and functional composition. This language paradigm ensures deterministic builds and reproducible environments, essential for modern software engineering requirements. Here we delve into key language features of Nix that distinguish it from traditional package management systems.

- **Higher-Order Functions**

At the core of Nix's functional programming capabilities are higher-order functions. These are functions that can take other functions as arguments or return them as results. This feature facilitates modular and reusable code by allowing functions to be composed, passed around, and manipulated during runtime.

Consider the following example of a higher-order function in Nix:

```
let
  map = f: list:
    if list == [] then []
    else [ f (head list) ] ++ (map f (tail list));
  addOne = x: x + 1;
in
  map addOne [1, 2, 3, 4, 5]
```

The 'map' function takes a function 'f' and a list 'list', applying function 'f' to each element of 'list'. In this instance, 'addOne' is a simple function that increments its argument by one. Applying 'map' with 'addOne' to the list '[1, 2, 3, 4, 5]' results in '[2, 3, 4, 5, 6]'. Higher-order functions in Nix are instrumental in operations such as data transformation and functional abstraction.

- **Lazy Evaluation**

Lazy evaluation is a strategy that delays the execution of an expression until its value is actually needed. This approach not only improves performance by avoiding unnecessary calculations but also supports handling potentially infinite data structures.

In Nix, lazy evaluation can manifest in several operations, ensuring calculations are deferred until absolutely necessary. Consider the following example where lazy evaluation is crucial:

```
let
  infiniteNumbers = listFrom: current:
    [current] ++ (listFrom (current + 1));
  take = n: list:
    if n <= 0 || list == [] then []
    else [ (head list) ] ++ (take (n - 1) (tail list));
in
  take 5 (infiniteNumbers 1)
```

Here, 'infiniteNumbers' generates an infinite list starting from a given number, while 'take' extracts a finite number of elements from any list. Thanks to lazy evaluation, Nix efficiently handles an infinite list without evaluating its elements until required. In this example, the outcome would be the list '[1, 2, 3, 4, 5]'.

- **Attribute Sets and Advanced Typing**

Attribute sets in Nix are dictionaries that map strings to values. They are central to defining packages and configurations, offering a structured way to organize complex data. Attribute sets support pattern matching and updates, thus enabling flexible data manipulation.

Consider the basic setup of an attribute set:

```
let
  config = {
    hostName = "example-host";
    user = "admin";
  };
in
  "${config.hostName} is managed by ${config.user}"
```

This example illustrates assigning values to 'config', which can be accessed directly using dot-notation. The encapsulated data can be updated using the '//' operator, allowing for immutable but easily modifiable structures.

Advanced typing in Nix leverages the explicitly declarative configuration model. Functions and operators in Nix deliver type checking at evaluation, ensuring functions are applied correctly. A simple function showcasing type safety is depicted here:

```
let
  sum = a: b: if (builtins.isInt a && builtins.isInt b) then a + b else throw "
      Arguments must be integers";
in
  sum 5 7
```

The 'sum' function summates two numbers while confirming they are both integers. If either argument is not an integer, an error message is thrown. This mechanism guarantees that inputs meet specified types, providing safer code and reducing runtime errors.

- **Modularity and Function Composition**

Functional composition is a powerful feature of Nix, facilitating modular and scalable configurations. By combining simple functions into more complex constructs, users achieve intricate configurations with clear logical steps.

Assuming the existence of two functions, 'double' and 'negate', one might compose them as follows:

```
let
  double = x: 2 * x;
  negate = x: -x;
  doubleNegate = x: (double (negate x));
in
  doubleNegate 4
```

Here, 'doubleNegate' is the composition of 'double' and 'negate', succinctly yielding '-8' when applied to '4'. Functional composition leverages the reusability and flexibility of code, ensuring users can build comprehensive configurations from simple building blocks.

- **Recursive Functions and Fixed Points**

Nix supports recursive functions, a critical aspect enabling users to define functions referencing themselves. Recursive definitions are often tied to fixed points, which represent inputs that remain unaltered by further transformations.

A classic recursive function is the factorial, which can be defined using a fix-point combinator:

```
let
  fix = f: (x: f (x x)) (x: f (x x));
  factorial = fix (fact: n: if n == 0 then 1 else n * fact (n - 1));
in
  factorial 5
```

The 'fix' function enables recursion without the function explicitly calling itself by name. Applying 'factorial' to '5' results in '120', demonstrating how recursive constructs can be elegantly expressed in Nix.

- **Nix Language and Domain-Specific Constructs**

The language's intrinsic domain-specific constructs provide the means to define package derivations precisely. Derivations are the building blocks for describing how packages are built and are composed using Nix's high-level abstractions.

The following example outlines a simple derivation:

```
let
  pkgs = import <nixpkgs> {};
in
  pkgs.stdenv.mkDerivation {
    name = "example";
    src = ./.;
    buildInputs = [ pkgs.gcc ];
    buildPhase = ''
      gcc -o hello hello.c
    '';
    installPhase = ''
      mkdir -p $out/bin
      cp hello $out/bin/
    '';
  }
```

This derivation clearly specifies inputs, build tools, and installation steps using expressive syntax. Such clarity helps maintain and extend packages with ease.

In addition, domain-specific constructs include Nix's API, which is rich in utility functions aiding in expression evaluation, derivation construction, and data manipulation. Familiarity with these constructs empowers users to develop robust configurations swiftly.

The exploration of advanced Nix language features reveals a highly flexible and powerful system for managing software builds and environments. Understanding higher-order functions, lazy evaluation, complex attribute sets, and functional composition are essential for leveraging the full potential of Nix. As practical applications of these language features expand, they enhance package management's precision, efficiency, and clarity, positioning Nix as a critical tool in modern software engineering practices.

10.2 Customizing Builds with Hooks and Patches

Customizing package builds in Nix involves leveraging hooks and patches — powerful tools that allow developers to modify and extend builds to suit specific requirements. This degree of customization accommodates unique deployment necessities and enhances the functionality of managed software environments. Understanding how to implement hooks and patches proficiently is essential for exploiting the modularity and flexibility that Nix offers.

Understanding Hooks in Nix Hooks in Nix specify additional instructions to be executed during different phases of the build process. Typically, these are shell commands or scripts executed before or after the main phases like configurePhase, buildPhase, or installPhase. Hooks allow seamless integration of custom scripts, helping to automate additional steps without altering the original build scripts extensively.

A Nix derivation can include hooks as follows:

```
let
  pkgs = import <nixpkgs> {};
in
  pkgs.stdenv.mkDerivation {
    name = "sampleHookedBuild";
    src = ./.;
    preBuild = ''echo "Running pre-build script..."'';
    postInstall = ''echo "Running post-install script..."'';
  }
```

In this example, the derivation utilizes preBuild and postInstall hooks to execute scripts automatically before the build and after the installation phase, respectively. Users can define any number of hooks to tailor the build process precisely, adapting package behaviors dynamically based on needs.

Common Use Cases for Hooks Hooks serve various practical purposes, such as applying custom configurations, setting environment variables, cleaning up files, or executing sanity checks. Some common examples include:

- **Setting Environment Variables:** Hooks can set or modify environment variables dynamically to adapt builds to different systems or deployment conditions.

```
preConfigure = ''
  export CXXFLAGS="-O2 -g"
  echo "C++ flags set to $CXXFLAGS"
'';
```

- **Custom Pre- or Post-Build Steps:** Hooks execute supplementary scripts or commands necessary for the builds.

```
preBuild = ''
  chmod +x customScript.sh
  ./customScript.sh || exit 1
'';
```

- **Patch Application:** Some hooks apply patches, as discussed below, directly integrating fixes or modifications at specific build stages.

The versatility of hooks contributes significantly to the granularity of control Nix offers during package setup and deployment.

Patches and Their Role in Customization Patches allow modifications in source code. They are diff files that apply changes to the codebase, often used to integrate bug fixes, security updates, or feature enhancements without waiting for the upstream release. In Nix, patches are directly specified within a derivation, streamlining the build modification process transparently.

A simple example of applying patches within a Nix derivation could be:

```
let
  pkgs = import <nixpkgs> {};
  myPatch = ./fix-bug.patch;
in
  pkgs.stdenv.mkDerivation {
    name = "patchedSoftware";
    src = ./.;
    patches = [ myPatch ];
  }
```

This derivation leverages myPatch, implementing modifications seamlessly during the build process. Utilizing patches allows developers and maintainers to implement crucial updates while maintaining consistent, reproducible environments.

Creating and Applying Patches Creating a patch involves generating a diff of the original and modified files. Tools such as diff in Unix-like systems facilitate this process. The command:

```
diff -u original_file.c modified_file.c > fix-bug.patch
```

produces a patch file fix-bug.patch containing necessary changes. To apply this patch during a Nix build, specify it within the patches attribute as demonstrated above.

In scenarios necessitating multiple patches, Nix efficiently manages and applies them in sequence:

```
let
  pkgs = import <nixpkgs> {};
  patchOne = ./fix-bug.patch;
  patchTwo = ./enable-feature.patch;
in
  pkgs.stdenv.mkDerivation {
    name = "multiPatchedSoftware";
    src = ./.;
    patches = [ patchOne patchTwo ];
  }
```

Each listed patch processes sequentially, with later patches potentially overwriting or complementing earlier ones. This ordering provides extensive control over how patches influence the final build.

Advanced Patch Techniques Advanced usage of patches entails conditional application, dynamically controlled through environmental setups. Consider the following conditionally applied patch:

```
let
  pkgs = import <nixpkgs> {};
  extraPatch = ./optional-feature.patch;
in
  pkgs.stdenv.mkDerivation {
    name = "conditionallyPatchedSoftware";
    src = ./.;
    patches = (if pkgs.stdenv.isDarwin then [ extraPatch ] else []);
  }
```

In this case, extraPatch applies only on Darwin-based systems. Such functionality ensures patches are relevant and optimized based on target environments, preventing unnecessary or harmful modifications in incompatible systems.

Additionally, some build systems require manual patch application through custom hooks. This might be accomplished using a custom prePatch hook:

```
prePatch = ''
  patch -p1 < ${./missing-include.patch} || exit 1
'';
```

This script manually applies a patch, integrating custom error handling or more nuanced patch strategies as necessary.

Interplay of Hooks and Patches The interaction between hooks and patches empowers developers to coordinate complex build processes proficiently. For instance, developers might apply patches and subsequently trigger specific configuration changes through hooks:

```
let
  pkgs = import <nixpkgs> {};
  featurePatch = ./new-feature.patch;
in
  pkgs.stdenv.mkDerivation {
    name = "fullyCustomizedBuild";
    src = ./.;
    patches = [ featurePatch ];
    postPatch = ''
      echo "Custom config adjustments post-patching..."
      ./configure --enable-new-feature
    '';
  }
```

This sequence ensures the system accommodates applied patches with necessary configurations, establishing coherence in complex derivations.

Case Study: Customizing Open Source Software Builds A real-world example involves customizing the build of a popular open-source project to include custom branding and optimization flags. This would encompass specifying hooks for environmental settings and applying patches for branding.

```
let
  pkgs = import <nixpkgs> {};
  brandingPatch = ./branding.patch;
in
  pkgs.stdenv.mkDerivation {
    name = "customizedOSS";
    src = pkgs.fetchFromGitHub {
      owner = "somerepo";
      repo = "opensourceproject";
      rev = "v1.0.0";
      sha256 = "...";
    };
    patches = [ brandingPatch ];
    preConfigure = ''
      export CFLAGS="-O2 -march=native"
    '';
    postInstall = ''
      echo "Build complete with custom branding"
    '';
  }
```

In this case, the build is tailored with performance-centric flags and specific branding modifications verified through subsequent scripts. Such adaptations demonstrate the utility of hooks and patches for actual deployment scenarios, significantly influencing the differentiation and specialization of software builds in product ecosystems.

The strategic deployment of hooks and patches in Nix permits substantial customization, enhancing the capacity for managing, extending, and optimizing packages. Mastery of these tools ensures precise control over build processes, fostering innovative and distinct software deployment solutions tailored to unique operational exigencies.

10.3 Leveraging Overlays for Package Management

Overlays in Nix enable users to extend and customize the Nixpkgs repository effortlessly, offering a way to incorporate new packages or modify existing ones without altering the original source. This functionality is vital for maintaining a clean separation between custom modifications and official Nixpkgs, facilitating collaboration, version control, and adaptability in package management. This section explores the structure, usage, and advantages of overlays, supplemented by detailed coding examples and analysis.

- Understanding Overlays

Overlays in Nix allow users to inject custom logic or packages into the Nixpkgs package ecosystem. They operate by layering additional package definitions or alterations over the original Nixpkgs definitions, similar to how filesystem overlays work in other contexts. This layered approach is highly beneficial as it preserves the integrity of upstream packages while enabling extensive customization.

Consider overlays as higher-level constructs that wrap around Nixpkgs, modifying or augmenting package expressions. Overlays are defined using Nix expressions within a conceptual framework that ties each package's modifications seamlessly into existing or new packages.

- Structure of Overlays

The structure of an overlay involves defining a function that takes an attribute set, usually containing existing package sets, and returns a new attribute set. This new set can contain modified versions of existing packages or new packages defined in terms of the original ones.

Here is an example demonstrating the basic structure of an overlay:

```
self: super: {
  foo = super.foo.overrideAttrs (old: {
    version = "2.0.0";
    src = self.fetchurl {
      url = "https://example.com/foo-2.0.0.tar.gz";
      sha256 = "...";
```

```
    };
  });
}
```

In this example, the overlay takes 'self' and 'super' as arguments:

- 'super' represents the original package set, serving as a basis for modification.
- 'self' provides access to the modified package set, enabling recursive definitions when necessary.

The package 'foo' is overridden using 'overrideAttrs', changing its version and source URL. This overlay illustrates how users can refine a package's attributes without directly modifying the original definition in Nixpkgs.

- Applying Overlays

To apply overlays, users typically employ them within a Nix expression that imports Nixpkgs with the overlay applied. The following code snippet exhibits overlay application:

```
let
  overlay = import ./my-overlay.nix;
  nixpkgs = import <nixpkgs> {
    overlays = [ overlay ];
  };
in
  nixpkgs.mkShell {
    buildInputs = [ nixpkgs.foo ];
  }
```

In this script, the user:

1. Defines 'overlay' by importing a local file named 'my-overlay.nix'.
2. Imports Nixpkgs and applies the overlay through the 'overlays' attribute.

The Nix environment, created with 'mkShell', includes the customized package 'foo', thereby making the new package attributes available for use or further modification.

- Complex Overlay Implementations

Overlays are not limited to simple attribute modifications. They can refactor entire package structures or add sophisticated logic conditions. A complex overlay example might involve conditional logic dependent on particular system features:

```
self: super: {
  bar = if self.stdenv.isDarwin then
    super.bar.overrideAttrs (old: {
      version = "3.0.0-darwin";
      buildInputs = old.buildInputs ++ [ self.libFoo ];
    })
  else
    super.bar;

  libFoo = self.fetchFromGitHub {
    owner = "someuser";
    repo = "libFoo";
    rev = "abcde";
    sha256 = "...";
  };
}
```

Here, the overlay defines package 'bar' with differing attributes based on the operating system. On Darwin systems, it modifies 'bar' with a specific version and an additional build input, 'libFoo', which is also defined as part of the overlay using 'fetchFromGitHub'.

- Use Cases and Benefits of Overlays

Overlays present numerous benefits and use cases within Nix package management. Key benefits include:

- Non-intrusive Customization: Overlays redefine packages without touching the original Nixpkgs, maintaining backward compatibility with upstream changes.
- Separation of Concerns: Distinct overlays permit easy toggling between different customization sets or experimentation with new configurations while keeping base package definitions clean.
- Collaboration and Sharing: Overlays can be shared among teams or communities, enabling collective enhancement of package sets without requiring central repository modifications.

- Isolated Experimentation: Developers can use overlays to experiment with new versions or optimizations independently from the main package repository.

- Exploring Real-World Overlay Scenarios

Scenario 1: Integrating New Dependencies

Consider a project requiring a library not currently included in Nixpkgs. An overlay provides a straightforward mechanism to introduce this dependency:

```
self: super: {
  newLibrary = super.stdenv.mkDerivation {
    name = "newLib";
    version = "1.2.3";
    src = self.fetchurl {
      url = "https://example.com/newLib-1.2.3.tar.gz";
      sha256 = "...";
    };
    buildInputs = [ super.zlib ];
    nativeBuildInputs = [ super.gnumake ];
    installPhase = ''
      mkdir -p $out/lib
      cp libnew.so $out/lib/
    '';
  };
}
```

This overlay defines a new library 'newLibrary', introduces it into the environment, ensuring compatibility with existing tools and dependencies seamlessly integrated within package construction.

Scenario 2: Performance Enhancements

One might seek performance enhancements through compiling optimizations for key packages:

```
self: super: {
  fastHTTP = super.fastHTTP.overrideAttrs (old: {
    CFLAGS = "-O3 -march=native";
    NIX_CFLAGS_COMPILE = "-DNDEBUG";
  });
}
```

Here, the 'fastHTTP' package is substantially optimized with compilation flags targeting enhanced performance on specific hardware architectures by setting aggressive optimization and native flags.

Scenario 3: Debugging and Development

Developers may use overlays to introduce debugging flags temporarily for development builds:

```
self: super: {
  debuggingApp = super.app.overrideAttrs (old: {
    buildInputs = old.buildInputs ++ [ self.debugTool ];
    CFLAGS = (old.CFLAGS or "") + " -g";
  });

  debugTool = self.fetchurl {
    url = "https://example.com/debugTool.tar.gz";
    sha256 = "...";
  };
}
```

The overlay here not only modifies build inputs by adding a downloadable debugging tool but also appends debugging flags, preparing the application for in-depth diagnostic sessions.

- Evolving Overlays in Nix Ecosystem

Overlays continue to evolve, supporting increasingly dynamic package management scenarios. They stand out as powerful facilitators of innovation and customization across diverse use cases from enterprise-grade system configurations to individualized development settings. The intrinsic flexibility they offer complements the broader Nix paradigms, providing mechanisms to optimize, experiment, and enhance software infrastructure without compromising on the benefits of immutability and declarative consistency that underpins Nix's design philosophy.

Overlays embody a strategic toolset for transcending the default boundaries of package management, enabling bespoke solutions that meet specific operational demands with elegance and precision. Whether adapting third-party software for particular organizational needs or conducting groundbreaking development cycles on cutting-edge technologies, overlays remain critical in ensuring developers can articulate their visions within the impactful framework that Nix affords.

10.4 Using Lib Functions for Simplified Configuration

Nix's built-in library functions, accessible through the lib attribute, offer an extensive suite of utilities and abstractions designed to streamline configurations. Utilizing these functions effectively improves code efficiency and clarity, facilitating the creation of complex environments with less effort and fewer errors. This section elucidates how to employ lib functions for simplified configurations, exploring their potential to mitigate complexity and enhance maintainability.

Overview of Lib Functions Within the Nix ecosystem, lib functions serve as reusable components, providing a rich set of functional programming utilities and abstractions. These utilities cover a wide range of operations, from list manipulation and set operations to string handling and attribute set processing. By harnessing these functions, Nixpkgs simplifies routine tasks, making configurations concise and robust against subtle bugs.

Lib functions are accessible via the lib attribute, typically passed to Nix expressions through the pkgs attribute. The modularity and adherence to functional programming principles inherent in these functions contribute to the composability of Nix expressions.

Functional Programming Utilities The library provides numerous utilities grounded in functional programming concepts, enabling developers to manage collections, strings, and data structures with precision.

- **List Manipulation**

  Functions for handling lists are fundamental, offering tools for map, filter, fold, and other common idioms. Here is an example of employing lib for list operations:

```
let
  pkgs = import <nixpkgs> {};
  lib = pkgs.lib;
  numbers = [1, 2, 3, 4, 5];
  evenNumbers = lib.filter (n: n % 2 == 0) numbers;
```

```
in
  evenNumbers
```

The filter function takes a predicate (n: n % 2 == 0) and a list (numbers), returning a list of even numbers [2, 4]. Through such concise expressions, lib functions diminish verbosity in list processing tasks.

- **Attribute Set Functions**

  Handling attribute sets, which form the crux of many package definitions, is another crucial area where lib functions excel:

```
let
  pkgs = import <nixpkgs> {};
  lib = pkgs.lib;
  initialSet = { a = 1; b = 2; c = 3; };
  overriddenSet = lib.attrsets.recursiveUpdate initialSet { b = 20; d = 4; };
in
  overriddenSet
```

  In this example, lib.attrsets.recursiveUpdate merges two attribute sets, resulting in a = 1; b = 20; c = 3; d = 4; . Attributes from the second set override or extend those in the first, which simplifies comprehensive modifications of existing configurations.

- **String Manipulation**

  String processing with lib functions is another area where Nix shines. Consider the use of lib.strings for concatenating and manipulating strings:

```
let
  pkgs = import <nixpkgs> {};
  lib = pkgs.lib;
  greeting = "Hello";
  subject = "World";
  message = lib.strings.concatStringsSep ", " [greeting subject];
in
  message
```

  Here, concatStringsSep concatenates a list of strings with a separator, producing the string "Hello, World". Such utilities minimize boilerplate code involved in string operations, improving readability and maintainability.

Configuration Simplification Beyond functional utilities, lib functions support high-level abstractions for efficiently managing larger configurations. They facilitate structured, scalable definitions while preserving readability.

- **Option Handling**

  Options and defaults in configurations often require meticulous handling; lib functions simplify this through convenience abstractions:

```
let
  pkgs = import <nixpkgs> {};
  lib = pkgs.lib;
  defaultConfig = { optionA = true; optionB = "default"; };
  userConfig = { optionB = "custom"; };
  finalConfig = lib.attrsets.recursiveUpdate defaultConfig userConfig;
in
  finalConfig
```

  Using lib.attrsets.recursiveUpdate, configurations are amalgamated, where user-specified options selectively override the defaults. This approach encapsulates best practices for merging configurations, reducing complexity and potential errors in large-scale setups.

- **Predicate Utilities**

  Conditional configurations benefit from predicate utilities provided by lib functions, enabling expressive and concise conditional logic:

```
let
  pkgs = import <nixpkgs> {};
  lib = pkgs.lib;
  isLinux = lib.systems.isLinux;
in
  if isLinux then "Building for Linux" else "Not a Linux build"
```

  In this case, lib.systems.isLinux conditionally influences the configuration flow, demonstrating the brevity and clarity achievable with predicate functions. Such constructs eliminate redundancy in condition evaluation, leading to more manageable conditional configurations.

Advanced Usage and Real-World Applications Leveraging these utilities extends beyond abstract examples, practically enhancing various real-world applications:

- **Building Modular Configurations**

  Complex systems often disaggregate configurations into modular components. Lib functions provide the architecture necessary for compositional consistency:

```
let
  pkgs = import <nixpkgs> {};
  lib = pkgs.lib;
  baseConfig = { enableFeatureX = true; };
  featureConfig = { enableFeatureY = true; };
  completeConfig = lib.attrsets.recursiveUpdate baseConfig featureConfig;
in
  completeConfig
```

  This principle of modular configurations enables composability, where extensions add features without duplication or modification of original constructs. Such designs facilitate scalability and adaptability over time.

- **Automation in Package Expressions**

  Automated tests or build conditions using lib functions demonstrate efficiency in adapting expressions based on runtime conditions:

```
let
  pkgs = import <nixpkgs> {};
  lib = pkgs.lib;
  needsTesting = lib.strings.contains "foo" pkgs.stdenv.buildPlatform;
in
  if needsTesting then pkgs.stdenv.mkDerivation {
    name = "testedPackage";
    buildInputs = [ pkgs.testDependency ];
  } else null
```

  Automatically adapting packages to build requirements exemplifies the utility of lib functions ensuring compliance with condition-driven environments, a routine requirement in continuous integration environments.

Case Studies and Implications **Case Study 1: Streamlined NixOS Configuration**

NixOS configurations, notorious for complexity, benefit sizably from lib functions. They encapsulate intricate setups, yielding configurations that remain readable despite their inherent depth and potential complexity.

Consider a simplified system configuration:

```
{ config, pkgs, ... }:

let
  lib = pkgs.lib;
  defaultPackages = [ pkgs.hello pkgs.cowsay ];
  extraPackages = config.extraPackages or [];
  finalPackages = lib.lists.flatten [ defaultPackages extraPackages ];
in
{
  environment.systemPackages = finalPackages;
}
```

This setup automatically augments default package lists with user-defined extras gracefully, exemplifying the elegance and simplicity that lib functions bestow upon otherwise cumbersome system configurations.

Case Study 2: Unified Development Environments

Creating consistent development environments across varying system landscapes underscores real-world usage. Imagine preparing a consistent environment structure using lib functions:

```
{ pkgs, lib, ... }:

let
  withPython = config.enablePython or false;
  basePackages = [ pkgs.git pkgs.curl ];
  pythonPackages = if withPython then [ pkgs.python39 ] else [];
  allPackages = lib.lists.concatLists [ basePackages pythonPackages ];
in
{
  environment.systemPackages = allPackages;
}
```

Here, configurations are automatically tailored based on the `withPython` flag, encapsulating base with optional functionality, highlighting ease of environment description lib functions afford.

Implications for Best Practices and Maintenance The strategic application of lib functions provides multiple advantages in Nix-based systems, notably:

- **Clarity and Maintainability**: Reducing verbosity through abstraction and simplifying intricate configurations leads to clearer, more maintainable systems.
- **Composability and Extensibility**: Emphasizing modular design paradigms ensures configurations are naturally extensible, a cornerstone of evolving codebases.
- **Reusability**: From small scripts to full-blown system definitions, lib functions enhance reusability, fostering a collaborative development approach.

Employing lib functions cohesively not only simplifies configurations but also offers durability and adaptability, ensuring sustainable growth and complexity management in diverse system architectures. Keeping lib functions integrally involved in solution recipes greatly eases both current codebase management and future modifications, standing as the clear means to foster richer, more efficient Nix infrastructure development.

10.5 Creating and Maintaining Private Repositories

Creating and maintaining private repositories is fundamental to managing proprietary or sensitive software packages within an organization. Nix provides robust support for private repositories, allowing developers to seamlessly integrate and distribute proprietary packages alongside public ones while maintaining a secure and efficient distribution process. This section explores the methodologies for setting up and managing private repositories, addressing security, integration, and best practice considerations.

Establishing a Private Repository Setting up a private repository in Nix involves selecting an appropriate storage mechanism, configuring access controls, and integrating it into your build and deployment workflows.

Storage Selection The storage back-end for a private repository can vary based on organizational infrastructure demands and resource availability. Options include:

- Self-hosted solutions: Using NGINX or Apache to serve a directory of Nix expressions and sources.
- Cloud-based storage: Leveraging services such as AWS S3, Azure Blob Storage, or GCS to host package directories.
- Dedicated package storage services: Services like Artifactory or Nexus, which provide robust file management and access control features.

Self-hosted solutions might offer greater control over deployment, whereas cloud-based solutions provide scalability and reduced maintenance overhead.

Directory Structure A private Nix repository typically mirrors the layout of Nixpkgs, which involves directories for individual packages. A typical structure might include:

```
my-private-repo/
    default.nix
    lib/
    pkgs/
        my-package/
            default.nix
            some-source-file.tar.gz
        another-package/
    overlay.nix
```

Each package maintains its directory with essential Nix expressions and source files. The 'default.nix' file often serves as an entry point, aggregating different package sets and lib functions.

Setting Up 'default.nix' The 'default.nix' file acts as the entry point to the private repository, potentially resembling:

```
{ nixpkgs ? import <nixpkgs> {} }:

{
```

```
  my-package = import ./pkgs/my-package;
  another-package = import ./pkgs/another-package;
  lib = import ./lib;
}
```

This script initializes the repository packages, delegating individual package configurations to specific expressions within the repository.

Security and Access Control Ensuring the security of a private repository is paramount. It involves configuring strict access controls, authentication measures, and audit capabilities.

Access Control Mechanisms

- Authentication: Implement basic authentication using HTTP authentication methods or more advanced token-based systems.
- Encryption: Leverage HTTPS for secure transmission of package data.
- Database/Service Permissions: For cloud services or dedicated package managers, ensure service-level access control using IAM permissions or similar constructs.

Example HTTP Basic Authentication in NGINX Configuring basic authentication in an NGINX server, as an example, could resemble:

```
server {
    listen 80;
    server_name private-nix-repo.example.com;

    location / {
        auth_basic "Protected Repository";
        auth_basic_user_file /etc/nginx/.htpasswd;
        root /var/www/my-private-repo;
    }
}
```

The file '/etc/nginx/.htpasswd' holds hashed username and password entries, created using tools like 'htpasswd'.

Maintaining and Updating Packages A vital aspect of managing private repositories is maintaining and updating packages seamlessly, ensuring smooth workflows and integration.

Automation and CI/CD Integrating continuous integration and deployment (CI/CD) tools can automate package updates and deployments. Platforms like Jenkins, GitLab CI, or GitHub Actions enable automating:

- Building packages: Ensuring that binaries or artifacts are prepared and stored in repository directories.
- Testing packages: Executing automated tests to validate package integrity and functionality.
- Deploying updates: Automating the deployment of package updates to staging or production environments.

Version Control and Branching Strategy Keeping source and Nix expressions under version control ensures easy rollback, auditing, and collaborative management. A typical branch strategy might include:

- Main branch: Hosting stable releases.
- Dev branch: STEM for ongoing development or testing.
- Feature branches: For individual features or fixes that eventually merge back to 'dev' or 'main'.

Example Git Setup Command Sequence To initialize a Git repository and push to a remote service:

```
git init
git add .
git commit -m "Initial commit of private repo"
git branch -M main
git remote add origin https://example.com/my-private-repo.git
git push -u origin main
```

With this setup, package updates merge into selected branches and subsequently build and deploy automatically via CI/CD.

Utilizing Private Repositories in Nix Expressions Enabling and utilizing packages from private repositories in Nix expressions involves straightforward integration steps.

Adding a Private Repository as an Overlay Within environments or specific projects, utilize overlays to integrate private repositories:

```
let
  privateOverlay = import <path-to-my-private-repo>/overlay.nix;
  nixpkgs = import <nixpkgs> {
    overlays = [ privateOverlay ];
  };
in
  nixpkgs.my-package
```

This configuration flexibly employs overlays, adding private repository packages seamlessly into larger package sets.

Environment Configuration For NixOS or shell environments, integrate private packages by including them directly in configurations:

```
{ config, pkgs, ... }:

let
  privatePkgs = import <path-to-my-private-repo> { inherit pkgs; };
in
{
  environment.systemPackages = with privatePkgs; [ my-package another-package ];
}
```

Such configurations incorporate private packages into broader system environments or shell-based setups.

Best Practices and Considerations Maintainability and Scalability

- Separate Concerns: Maintain distinct separation between public and private repositories to ease upgrading Nixpkgs versions without affecting private modifications.
- Audit Practices: Regularly audit access and usage logs, ensuring adherence to organizational security policies.

- Package Naming: Prefix private packages with organization-specific identifiers to avoid name clashes (e.g., 'myorg-myapp').

Compliance and Licenses

- License Management: Ensure compliance with open-source or proprietary licenses when integrating diverse packages into the private repository.
- Policy Enforcement: Implement policies for package inclusion, such as coding standards or security requirements.

Contingency Planning

- Backup Solutions: Regularly back up repository contents to provide resilience against data loss.
- Reproducibility Checks: Periodically verify that package builds remain reproducible by rebuilding from scratch on a clean environment.

Through effective creation, management, and integration of private repositories, Nix offers an enterprise-ready platform for securely distributing internal packages alongside public offerings. With precise controls and automated workflows, organizations can optimize package management for proprietary software solutions while leveraging the flexibility, scalability, and security inherent in Nix's design philosophy. This comprehensive approach ensures efficient software delivery pipelines that readily adapt to evolving enterprise needs, maintaining consistency and reliability across complex systems.

10.6 Integrating Nix with Other Development Tools

Integrating Nix with other development tools unlocks the full potential of a modern development workflow. By combining the deterministic build and reproducible environment capabilities of Nix with tools like

Docker, Vagrant, and CI/CD pipelines, developers can achieve streamlined processes, enhance productivity, and ensure consistency across different stages of software development. This section details methods and best practices for integrating Nix with popular development tools, providing insights and practical code examples to facilitate seamless integration.

Using Nix with Docker Docker provides containerization capabilities that encapsulate software environments in isolated units, ensuring that software runs consistently across different computing environments. Nix complements Docker by supplying a reproducible base environment:

Building Docker Images with Nix Utilizing Nix to build Docker images guarantees that every image build is identical, based on a Nix package definition:

```
{ pkgs ? import <nixpkgs> {} }:

pkgs.dockerTools.buildImage {
  name = "my-nix-image";
  fromImage = "alpine";
  contents = [ pkgs.hello ];
  config = {
    Cmd = [ "${pkgs.hello}/bin/hello" ];
  };
}
```

The script uses 'dockerTools.buildImage', creating a Docker image from the Alpine base, with the 'hello' package included. The 'Cmd' parameter sets the default command in the container to the 'hello' executable.

Advantages of Nix-Docker Integration

- Reproducible Environments: Ensures that Docker images remain consistent across different builds.
- Dependency Isolation: Encapsulates dependencies within the images, reducing conflicts and compatibility issues.

- Simplified Declarative Configuration: Leverages Nix's declarative syntax to define the entire build process.

Integrating Nix with Vagrant Vagrant provides a platform for creating and managing virtualized environments. By using Nix, developers can achieve reproducible environments that Vagrant manages seamlessly.

Setting up Vagrant with Nix Provisioning Configure a Vagrantfile to use Nix for provisioning virtual machines:

```
Vagrant.configure("2") do |config|
  config.vm.box = "ubuntu/bionic64"

  config.vm.provision "nix-shell", type: "shell" do |s|
    s.name = "Install Nix Packages"
    s.inline = <<-SHELL
      curl -L https://nixos.org/nix/install | sh
      source /home/vagrant/.nix-profile/etc/profile.d/nix.sh
      nix-env -iA nixpkgs.git
    SHELL
  end
end
```

This configuration sets up an Ubuntu box and provisions it with Nix, subsequently installing 'git' via 'nix-env'.

Benefits of Nix-Vagrant Integration

- Consistency: Vagrant environments behave consistently due to Nix's reproducibility.
- Simplified Ubuntu and Nix Integration: Simplifies integrating Ubuntu-based virtual environments with Nix package management.

Nix in Continuous Integration/Continuous Deployment (CI/CD) Pipelines CI/CD pipelines are instrumental in automating the testing, building, and deploying of applications. Integrating Nix into these workflows brings uniformity and reliability:

Implementing Nix in CI/CD Workflows Below is an example configuration using GitHub Actions to run tests within a Nix-provisioned environment:

```
name: CI

on: [push, pull_request]

jobs:
  build:
    runs-on: ubuntu-latest
    steps:
    - uses: actions/checkout@v2
    - name: Install Nix
      run: |
        curl -L https://nixos.org/nix/install | sh
        source ~/.nix-profile/etc/profile.d/nix.sh
    - name: Build with Nix
      run: nix-build

    - name: Run Tests
      run: nix-shell --run 'pytest tests'
```

This configuration performs the following:

1. Checks out the latest code. 2. Installs Nix on the runner using GitHub Actions. 3. Executes 'nix-build' to compile the application. 4. Runs tests using pytest within a Nix shell environment.

The integration ensures reproducible builds and a consistent testing environment across all pull requests and pushes.

Advantages in CI/CD Environments

- Reproducible Builds: Guarantees that artifacts are consistent over time.
- Simplified Environment Setup: Reduces dependencies and complex setup scripts, as environments exist declaratively.
- Improved Test Reliability: Ensures tests run in identical environments, reducing false negatives or positives.

Integrating Nix with Development Environments Beyond runtime environments, Nix can optimize local development setups by integrating with IDEs and editors:

Using Nix with Visual Studio Code VS Code, a popular development environment, can leverage Nix for configuration management:

1. **Setting Up a DevShell**: Create a 'shell.nix':

```
{ pkgs ? import <nixpkgs> {} }:

pkgs.mkShell {
  buildInputs = [ pkgs.nodejs pkgs.python3 ];
}
```

2. **Configuring VS Code**: Point VS Code's integrated terminal to begin with Nix shell:

Ensure the workspace uses the Nix shell environment by configuring '.vscode/settings.json':

```
{
    "terminal.integrated.shell.linux": "/bin/bash",
    "terminal.integrated.shellArgs.linux": ["--rcfile", "/home/user/project/.envrc"]
}
```

3. **Launching and Developing**:

Through these configurations, developers launch VS Code terminals within the Nix environment, accessing all configured dependencies seamlessly.

Benefits in Development Environments

- Dependency Management: Simplifies handling of dependencies across projects.
- Portability: Ensures environments can be recreated anywhere, fostering collaborative consistency.
- Efficiency: Reduces setup and teardown times for development environments.

Collaborative Benefits and Challenges Successfully integrating Nix with other tools holistically improves team collaboration and deployment practices:

Streamlined Onboarding New team members configure and launch consistent development environments quickly, bypassing complex setup steps traditionally associated with multi-tool environments.

Uniformity Across Stages From development to deployment, Nix guarantees that environments and behaviors are uniform, reducing discrepancies that typically occur between different system setups.

Challenges and Mitigation Strategies As with any integration, merging Nix with existing tools presents challenges:

Learning Curve The unique paradigm Nix introduces demands significant upfront learning, particularly for developers familiar only with imperative package managers.

Mitigation: Training sessions and documentation should outline Nix fundamentals, accompanied by practical workshops where team members learn through tailored, role-relevant examples.

Existing Infrastructure Integration Legacy infrastructure may resist seamless Nix integration, especially where tightly coupled or complex tool chains exist.

Mitigation: Gradually integrate Nix through staged rollouts in non-critical systems, using feedback to address integration issues before wider application.

Conclusion: Integrating the Future with Flexibility Nix stands at the confluence of modern development practices, marked by its flexibility and reproducibility. Making it a core component alongside tools like Docker, Vagrant, and CI/CD systems extends its benefits throughout development pipelines, emphasizing environment consistency and reducing errors inherent in dynamic systems. As organizations continue to embrace complex cloud-native architectures, harnessing Nix offers a pathway to cohesion, predictability, and ultimately, success in software delivery.

10.7 Performance Tuning and Optimization

Performance tuning and optimization of Nix builds are pivotal for reducing build times and maximizing resource efficiency. This involves an analysis of both the internal workings of the Nix package manager and the external hardware and software environments. Strategies extend across various dimensions, including derivation efficiency, parallel execution, system resource allocation, and intelligent caching. This section provides a comprehensive exploration of methods to optimize Nix performance, highlighted by examples and best practices.

Understanding the Nix build mechanics is crucial for effective optimization of builds. Nix employs derivations, which are low-level representations of package build instructions, to methodically establish reproducible environments. This process revolves around a few key operations:

- Derivation Evaluation: Translating high-level package expressions into derivations.
- Dependency Resolution: Constructing a build graph based on package dependencies.
- Build Execution: Sequentially or concurrently building derivations on isolated sandboxes.
- Caching: Storing build outputs to avoid redundant computations when the same inputs are evident.

Each phase comprises potential bottlenecks or opportunities for improvement.

Optimizing derivation efficiency involves mitigating the overhead associated with derivation evaluation by employing concise and efficient expressions. Consider applying the following strategies:

- **Simplifying Expressions:** Trivializing package expressions reduces overhead. Simplifying derivation logic through avoidance of redundant operations aids performance optimization:

```
let
  inherit (import <nixpkgs> { }) stdenv writeTextFile;
in
  stdenv.mkDerivation rec {
    name = "optimized-example";
    src = ./source;
    installPhase = ''
      mkdir -p $out/bin
      cp ${src}/example $out/bin/
      sed -i 's/DEBUG/NODEBUG/' $out/bin/example
    '';
  }
```

Here, the 'installPhase' uses simplified string manipulations, reducing computation complexity during build execution.

- **Minimizing Dependency Chains:** Overprocessed dependency chains exacerbate build times. Reevaluate necessity by pruning extraneous dependencies and optimizing package inputs:

```
buildInputs = [ pkgs.gcc pkgs.make ]; # Avoid unnecessary packages
```

Use lightweight alternatives for dependencies where possible, avoiding comprehensive libraries when only subsets are needed.

Nix supports parallel builds, enhancing throughput by harnessing multiple CPU cores concurrently. Proper configuration of parallelism expands the effective use of system resources.

- **Configuring Parallel Builds:** Parallelism is configurable through the 'nix.conf' file, enabling concurrent derivation builds:

```
build-cores = 0           # Automatically use all available cores
max-jobs = auto             # Set based on system infrastructure
```

Setting 'build-cores' to zero allows Nix to determine optimal core usage, while 'max-jobs' adapts runtime job counts to suit available system resources.

- **Analyzing Build Performance:** Use Nix tools to monitor build efficiencies and identify bottlenecks:

```
nix log $(nix-store -r '<derivation-path>' -l)
```

Reviewing the log for a given derivation reveals potential inefficiencies and helps guide further optimization efforts.

Caching mechanisms in Nix leverage both local storage and remote caches to facilitate the reuse of existing binaries. However, managing cache effectively ensures builds draw from the latest optimized outputs.

- **Enabling and Utilizing Binary Caches:** Binary caches store pre-compiled binaries to expedite subsequent builds of identical derivations:

```
substituters = https://cache.nixos.org/
trusted-public-keys = nix-cache.s3.amazonaws.com-1:3VAnUr+NUggvd82nbdhijiM8j/Mi9G0Oooib
```

Configuring appropriate substituters and trusted keys ensures access to verified binary caches.

- **Automated Build Output Management:** Use the Nix garbage collection and pruning commands for effective cache management:

```
nix-collect-garbage -d # Delete all older than 14 days
```

This practice maintains storage hygiene and optimizes cache efficiency by purging unused artifacts.

Nix can further benefit from specific system-level optimizations, leveraging virtualization features, memory enhancements, and advanced I/O configurations.

- **Optimizing Virtualized Environments:** Ensure virtualized environments are provisioned with sufficient CPU, memory, and networking capabilities, maximizing virtual resource availability. Leverage virtualization tools' CPU pinning options to pin builds to specific cores, isolating computational tasks.

- **Memory and I/O Enhancements:** Improving memory and I/O speeds can drastically reduce the time intensive operations can bottleneck left unchecked:

- Consider enabling fast in-memory filesystem overlays ('/dev/shm') for reduced disk I/O during build operations.
- Equip systems with higher-speed NVMe or SSD storage, cutting down on read-write wait times during heavy cache operations.

Case studies can illustrate effective optimization techniques:

- **Case Study 1: Large-Scale Nix Deployment**

In a scenario where hundreds of packages undergo nightly builds, optimizations included:

- Dedicated Build Infrastructure: Provisioning dedicated CI/CD servers with optimized hardware (SSD, ample RAM).
- Strategic Cache Utilization: Reliance on both distributed team-local caches and the official Nix binary cache.
- Throttled Parallel Computing: Tuning parallelism relative to server load ensured no resource saturation, maintaining throughput consistency.

These actions propagated build time reductions by approximately 40%, signifying the impact of targeted optimizations.

- **Case Study 2: Micro-Optimization in Development**

A project involving compute-intensive simulations benefited from localized optimizations:

- Dependency Slimming: Evaluated and reduced package dependencies, relieving build overhead.

- Custom Wrapper Scripts: Scripts tailored execution environments, appending dynamic memory allocation flags to simulators.

This focused approach to performance resulted in over 20% execution speed improvements.

- **General Best Practices for Performance Tuning**

- Iterative Profiling: Regularly profile and optimize builds, establishing benchmarks to identify regression points.
- Documentation of Changes: Document architectural changes and environment-specific optimizations, fostering reproducibility.
- Feedback from Real Users: Collect performance insights directly from build users or environments, aligning developmental optimizations with real-world usage demands.

Performance tuning for Nix requires a harmonious balance between Nix's build mechanisms and extrinsic system capabilities. By integrating optimization strategies at multiple levels—code simplification, parallel execution configuration, system resource deployment, and caching—developers can drastically influence the efficiency and reliability of Nix-managed environments. This enduring pursuit of optimization not only underpins operational resilience but also sets the stage for scalable, high-performance software delivery.

Chapter 11

Continuous Integration and DevOps with Nix

Continuous integration and DevOps practices with Nix leverage its reproducibility and consistency to streamline development workflows. Nix facilitates the creation of reliable and consistent build environments, ensuring that code behaves the same way across development, testing, and production stages. By integrating Nix into CI/CD pipelines, teams can automate software builds and deployments with confidence, minimizing configuration drift and simplifying dependency management. This chapter focuses on how Nix enables efficient orchestration in DevOps, promoting robust, scalable systems and enhancing collaboration through precise and predictable software delivery processes.

11.1 Nix in the DevOps Lifecycle

Incorporating Nix in the DevOps lifecycle introduces a fundamental enhancement to both the reproducibility and consistency of software systems, crucial aspects in the contemporary continuous integration (CI) and continuous deployment (CD) processes. This section delves into the significant role that Nix plays within these domains, outlining its contributions to enhancing systems' dependability and streamlining collaborative development efforts.

Nix's participation in the DevOps lifecycle begins with its core strengths in package management, which are distinguished by ensuring that software builds and execution environments can be reproduced exactly, independent of the underlying hardware, operating system, or external states. In the CI/CD context, these features address persistent challenges related to environment configuration drift—a phenomenon whereby discrepancies in environments lead to divergences in application behavior across development, testing, and deployment stages.

The exact versioning control and dependency management capabilities of Nix form a foundational component of system consistency. By employing a purely functional language to specify build instructions, known as Nix expressions, it mandates that dependency graphs be explicit. Any mutation within the environment necessitates a redefinition through Nix expressions, precluding any unintended side-effects that typically occur in traditional mutable environments.

```
# Example of a Nix expression for a package
{ pkgs ? import <nixpkgs> {} }:

pkgs.stdenv.mkDerivation {
  name = "examplePackage";
  src = <url-to-source>;

  buildInputs = [ pkgs.dependency1 pkgs.dependency2 ];

  buildPhase = ''
    ./configure
    make
  '';

  installPhase = ''
    make install
  '';
}
```

The deterministic nature of these builds is central to the effectiveness of CI/CD pipelines. During continuous integration, when code repositories are frequently merged and systems are rebuilt, Nix ensures that every build artifact is a direct manifestation of its input source and dependencies. This fidelity mitigates the "it works on my machine" syndrome, with Nix's immutability properties preventing the silent and inadvertent drift that often complicates testing and integration.

Moreover, in the continuous deployment stage, Nix's reproducibility ensures that deployment environments and application artifacts are consistently aligned with earlier testing stages. The predictable behavior fostered by Nix not only aids in eliminating runtime discrepancies but also simplifies error tracking and extends the robustness of deployments across varied infrastructure environments.

For example, deploying an application in a staging or production setting using Nix involves a straightforward adaptation of the same Nix expressions used during development, eliminating the need for environment-specific scripts that often become sources of subtle bugs and operational overhead.

```
# Deploying with Nix
nix-build -E 'with import <nixpkgs> {}; callPackage ./default.nix {}'
```

This command produces a build artifact that can be deployed confidently across any system with the Nix toolchain installed. It encapsulates both application binaries and their dependencies, ensuring exact fidelity to the tested outcomes.

Nix's utility further amplifies in its ability to manage system configurations as code. This is illustrated by NixOps, a tool for deploying NixOS systems, which uses declarative specifications for infrastructure deployment and maintenance, reinforcing the principles of Infrastructure as Code (IaC). NixOps provisions and manages resources across multiple cloud providers while maintaining system state consistency through Nix expressions.

```
# A simple NixOps configuration
{
  network.description = "Simple NixOps network";

  webserver = {
    deployment.targetEnv = "ec2";
    ec2.instanceType = "t2.micro";
    ec2.region = "us-west-2";

    services.httpd.enable = true;
  };
}
```

Such capabilities allow teams to define whole application stacks, including network configurations, operating systems, and application dependencies, within a singular, reproducible, and version-controlled environment description. This eliminates not only configuration drift but also facilitates parallel development and operational practices across diverse teams and geographies.

The integration of Nix within the CI/CD pipelines also provides valuable improvements to both time and resource efficiencies. Given the atomic nature of Nix builds and deployments, layers that replicate existing builds are cached, dramatically reducing the time and computational resources typically expended on repeated build processes. As a consequence, Nix supports a rapid iteration cycle, advocating a fail-fast, fix-fast mentality that is crucial in agile development environments.

Additionally, Nix empowers developers by decoupling application logic from system settings, allowing individual development environments to be personalized without affecting shared environments. Developers can operate within personalized configurations knowing such modifications are localized and reversible, thereby fostering a productivity-enhancing comfort without jeopardizing system integrity.

From an operational perspective, the reproducibility bestowed by Nix underpins not only build-time consistency but is crucial for ensuring systemic reliability in production. Downtime incidents due to configuration errors or dependency issues are minimized, easing the burden on operational teams and reducing the total cost of ownership.

Finally, Nix plays a pivotal role in enabling collaborative software development. By standardizing environments across all stages of development and deployment, it mitigates integration risks commonly encountered in collaborative projects involving cross-functional teams. The use of a shared vocabulary through Nix expressions harmonizes understanding, enhancing the clarity and communicability of build processes and infrastructure requirements.

Within the context of a modern DevOps workflow, Nix not only facilitates seamless integration and deployment cycles but also aligns organizational processes to operate in concert with best practices, promoting continuous delivery of high-quality software artifacts with confidence.

The role of Nix in the DevOps lifecycle embodies a significant shift towards highly reproducible and reliable software systems. By leveraging its deterministic and declarative paradigms, organizations can attain streamlined integration and deployment processes characterized by unprecedented consistency and flexibility. This empowers teams to focus on feature development and improvements, securing stakeholder value through improved software quality and delivery timelines.

11.2 Setting Up Nix for CI/CD Pipelines

Integrating Nix into continuous integration and continuous deployment (CI/CD) pipelines revolutionizes the efficacy and dependability of software delivery processes. This section provides a comprehensive guide on how to set up Nix within CI/CD environments, encompassing key infrastructure configurations, best practices for achieving optimal performance, and maximizing the potential of Nix's reproducibility features.

The primary rationale for utilizing Nix in CI/CD pipelines is its ability to guarantee environment consistency across all stages of development, testing, and deployment. This consistency eliminates many traditional pipeline issues related to environment discrepancies and configuration management. When configuring these pipelines, a systematic approach is essential to harness Nix's capabilities effectively.

Installing Nix

Setting up Nix starts with its installation across all pertinent build agents and deployment servers in the CI/CD environment. Installation ensures that all nodes in the pipeline can leverage Nix's build isolation and dependency management features. Installation can be achieved by executing the following command, which fetches and installs Nix from the canonical Nix package repositories:

```
curl -L https://nixos.org/nix/install | sh
```

It is important to verify that the installation was successful by confirming the version of Nix installed using:

```
nix-env --version
```

Subsequent steps involve the configuration of the Nix daemon service to run builds in isolated sandboxes. This configuration ensures builds are environment-independent, a critical advantage in providing reproducible build artifacts. This can be achieved by editing the /etc/nix/nix.conf file to include:

```
build-users-group = nixbld
sandbox = true
```

Integrating Nix in CI/CD Tools

A wide range of CI/CD tools support or can be configured to support Nix, including Jenkins, GitLab CI, and GitHub Actions, among others.

Using Nix in Jenkins

To begin with Jenkins, the addition of the Nix suite involves the setup of build environments through scripted pipelines, as Jenkins does not have native support for Nix. Incorporating Nix seamlessly involves:

- Selecting a strategy for Nix installation across Jenkins agents.
- Configuring Jenkins jobs or pipelines to utilize Nix builds.

A Jenkins pipeline can be defined to utilize Nix for isolated builds and installations as follows:

```
pipeline {
    agent any
    stages {
        stage('Install Nix') {
            steps {
                sh '''
                   curl -L https://nixos.org/nix/install | sh
                   source $HOME/.nix-profile/etc/profile.d/nix.sh
                   '''
            }
        }
        stage('Build with Nix') {
            steps {
                sh 'nix-build default.nix'
            }
        }
        stage('Deploy') {
            steps {
                sh 'nix-env -i ./result'
            }
        }
    }
}
```

Using Nix in GitLab CI

For GitLab CI, adjustments to the .gitlab-ci.yml configuration file allow Nix integration. GitLab runners can be tweaked to run builds within Nix environments, by specifying:

```
image: nixos/nix

build-job:
  script:
    - nix-build default.nix
    - nix-env -i ./result
```

This configuration uses a Docker image pre-configured with Nix, ensuring that all the GitLab runners execute the scripts in a standardized and reproducible fashion.

Using Nix in GitHub Actions

For GitHub Actions, integration with Nix again revolves around scripted workflows, parsed by YAML files:

```
name: CI

on: [push, pull_request]

jobs:
  build:
    runs-on: ubuntu-latest
    steps:
      - uses: actions/checkout@v2
      - name: Install Nix
        run: curl -L https://nixos.org/nix/install | sh
      - run: source $HOME/.nix-profile/etc/profile.d/nix.sh
      - name: Build Package
        run: nix-build default.nix
```

This script defines the atomic steps of a CI pipeline using GitHub Actions to verify, compile and test applications in a controlled Nix-provided environment.

Best Practices for Configuration

A successful CI/CD integration with Nix demands adherence to several disciplined practices:

- **Stateless Builds**: Configure Nix to utilize the sand-boxed state, ensuring all builds are deterministic. This involves setting up builds in isolation, pushing for the maximization of reproducibility.

- **Caching**: Use caching capabilities to store derivations and results. Tools like Cachix can be integrated to cache build results, reducing computational overhead and speeding up pipeline executions.
- **Declarative Configurations**: Define CI pipelines rigorously using declarative styles. By utilizing Nix expressions universally, whether for build instructions or application configurations, the CI/CD process remains transparent and verifiable.
- **Parallelization**: Leverage job parallelization techniques by breaking down pipeline stages, allowing multiple, independent, Nix build processes to occur simultaneously.

Challenges and Considerations

While integrating Nix provides immense benefits, practitioners must also address challenges such as:

- **Learning Curves**: Considerable time investment is needed for teams unfamiliar with functional languages, to fully grasp Nix syntax and semantics.
- **Platform Compatibility**: Ensure that all build agents and environments are compatible with the Nix system, which might entail additional configuration or replacement of incompatible services.
- **Security Concerns**: Although Nix improves security by not having mutable dependencies, care must be taken with network accessibility settings to avoid unintended vulnerabilities.

Setting up Nix in CI/CD pipelines involves a detailed orchestration of tool installations, environment configurations, and script-driven automation. By embracing the specificity, declarativism, and robust dependency management that Nix offers, CI/CD environments can achieve unparalleled reproducibility and reliability, laying a strong foundation for the robust delivery of software through continuous integration and deployment processes. The integration of Nix not only resolves traditional development and deployment gaps but inherently fosters a culture of shared responsibility and quality assurance in the software development lifecycle.

11.3 Building Reliable Dev Environments

The creation of reliable development environments is pivotal for the successful execution of software projects, ensuring that all team members work within consistent and reproducible settings. Nix, with its innovative approach to package management and environment configuration, provides the tools necessary to establish development environments that are stable and identical across diverse platforms, thereby reducing integration issues and enhancing productivity.

At the core of Nix's capability to build reliable development environments is its foundation on purely functional paradigms. This ensures that environments are immutable and deterministic, characteristics that are essential when the goal is to minimize discrepancies and runtime failures in software builds and execution. The process of creating these environments involves crafting Nix expressions and configurations that accurately define all dependencies, build inputs, and environmental variables necessary for software development.

Nix enforces several core principles that underpin the construction of reliable development environments, namely:

- **Immutability**: Environments created using Nix are immutable, meaning that once they are instantiated, they cannot be altered inadvertently. Each change mandates an explicit reconfiguration and rebuild within the Nix system, preventing accidental drift that can lead to inconsistencies.

- **Reproducibility**: Regardless of the host infrastructure, a Nix-defined environment can be recreated provided the Nix expression file is available. This is achieved through the atomic nature of Nix builds, which are driven by explicitly defined input files and dependencies.

- **Minimal Dependency Hell**: By constructing dependency graphs explicitly within a functional language, Nix avoids the common "dependency hell" observed in software development. Each package or library exists in a distinct path, reducing conflicts.

- **Granular Version Control**: Nix allows the definition of precise package versions in its expressions, facilitating fine-grained control over dependencies and software components.

To construct a Nix-based development environment, a user typically creates a default.nix file, which defines the software dependencies and configuration needed for a project. An example of a default.nix file for a Python development project might resemble:

```
{ pkgs ? import <nixpkgs> {} }:

let
  pythonPackages = pkgs.python3.pkgs;
in
with pkgs; mkShell {
  buildInputs = [
    pythonPackages.numpy
    pythonPackages.scipy
    pythonPackages.matplotlib
  ];

  shellHook = ''
    export PYTHONPATH=$PWD:${PYTHONPATH}
    alias start_notebook='jupyter-notebook --no-browser'
  '';
}
```

In this example, a Nix shell environment is formulated to incorporate specific Python packages. This preparation involves:

- The use of mkShell to define a shell environment.

- Specification of buildInputs, which enumerates all required packages.

- Definition of a shellHook to provide environment-specific variables and actions, thereby enhancing the utility and accessibility of the Nix shell for developers.

To instantiate this environment, a developer executes:

```
nix-shell
```

Upon execution, the command spawns a development shell, laden with the specified dependencies and configurations, ensuring that every developer operates in an environment mirroring the one defined by the default.nix file.

A notable advantage of Nix-driven environments is their inherent scalability and flexibility, which extends to applications beyond personal development machines to entire teams and even production systems. These features are particularly advantageous to remote teams operating across different platforms, where maintaining consistency can be challenging.

For scalable enterprise applications, it is possible to encapsulate entire service architectures via Nix, enabling deployment environments that are verifiably consistent and straightforward to instantiate across new infrastructure.

Consider a multi-service application involving a web server, database, and caching layer. Each component can be individually defined and controlled using Nix expressions, facilitating ease of deployment and scalable redundancy:

```
{ pkgs ? import <nixpkgs> {} }:

let
  webServer = pkgs.nginx.override {
    configFile = ./nginx.conf;
  };

  database = pkgs.postgresql.override {
    dataDir = "/var/lib/postgres/data";
  };

  cache = pkgs.redis.override {
    configArgs = ["--maxmemory 256mb"];
  };
in
pkgs.stdenv.mkDerivation {
  name = "my-environment";
  buildInputs = [ webServer database cache ];

  shellHook = ''
    echo "Starting services..."
    systemctl start nginx
    systemctl start postgresql
    systemctl start redis
```

```
";
}
```

Several best practices should be adhered to when managing Nix-based development environments, including:

- **Version Pinning**: Use specific versions of dependencies to ensure reproducibility across time and contributors.
- **Incorporate Testing Frameworks**: Integrate testing frameworks and scripts within the Nix expression to perpetuate continuous testing during development. This integration can ensure functionality is preserved as changes occur.
- **Leverage Continuous Integration**: Synchronize Nix environments with CI tools to guarantee that the exact development environment is utilized during integration and testing phases.
- **Documentation**: Adequately document the setup and usage of Nix expressions to facilitate onboarding and maintenance.
- **Shared Nixpkgs Channel**: Use a shared or team-specific channel of nixpkgs to avoid inconsistencies stemming from divergent package versions.

Reliable development environments play a critical role in reducing errors that typically arise from discrepancies between developer configurations. The ability of Nix to encapsulate and enforce precise dependency versions and environment settings addresses one of the most common sources of integration failures.

Moreover, reproducibility is on its foundational strength. Unifying development and deployment environments using identical Nix expressions allows for environments that can be consistently duplicated elsewhere, vastly reducing the potential for errors attributed to environment differences during the software lifecycle.

The transparency provided by Nix expressions also contributes to error reduction by making environmental assumptions explicit and analyzable. This elevates the predictability of system behaviors and reduces uncertainties during debugging or extending applications.

Building reliable development environments using Nix ensures that software teams can develop and collaborate in determined, consistent settings. By capitalizing on Nix's immutable and reproducible nature, converged efforts on software builds and deployments become more coordinated, hence diminishing risks and potential downtime. Nix's intricate control over every aspect of the environment, from system libraries to programming-language-specific packages, provides a holistic solution that emphasizes simplicity congruent with powerful environment control. The adaptability of Nix further recommends its integration into CI/CD systems, spanning development to production environments, thereby supporting a streamlined and error-resistant software delivery process.

11.4 Using Nix to Manage Environment Dependencies

Managing environment dependencies effectively is a critical aspect of modern software development, ensuring that applications maintain consistency and stability across different stages of development, testing, and deployment. Nix stands out as a powerful tool in managing these dependencies due to its unique approach to package management, which is characterized by declarative specifications, immutability, and reproducibility. This section explores how Nix facilitates the management of environment dependencies, minimizes conflicts, and enhances overall system reliability.

At the heart of Nix's approach to dependency management is its functional programming paradigm, where environments and packages are described in Nix expressions. These expressions explicitly state the package requirements, along with their exact versions and any configurations necessary for the package to operate correctly within an environment. This clear specification prevents issues related to dependency drift and ensures that the same environment configuration can be reproduced multiple times on different systems.

- **Exact Reproducibility**: The ability to recreate environments precisely as they were developed initially is one of Nix's most significant advantages. This is achieved through deterministic builds facilitated by Nix expressions, which specify the exact versions and conditions of all dependencies.

- **Elimination of Dependency Hell**: By providing isolated package paths and preventing side-by-side installation conflicts, Nix effectively resolves dependency hell. Each package is installed in its unique store path, preventing interference between packages.
- **Flexibility and Compatibility**: Nix operates consistently across various Linux distributions and macOS. This cross-platform compatibility ensures that dependencies behave the same way regardless of the underlying system, promoting seamless development workflows.
- **Easy Rollbacks and Upgrades**: Nix allows precise version control over all components. It supports easy rollbacks to previous versions if upgrades introduce issues, and reproducible system upgrades, ensuring minimal disruption.

Example of Managing Dependencies with Nix

Consider a project that requires specific versions of several libraries and tools for development in a Python environment. The following Nix expression provides such an environment:

```
{ pkgs ? import <nixpkgs> {} }:

pkgs.mkShell {
  buildInputs = [
    pkgs.python3
    pkgs.python3Packages.virtualenv
    pkgs.python3Packages.requests
    pkgs.python3Packages.numpy
    pkgs.git
  ];

  shellHook = ''
    echo "Activating Python environment..."
    virtualenv venv --no-site-packages
    source venv/bin/activate
  '';
}
```

In this example, a Nix shell environment is created. The mkShell function is used to set up build inputs, specifically listing the Python package, several essential libraries, and the Git version control tool. The shellHook script ensures that a Python virtual environment is created and activated upon entering the shell, further isolating Python dependencies.

Advanced Dependency Management Techniques

Nix offers several advanced techniques and tools for managing complex dependencies in larger projects:

- **Overriding Dependencies**: To customize a package build, Nix allows the overriding of package attributes. This is useful when modifying specific aspects of package builds without altering the entire package or duplicating its entire Nix expression.

```
{ pkgs ? import <nixpkgs> {} }:

let
  myCustomPython = pkgs.python3.override {
    packages = self: with self; [ numpy pandas ];
  };
in
pkgs.mkShell {
  buildInputs = [ myCustomPython ];
}
```

  This snippet overrides the default python3 package, so that it automatically includes numpy and pandas. This custom override reduces verbosity and the potential for errors in specifying package dependencies repeatedly.

- **Pinning Nixpkgs**: To ensure consistency across builds, developers can pin the Nix channel to a specific revision, ensuring that the package set remains unchanged until explicitly updated.

```
# Pinning a Nixpkgs version
nix-channel --remove nixpkgs
nix-channel --add https://nixos.org/channels/nixos-21.05 nixpkgs
nix-channel --update
```

  This approach stabilizes the entire project's package dependencies to a known state, thereby eliminating variables introduced by upstream Nixpkgs changes.

- **External Dependency Management**: Nix also integrates well with external tools and languages. For instance, using bundix for Ruby projects or poetry2nix for Python enriches Nix's ecosystem interoperability:

```
# Using poetry2nix for Python dependency resolution
poetry2nix > default.nix
nix-build default.nix
```

Generated Nix expressions automatically resolve dependencies defined in pyproject.toml, providing tight alignment with language-specific dependency tools while retaining Nix's reproducibility.

Best Practices for Effective Nix Dependency Management

To maximize the benefits of Nix in managing dependencies, several best practices should be observed:

- **Consistent Environment Definitions**: Always define environments explicitly using Nix expressions to ensure that the same set of packages are produced on every build.
- **Team-wide Nix Configurations**: Share common Nix setups and configurations across the team to prevent version mismatches and undefined behavior between different development setups.
- **Regularly Review Pinning Strategies**: Evaluate pinned package versions for security vulnerabilities and performance issues, refreshing them periodically while maintaining backward compatibility.
- **Automation and CI Integration**: Integrate Nix with CI pipelines, ensuring that environments are automatically built and tested, thereby instantly highlighting discrepancies or dependency failures during integration stages.
- **Documentation**: Thoroughly document any custom Nix expressions or overrides used to manage dependencies, making it simpler for team members to understand, adapt, and extend configurations as needed.

Challenges in Dependency Management with Nix

While Nix offers robust solutions for dependency management, it also introduces potential challenges developers must address:

- **Learning Curve**: Nix's functional language and declarative style can be unfamiliar to new users, requiring a learning curve before proficiency is achieved.
- **Binary Cache Mismatches**: When collaboratively working on a project, mismatches between team members' binary caches can cause unexpected behavior. Solutions involve settling on common cache configurations.
- **Cross-Compatibility Issues**: While Nix is highly portable, there may be edge cases involving non-standard platforms or exotic dependencies that challenge the system's out-of-the-box solutions.

Managing environment dependencies with Nix empowers developers to create robust, reproducible, and scalable software systems. By leveraging Nix's declarative expressions, developers eliminate environmental inconsistencies and maintain precise control over software components. As projects grow in size and complexity, Nix provides the tools and methodologies necessary to handle intricate dependency graphs, facilitate teamwork, and automate deployment processes seamlessly in any configuration. Through consistent application of best practices and ongoing evaluations of setup and configuration practices, teams can harness Nix's full potential to deliver high-quality software with improved reliability and reduced operational overhead.

11.5 Automating Builds and Tests with Nix

Automating builds and tests is a cornerstone of efficient software development processes. Nix is particularly well-suited for this task, offering unmatched consistency and reliability through its functional approach to package management and environment configuration. By leveraging Nix for automated builds and testing, developers can ensure that software components behave predictably across each stage of the continuous integration and continuous delivery (CI/CD) pipeline, significantly reducing human error and enhancing productivity.

This section delves into the strategies and methodologies for automating builds and tests using Nix, focusing on the formulation of reproducible build scripts, integration with CI/CD systems, and advanced techniques to further optimize the automation process.

- **Fundamentals of Nix Automation**

Nix uses a combination of descriptive Nix expressions and a robust package store to automate both build and test processes:

- **Nix Expressions**: These form the blueprint for every build process, describing precisely how software should be compiled and which dependencies are required. They encapsulate build instructions in a declarative format.
- **The Nix Store**: An append-only data store where all packages are kept, ensuring that each build output and its dependencies are stored uniquely, nixing the common problem of file overwriting seen in traditional systems.
- **Execution Sandboxing**: Builds are conducted in isolated environments, preventing external systemic influences and guaranteeing that results are independent of changes in the user's home directory or other mutable system states.

- **Writing Build Scripts with Nix**

To automate a build with Nix, a .nix file is created which contains the necessary build instructions and dependency specifications. Consider the example of automating the build of a C program:

```
{ pkgs ? import <nixpkgs> {} }:

pkgs.stdenv.mkDerivation {
  name = "hello";
  version = "2.10";
  src = pkgs.fetchurl {
    url = "http://ftp.gnu.org/gnu/hello/hello-${version}.tar.gz";
```

```
    sha256 = "sha256-value";
  };

  buildInputs = [ pkgs.gcc ];

  buildPhase = "make";
  installPhase = ''
    make install
    mkdir -p $out/bin
    cp src/hello $out/bin/hello
  '';
}
```

This expression uses the 'stdenv.mkDerivation' function, which takes several arguments:

- **name** and **version**: The name and version of the package.
- **src**: Specifies where to obtain the source code, in this case fetching it from a URL.
- **buildInputs**: Lists the dependencies required for the build, demonstrating how to leverage the GCC compiler.
- **buildPhase** and **installPhase**: High-level phases where the compilation and installation are defined.

Upon executing 'nix-build' with this Nix expression, Nix will download the required source code, compile the package in a reproducible manner and place the result in a hashed directory within the Nix store.

- **Automating Tests with Nix**

Automating tests within Nix follows a similar paradigm as builds. The test scripts form part of the derivation, ensuring that every build's validity is immediately verifiable. Nix supports various test frameworks, integrated directly into the build process.

Consider adding a simple test to the previous build expression:

```
{ pkgs ? import <nixpkgs> {} }:

pkgs.stdenv.mkDerivation {
  name = "hello";
  version = "2.10";
  src = pkgs.fetchurl {
```

```
    url = "http://ftp.gnu.org/gnu/hello/hello-${version}.tar.gz";
    sha256 = "sha256-value";
  };

  nativeBuildInputs = [ pkgs.gcc pkgs.bash ];

  buildPhase = "make";
  checkPhase = ''
    make check
  '';
  installPhase = ''
    make install
    mkdir -p $out/bin
    cp src/hello $out/bin/hello
  '';
}
```

In this expression, the 'checkPhase' is introduced to run the tests, enhancing the build's integrity check. By using 'make check', any included test files in the source are executed, ensuring the compiled program meets expected behaviors before proceeding with installation.

- **Integration with CI/CD Systems**

Nix integrates seamlessly with CI/CD systems, due to its declarative and reproducible nature, allowing automated builds and tests to be part of the continuous development pipeline. Here's how:

- **Jenkins**: Jenkins pipelines can be configured to run 'nix-build' commands as part of the build step. By integrating Nix, Jenkins workflows maintain consistency across builds and can quickly roll back to previous known good states if issues arise in new changes.

```
pipeline {
    agent any
    stages {
        stage('Build') {
            steps {
                sh 'nix-build hello.nix'
            }
        }
        stage('Test') {
            steps {
                sh './result/bin/hello'
            }
        }
    }
}
```

- **GitLab CI**: Similarly, GitLab CI runners execute Nix shell environments for builds, as instructed within the '.gitlab-ci.yml' configuration:

```
image: nixos/nix

build-job:
  script:
    - nix-build hello.nix
    - ./result/bin/hello
```

- **GitHub Actions**: For GitHub Actions, packages are built using automated workflows defined in the '.github/workflows' directory. The workflow might look like:

```
name: C Build

on: [push, pull_request]

jobs:
  build:
    runs-on: ubuntu-latest
    steps:
      - uses: actions/checkout@v2
      - name: Install Nix
        run: curl -L https://nixos.org/nix/install | sh
      - run: nix-build hello.nix
      - name: Execute Binary
        run: ./result/bin/hello
```

These automation scripts ensure that all parts of the software development lifecycle exploit Nix's deterministic build environment, providing confidence and predictability in delivering high-quality software.

- **Advanced Automation Techniques**

- **Binary Cache Utilization**: Using Nix's ability to cache build outputs, systems like Cachix can be set up to share build artifacts between CIs, integrating faster build processes through cache sharing.

- **Custom Derivations**: Build more complex pipelines involving specific custom derivations that leverage external scripts or other languages, embedding test scripts directly into builds.

- **Cross-Platform Builds**: Utilize Nix to automate the generation of cross-platform builds by specifying target architectures within derivations, ensuring comprehensive test coverage and deployment on multiple systems.
- **Parallel Builds**: Optimize builds by deploying Nix's capability to perform parallel package constructions, accelerating the build process without sacrificing consistency.

- **Challenges and Considerations**

Automating builds and tests with Nix, while powerful, requires careful consideration of several aspects:

- **Complex Configuration**: For those new to Nix, the configuration might seem complex. However, investing the time in understanding how to efficiently write and manage Nix expressions pays dividends in reliable and quick-to-repeat builds.
- **Outdated or Nonexistent Nixpkgs**: Depending upon Nixpkgs for dependencies can pose challenges if desired versions do not exist in the package set. Consider maintaining a local overlay if specific patches or versions are critical.
- **Tooling Integration**: Despite growing support, some CI/CD tools might not natively integrate Nix. Workarounds, such as using containers that preinstall Nix, facilitate its usage until official support arrives.

Automating builds and tests with Nix provides a robust framework for ensuring software quality and reliability across the development lifecycle. By deploying immutable and reproducible build scripts, Nix minimizes discrepancies that often arise in multi-developer projects, contributing significantly to seamless test automation. As organizations increasingly adopt CI/CD methodologies in pursuit of increased agility and reduced cycle times, embracing Nix as a core component enables predictable, repeatable outcomes that form the backbone of effective deployment pipelines. Implementing Nix, with an understanding of its capabilities and limitations, offers a path towards more efficient and transparent software delivery mechanisms, which is essential in today's fast-paced development environment.

11.6 Deploying Applications Using Nix

Deploying applications in a reliable and efficient manner is a fundamental aspect of modern software delivery, ensuring that applications transition smoothly from development through to production environments. Nix emerges as a powerful tool in this domain, leveraging its unique properties of reproducibility and immutability to offer unparalleled consistency in deployments. This section explores the methodologies and best practices for deploying applications using Nix, highlighting its advantages, integration with various infrastructure setups, and the challenges that may arise.

Nix's deployment mechanism is built upon its capability to create exact replicas of development environments in production settings, thereby preventing discrepancies that could adversely affect application functionality. The deployment process begins with the encapsulation of an application and its dependencies into a Nix expression, which serves as a recipe for constructing the entire runtime environment.

- **Packaging Applications**: The initial step in deploying applications using Nix involves packaging the application into a Nix environment. This encapsulation includes all the necessary libraries and configuration settings required for the application to operate correctly. The result is a binary artifact that is immutable and self-contained.
- **Transfer and Deployment**: Once packaged, the application can be transferred to a deployment target, whether a physical server, virtual machine, or container, without the risk of environmental drift. The packaged application and its dependencies are stored in the Nix store, facilitating rapid transfer and deployment processes.
- **Activation and Execution**: Deployments leverage Nix's execution isolation to maintain application integrity, executing the packaged application within a sandboxed environment. By utilizing Nix's built-in features, deployments can be atomic, scriptable, and repeatable.

Example of Deploying an Application with Nix

Consider a scenario where the objective is to deploy a web application built with Node.js. This involves creating a Nix expression that specifies the runtime environment and dependencies:

```
{ pkgs ? import <nixpkgs> {} }:

pkgs.stdenv.mkDerivation {
  name = "my-web-app";
  src = ./source; # Path to the project's source code

  buildInputs = [ pkgs.nodejs ];

  buildPhase = "npm install";

  installPhase = ''
    npm run build
    mkdir -p $out
    cp -r dist/* $out
  '';

  meta = {
    description = "A simple web application built with Node.js";
  };
}
```

This Nix expression fetches the application's source code, utilizes Node.js as a build dependency, runs 'npm install' to resolve packages, and copies the build output to the Nix store. When executed with 'nix-build', the command generates a deployable artifact.

Deploying in Diverse Environments

Deployments in varying environments require flexibility, a hallmark of Nix's capabilities. Nix facilitates multiple deployment strategies:

- **Deployment on Physical Servers and Virtual Machines**: Nix supports native installations, allowing applications to be deployed directly onto servers or VMs, provided the Nix environment is set up on these machines. Deployments are performed by replicating the build artifact and executing it within an appropriately configured environment.
- **Docker Containers**: Leveraging Docker with Nix extends deployment versatility. A Docker image can be built by including the Nix package, enabling applications to be run as containers. The following illustrates how a Dockerfile might leverage Nix:

```
FROM nixos/nix
```

```
COPY . /app
WORKDIR /app

RUN nix-env -iA nixpkgs.nodejs \
    && npm install \
    && npm run build

CMD ["node", "./dist/server.js"]
```

This approach installs Node.js via Nix, ensuring that the build and runtime environments inside the Docker container are consistent with expectations.

- **Cloud-Based Deployments**: NixOps, a Nix-based tool, simplifies cloud deployments, abstracting infrastructure management using Nix expressions. Here's a simple example of deploying an application to AWS with NixOps:

```
{
  server1 = { config, pkgs, ... }: {
    deployment.targetEnv = "ec2";
    deployment.ec2.region = "us-west-1";

    services.httpd.enable = true;
    services.httpd.documentRoot = "/var/www/htdocs";

    users.users.myuser = {
      isNormalUser = true;
      home = "/home/myuser";
      extraGroups = [ "wheel" ];
    };
  };
}
```

Using this configuration file, NixOps provisions an EC2 instance, configures necessary services, and deploys the application, ensuring comprehensive environment control and consistency.

Best Practices for Deploying with Nix

To harness the full potential of Nix in deployments, adhere to the following best practices:

- **Pin Dependencies**: Ensure that all dependencies are explicitly defined in the Nix expressions, including specific versions of libraries and tools, to guarantee reproducibility across deployments.

- **Utilize Binary Caches**: Caching mechanisms such as Cachix can be leveraged to reduce build times by storing and sharing pre-built binaries across different deployment targets.
- **Testing Before Deployment**: Implement automated tests to validate that each build behaves as expected in its target deployment environment, leveraging Nix's reproducibility to mirror production settings in testing stages.
- **Employ Version Control for Nix Expressions**: Treat Nix expressions as first-class citizens in version control systems, managing them alongside application source code changes to track and reproduce environments historically.
- **Continuous Integration**: Integrate Nix deployments with CI/CD tools for automatic deployment triggering, resulting in fast feedback loops and reducing manual intervention.

Challenges and Considerations

While deploying applications using Nix offers numerous advantages, it also necessitates considered strategies to overcome potential obstacles:

- **Initial Setup Complexity**: For teams new to the functional paradigm, initial set-up can be challenging. Comprehensive documentation and onboarding sessions can smooth this learning curve.
- **Environmental Dependencies**: Applications with dependencies on specific hardware features or legacy systems might require additional configurations or workarounds to align with Nix's immutable and isolated execution model.
- **Network and Security Configurations**: Deploying in production environments often requires robust network configurations. Ensure that security protocols are well-integrated into Nix-based deployment tools to protect application data and integrity.

Deploying applications using Nix provides a powerful framework for establishing consistent, reproducible, and reliable environments. By leveraging its unique functional and declarative approach, Nix enables developers to mitigate the risks associated with traditional deployment methodologies, reducing systemic errors and aligning deployed applications closely with their development and testing counterparts. The integration of Nix into deployment pipelines empowers teams to focus on feature development and scaling, knowing that their deployment framework is stable and efficient. As a result, Nix facilitates the creation of high-quality software delivered seamlessly to production environments, ensuring consistent performance and reliability across diverse deployment scenarios. As teams continue to scale and the complexity of infrastructures grows, Nix represents a foundational tool for modern software delivery, encapsulating the principles of reproducibility and determinism at every step of the deployment process.

11.7 Monitoring and Optimizing CI/CD Workflows

Continuous Integration and Continuous Deployment (CI/CD) workflows are essential for modern software development, facilitating rapid delivery and ensuring that integrations and deployments remain error-free. While CI/CD workflows streamline software delivery, their efficacy greatly depends on rigorous monitoring and optimization strategies. This section explores how to monitor and optimize CI/CD workflows, focusing on performance metrics, bottleneck identification, and best practices for maintaining efficient and scalable pipelines.

At the core of efficient CI/CD workflows lies their ability to provide fast feedback and maintain consistent environments across all stages of development. Effective monitoring techniques are vital for maintaining smooth operation and timely delivery in CI/CD pipelines. Furthermore, optimization strategies ensure that these pipelines are not only efficient but also scalable and resilient to varying workloads.

The Importance of Monitoring in CI/CD Workflows

Monitoring CI/CD workflows is a multi-faceted challenge that involves observability at various stages: from the initial code commits to the final production deployment. Key aspects of monitoring include:

- **Build Health**: Monitoring the success and failure rates of builds provides insight into the stability of source code and identifies potential trends warranting investigation.

- **Deployment Frequency and Success**: Understanding the frequency and success rate of deployments can indicate the pace of delivery and identify thresholds at which further capacity or changes might be necessary.
- **Resource Utilization**: By observing how much processing power, memory, and other resources builds and deployments consume, teams can adjust their resources to optimize costs and performance.
- **Lead Time for Changes**: Monitoring the time it takes for a committed change to reach production is crucial for understanding the efficiency of a CI/CD process.
- **Feedback and Error Rates**: Feedback from automated tests and error reporting systems ensures that potential issues are caught early in the pipeline, reducing downstream debugging and rework.

Tools for Monitoring CI/CD Workflows

Several tools are available that integrate seamlessly into CI/CD pipelines for monitoring purposes. These tools provide detailed insights into workflow efficiency and help identify areas for improvement:

- **Prometheus and Grafana**: Prometheus is a powerful open-source monitoring tool that can collect metrics from CI/CD systems. Grafana builds on Prometheus by providing visualization dashboards that make interpreting these metrics easier.

  A simple Prometheus configuration to collect metrics from a Jenkins server might look like this:

```
scrape_configs:
  - job_name: 'jenkins'
    static_configs:
      - targets: ['localhost:8080']
```

With metrics collected, Grafana can be configured to display these metrics, offering visualization capabilities that highlight trends and anomalies in the CI/CD process.

- **New Relic and DataDog**: These commercial solutions provide powerful analytics and monitoring capabilities, offering tailored dashboards and alerts that ensure teams are aware of critical issues in real-time.

- **Custom Logging and Alerting**: Infrastructure scripts can be customized to log critical events and system performance metrics, setting up alerts for thresholds that signify potential issues.

  Example logging script in a CI environment:

```
# Log build time and output
start=$(date +%s)
if nix-build myproject.nix > build.log 2>&1; then
    echo "Build succeeded"
else
    echo "Build failed" | mail -s "Alert: Build Failure" devops@example.com
fi
end=$(date +%s)
echo "Build duration: $(($end - $start)) seconds" >> build.log
```

  The script captures build success or failure and alerts team members via email if a problem arises, ensuring that issues are swiftly addressed.

Optimizing CI/CD Workflows

Continuous optimization of CI/CD workflows ensures their efficiency, robustness, and scalability. The following strategies are instrumental in achieving this:

- **Parallelizing Jobs**: Where possible, structure CI jobs to run in parallel, reducing total pipeline execution time and improving resource utilization.

  An example GitLab CI configuration with parallel jobs:

```
stages:
  - build
  - test

build:
  stage: build
```

```
    script:
      - make build

  test:
    stage: test
    parallel: 5
    script:
      - make test
```

- **Caching Dependencies and Artifacts**: Use caching mechanisms to store intermediate build artifacts and dependency libraries, avoiding time-consuming re-calculations and downloads between builds.

- **Reducing Complexity**: Simplify the CI/CD pipeline where possible by minimizing conditional logic and dependencies across stages. Aim for a clear and straightforward flow of actions.

- **Automating Environment Provisioning**: Use Infrastructure as Code (IaC) tools like Terraform to automate the setup and teardown of environments used in CI/CD pipelines, ensuring consistent and reliable infrastructure.

- **Enhancing Feedback Mechanisms**: Optimize the feedback loop by integrating more granular logging and error reporting. This transparency allows developers to rapidly respond to integration issues.

- **Continuous Review and Adjustment**: Regularly evaluate the CI/CD process by analyzing metrics and system logs, iterating upon areas identified as bottlenecks or inefficiencies.

Best Practices for Monitoring and Optimization

To effectively monitor and optimize CI/CD workflows, adhere to these best practices:

- **Define Key Metrics**: Establish which metrics are most important to your workflow's success and monitor these consistently. Common key performance indicators (KPIs) include build time, deployment frequency, and error rates.

- **Automate Alerts**: Implement automated alerting systems that notify teams immediately upon detecting thresholds or anomalies, ensuring timely intervention and resolution.
- **Scalable Infrastructure**: Design pipelines and deployments with scalability in mind, selecting infrastructure solutions that can adapt as the organization or project requirements grow.
- **Backtrace Issues**: Ensure thorough root cause analysis for any repeated workflow issues, implementing fixes and adjustments to prevent their recurrence.
- **Iterate Continuously**: As a part of the DevOps culture, reinforcing a cycle of continuous improvement, applying feedback, and refining processes in light of new insights.

Challenges and Considerations

Monitoring and optimizing CI/CD workflows also face specific challenges that must be navigated:

- **Alert Fatigue**: Too many alerts can lead to desensitization among team members. Establish clear priority levels for alerts to ensure attention is focused on significant issues.
- **Integration Complexity**: Synchronizing varied CI/CD tools with monitoring frameworks can be complex. Aim to choose solutions with native integrations or open APIs to simplify assimilation.
- **Scalability Hurdles**: As workflows scale, resource consumption may increase exponentially. Aim to automate scaling or define bursting policies to handle these spikes effectively.

Monitoring and optimizing CI/CD workflows is a complex but essential component of maintaining an effective software delivery pipeline. The ability to observe, analyze, and refine these processes is critical in sustaining a rapid feedback loop, efficient resource allocation, and continuous delivery of high-quality software. By embedding effective monitoring tools and strategies across their CI/CD infrastructure, organizations can anticipate potential issues, streamline complex processes, and ensure that their pipelines scale gracefully as their operational demands evolve. Embracing monitoring and optimization as iterative, integral parts of the CI/CD framework not only enhances software performance but also fortifies the entire system against unforeseen challenges, paving the way for sustainable growth and innovation. Through disciplined execution of best practices and attentive evaluation of metrics, teams can sustain and refine workflows that offer unwavering support to developers, operations, and end-users alike.

Chapter 12

Reproducible Builds Using Nix

Reproducible builds using Nix focus on creating identical binaries from the same source code, regardless of the environment, ensuring reliability and transparency in software development. Nix achieves this by tracking all dependencies and build instructions, enabling complete control over the build process. This approach enhances security by allowing verification of build outputs and mitigates issues related to discrepancies between environments. By fostering a system where software can be rebuilt consistently, Nix supports robust quality assurance and auditability, essential for both open-source contributions and enterprise-level software deployments.

12.1 Understanding Reproducible Builds

Reproducible builds are a critical concept in software engineering, concentrating on ensuring that the build process produces identical binary outputs when given the same source input, independent of the environment in which they are built. This principle is particularly paramount due to the inherent variability associated with different environments where software may be compiled and executed.

The essence of reproducible builds lies in guaranteeing that anyone can verify that a given source code indeed corresponds to the binaries distributed and executed. This assurance fosters transparency, enhances security, and cultivates trust in software products. In this section, we delve into the nuances of reproducible builds, exploring the rationale behind their necessity, the challenges encountered, and methodologies for achieving such builds.

A reproducible build is constituted through several phases including preprocessing, compiling, linking, and packaging, each of which must contribute deterministically to the final output. Thus, it is crucial that the entire toolchain used in these processes is deterministic. Any variation, be it in timestamps, file paths, or version of the tools employed, must be neutralized to ensure consistency.

For example, consider the following simple C program aimed to demonstrate the basic build process:

```
#include <stdio.h>

int main() {
    printf("Hello, World!\\n");
    return 0;
}
```

Compiling this with a typical command such as:

```
gcc hello.c -o hello
```

could yield different binaries under varying circumstances. Aspects like the compiler version, flags used, or even the system's environment variables could potentially alter the executable's hash, breaching reproducibility.

To achieve reproducibility, it's imperative to address several core components:

- **Version Control and Consistency**: Using precise versions of compilers, libraries, and dependencies ensures that the build process always uses the same tools. This demands rigor in managing package versions, achievable through configuration management tools like Nix.

- **Deterministic Compilation**: Compilers sometimes inject metadata like timestamps into binaries, which could vary across builds. It is vital to either disable such aspects or ensure their consistency. Compilers such as GCC and Clang offer specific flags to mitigate these effects (e.g., –enable-deterministic-archives).
- **Controlled Environment**: A build sourced from an uncontrolled environment can introduce non-deterministic factors. Tools like Docker or virtual machines can be employed to encapsulate the build environment, but for ultimate precision, Nix stands out by managing dependencies and environments declaratively.
- **Build Scripts Standardization**: Ensuring build scripts themselves are version controlled and uniform across environments prevents variability. Shell scripts or makefiles should be audited and crafted meticulously to avoid any ambiguous command that may react differently in diverse syntactic environments.

Let us consider an expanded example using the Nix package manager to establish a reproducible build environment. Assume a project with the following directory setup:

```
project/
  hello.c
  default.nix
```

The key file here is default.nix, the Nix expression file responsible for declaring the build environment and instructions:

```
{ stdenv, lib }:

stdenv.mkDerivation {
  name = "hello-world";
  src = ./.;
  buildInputs = [ ];
  buildPhase = ''
    gcc hello.c -o hello
  '';

  installPhase = ''
    mkdir -p $out/bin
    cp hello $out/bin/
  '';
}
```

This Nix expression directly impacts how reproducible builds are obtained. It relies on stdenv.mkDerivation, Nix's fundamental approach to package derivation, ensuring all inputs, including the C compiler and other tooling, are deterministically controlled by Nix.

Executing:

```
nix-build
```

results in a build environment where every variable— from the compiler version to library dependencies— is specified by Nix, facilitating a reproducible build.

Exploring further, a key factor is metadata such as randomization seeds utilized during kernel builds or build machine information that occasionally is encapsulated in binaries. For libraries like those built with Autotools, ensuring constructs like build timestamps utilize SOURCE_DATE_EPOCH is vital.

The impact of reproducible builds transcends personal assurance, offering industry-wide reliability, especially in open-source and critical dependency scenarios. For instance, consumer-developers are empowered to verify that no illicit changes transpired between compilation and distribution. Reproducible builds hence play an indispensable role in systems where cryptographic verification and security are paramount.

Understanding and implementing these practices involve knowledge of the artifact's hash or digital footprint at build completion versus checking for congruence with another system. Assurance and verification processes present themselves through checksum validation or binary inspection, accurately tracing stored metadata and confirming adherence to source input.

While reproducible builds introduce a demanding specification into processes, their long-term benefits in auditing, verification, and assurance hold significant merit. Building upon this foundation, subsequent sections will explore how tools like Nix not only enable these builds but enhance them, contributing robust reproducibility solutions across diverse development landscapes.

12.2 Nix's Role in Ensuring Reproducibility

Understanding reproducible builds sets the stage for exploring how Nix contributes significantly to achieving this goal through its unique design and functionalities. Nix, a purely functional package manager, implements a system distinct from traditional package managers, concentrating on declarative and stateless attributes conducive to reproducible builds.

At the heart of Nix's efficiency lies its treatment of packages and dependencies as outputs of functions. The entire approach revolves around the principle that the output of a function should be determined solely by its input, a concept known as referential transparency. This functional paradigm guarantees that whenever the same input is provided to Nix, the corresponding output remains consistent irrespective of the build environment.

Nix manages packages by creating isolated environments called derivations. Each derivation is a self-contained unit, constructed with explicit dependency declarations. A typical Nix expression (file with a .nix extension) dictates how software is built and packaged. This expression encapsulates all necessary dependencies, ensuring that any variation or update in the system does not disrupt the reproducibility guarantee.

Consider an example of a simple Nix package definition:

```
{ stdenv, fetchurl }:

stdenv.mkDerivation {
  pname = "example";
  version = "1.0";

  src = fetchurl {
    url = "https://example.com/example-1.0.tar.gz";
    sha256 = "0vxyk6sqh3imh2zmf8nsy793bdk6znskhm83sg44f6b8bg7y7yy7";
  };

  buildInputs = [ ];

  buildPhase = ''
    ./configure --prefix=$out
    make
  '';
```

```
  installPhase = ''
    make install
  '';
}
```

This expression is a functional definition, employing ‘stdenv.mkDerivation‘ to outline a reproducible build process. The expression fetches a source tarball using ‘fetchurl‘, which also checks for the source’s integrity using a SHA256 sum. The ‘buildPhase‘ and ‘installPhase‘ explicitly declare the compilation and installation steps, ensuring that external variations like untracked environment variables remain excluded from the build process.

Nix builds all packages in isolated environments. The sandboxing ensures that builds do not accidentally access system-wide packages or configurations. By default, builds occur in a controlled sandbox, where only those dependencies explicitly declared in the Nix expression can affect the build, further safeguarding against discrepancies from external influences.

- In traditional package systems, dependencies can sometimes be a source of indeterminism due to untracked or uncontrolled updates. However, Nix combats this through a unique mechanism: the Nix store. Each package or derivation resides in the store, located by default at /nix/store, structured in a manner reflecting a hash of all inputs from which it derives.

- Every component, from build scripts to library dependencies, directly influences this hash, eliminating any chance for unnoticed variations. Consider a package configuration change; Nix treats this as a new input, generating a new unique path and thus a new build, leaving the previous build intact. This immutability within the Nix store amplifies reproducibility, as changing an input automatically requires rebuilding the affected packages.

- Moreover, Nix can construct a precise dependency graph for any build, facilitating troubleshooting and ensuring all inputs are accounted for during builds. Invoking ‘nix-build‘ on a given expression will trace this graph, recreating the complete environment deterministically.

- Nix's innovative handling of package versioning and history provides additional edge by supporting automatic rollbacks. Suppose a more recent build introduces undetected anomalies; reverting to the previous version is straightforward. Since the Nix store retains older builds unless explicitly removed (via garbage collection), developers can seamlessly transition between different software versions without losing the reproducibility aspect.

- Garbage collection in Nix is another notable mention. Although Nix keeps every build intact to preserve reproducibility, it periodically purges unreferenced builds to conserve disk space. If a build or a specific configuration becomes unnecessary, marking its output as collectable allows the garbage collector to eliminate it without compromising reproducibility.

- In continuous integration environments where builds are frequent, stable, and reproducible, pipeline efficiency hinges greatly on well-managed dependencies. Nix simplifies this by ensuring consistent environments aligned across all stages of the software lifecycle. Developers align local environments with build and deployment servers using shared Nix expressions, thus maintaining functional parity and consistency throughout.

- The Nix approach aligns seamlessly with Docker-like images as well, allowing efficient creation of build environments where intended reproducibility and environment-specific dependencies are encapsulated and shared across development, staging, and production pipelines. This capability alleviates integration concerns, ensuring developers deploy exactly what was built and tested.

Let's revisit a more comprehensive example employing Nix in a continuous integration scenario using a 'ci.nix' configuration:

```
let
  pkgs = import <nixpkgs> {};
in
pkgs.stdenv.mkDerivation {
  name = "ci-build-example";

  src = ./.;

  buildInputs = [ pkgs.cmake pkgs.gcc ];
```

```
  buildPhase = ''
    cmake . -DCMAKE_BUILD_TYPE=Release
    make
  '';

  installPhase = ''
    mkdir -p $out/bin
    cp ./build/bin/ci-example $out/bin/
  '';
}
```

In this scheme, a CI configuration articulates native dependencies—here, cmake and gcc—necessary for the build. The build script, encapsulated within the 'buildPhase' and 'installPhase', ensures that each CI worker can rebuild the entire environment independently, ensuring builds retrieved, tested, and verified on any machine remain unchanged.

Understanding the essence of Nix as a tool for reproducibility illustrates its strategic advantage poised towards modern package management, ensuring builds are canonical and safe from external perturbations. Within built environments where integrity and determinism define success, Nix's methodology for reproducible builds stands out as a powerful resource, joining together ease of use, robustness, and clear governance over software dependencies and behaviors.

12.3 Creating Reproducible Environment Configurations

In the pursuit of software development consistency, creating reproducible environment configurations is essential for minimizing discrepancies across various development, testing, and production setups. Nix, leveraging its functional approach, provides a robust mechanism for describing environment configurations reproducibly and declaratively. This extends beyond mere package management to defining comprehensive development environments, right down to the specific versions of tools and libraries used.

Creating reproducible environment configurations ensures that developers can predictably recreate the same setup across all machines, thus eliminating the "it works on my machine" syndrome. With Nix, these environments are described explicitly in Nix expressions, promoting transparency and ease of audit.

Defining Environment Sources with Nix

A reproducible environment configuration in Nix is constructed from a set of requirements articulated in a Nix expression. This expression defines the environment's components and their exact configurations, including compilers, libraries, and applications, all specified deterministically.

To illustrate, consider a project requiring both Python and NodeJS:

```
{ pkgs ? import <nixpkgs> {} }:

pkgs.mkShell {
  buildInputs = [
    pkgs.python39
    pkgs.nodejs
  ];

  shellHook = ''
    export NODE_ENV=production
  '';
}
```

In this shell.nix example, we create a development shell that ensures python39 and nodejs are available within the tooling environment. The mkShell construct provides a framework to bring together dependencies under a single umbrella, where the shellHook enables configuration of environment-specific variables or settings.

Launching this environment via:

```
nix-shell
```

results in the instantiation of an isolated shell containing precisely these components and configurations. This means any developer checking out this codebase can execute nix-shell and gain access to an identical environment.

Advanced Techniques for Environment Management

For larger and more complex projects, further environment modularization may be required. Splitting configurations into multiple files is a profound pattern, maintaining clarity and reducing redundancy.

Imagine a project with different dependencies for frontend and backend development:

```
project/
  default.nix
  backend.nix
  frontend.nix
```

A default.nix might integrate these:

```
{ pkgs ? import <nixpkgs> {} }:

let
  common = import ./common.nix { inherit pkgs; };
  backendEnv = import ./backend.nix { inherit pkgs; };
  frontendEnv = import ./frontend.nix { inherit pkgs; };
in

pkgs.mkShell {
  buildInputs = backendEnv.buildInputs ++ frontendEnv.buildInputs ++ common.
        buildInputs;
}
```

This approach facilitates the independent management of module dependencies. The common.nix can contain shared dependencies like development tools, linters, or testing frameworks, while backend.nix and frontend.nix focus on their respective, unique requirements.

Reproducibility in Complex Systems

Integrating reproducibility into broader, polyglot systems, particularly those involving microservices or multiple teams, employing Nix supports cross-compatibility and cohesion. Such integration often involves orchestrating configurations across several nodes or services. Docker containers, in combination with Nix, provide a path toward stable and reproducible deployments.

Here's an illustration of configuring a container environment reproducibly using Nix and Docker:

```
{ pkgs ? import <nixpkgs> {} }:

pkgs.dockerTools.buildImage {
  name = "my-container";
  contents = [ pkgs.python39 pkgs.postgresql ];
  config = {
    Cmd = [ "python" "-m" "http.server" ];
    Env = [ "PORT=8000" ];
  };
}
```

Running this through

```
nix-build
```

yields a Docker image capturing an environment with Python3.9 and PostgreSQL, leaving no room for ambiguities introduced by host system changes or updates outside the control of the project team.

NixOS: Beyond Development into System-Wide Reproducibility

While Nix itself concerns development environments, NixOS expands reproducibility into operating system configurations. NixOS functionalities enable system-level configurations sharing the same deterministic principles as Nix. Entire systems, from the kernel to installed applications, are descriptively outlined in a configuration.nix file.

```
{ config, pkgs, ... }:

{
  boot.loader.grub.device = "/dev/sda";
  fileSystems."/" = {
    device = "/dev/sda1";
    fsType = "ext4";
  };

  environment.systemPackages = with pkgs; [
    vim
    wget
  ];

  services.httpd.enable = true;
  networking.firewall.allowedTCPPorts = [ 80 443 ];
}
```

This configuration prescribes an entire machine setup, further embedding reproducibility as even the exact system services and network configurations are described functionally.

Collaborative Development and Reproducible Research

The implications of reproducible environment configurations extend into collaborative domains, enhancing both team productivity and scientific research reproducibility. Shared Nix expressions eliminate guesswork across teams, aligning all contributors with a common environment baseline.

For open-access projects and scientific endeavors, using Nix for reproducibility ensures results are validated independently without environmental concerns. Supplemental data analyses can rely on the specified environment, ensuring results are not only repeatable by the original authors but can be comprehended, tested, and built upon by the wider community.

The strategic crafting of reproducible environment configurations with Nix is a leap forward in software development discipline. It transcends local development headaches, ensuring contributions across diverse teams and machines remain uniform and accountable. Incorporating environment declarations into project repositories solidifies the notion of "environment as code," benefitting both immediate tasks and establishing a futureproof foundation for adaptable and resilient software systems. Nix, while delivering precise configurations, broadens its value proposition by uniting development, deployment, and research through an unyielding consistency in reproducibility.

12.4 Managing Dependencies for Reproducibility

Effective dependency management forms the backbone of reproducible builds. Any discrepancy in dependencies directly jeopardizes the consistency of build outputs. In software systems, dependencies encompass libraries, tools, system packages, and any component utilized during the build and execution phases. Managing these dependencies deterministically allows developers to obtain identical outputs from the same source code.

Nix provides a robust framework to achieve reproducible dependency management, due to its functional, declarative nature. By treating software builds as functions of their dependencies, Nix ensures that variations in these dependencies are thoroughly managed, governed precisely by the Nix expression language.

The Functional Nature of Nix Dependency Management

In Nix, dependencies are expressed explicitly, breaking from traditional, implicit management. Each package described in a Nix expression enumerates its input dependencies, ensuring transparency. This explicitness demands that each input a package employs during its build is determined and hashed directly from the package definition, securing a deterministic build output.

Consider creating a package relying on specific external libraries. The dependencies must be declared within the Nix expression, ensuring the version and configuration are preserved:

```
{ stdenv, fetchurl, zlib, bzip2 }:

stdenv.mkDerivation {
  name = "myapp";
  version = "1.0";

  src = fetchurl {
    url = "https://example.com/myapp-1.0.tar.gz";
    sha256 = "0abcxyz3lmpk2azf88snryyvlskfnfhsllk29s5w40bh9x1mbs6r";
  };

  buildInputs = [ zlib bzip2 ];

  buildPhase = ''
    ./configure --with-zlib=${zlib} --with-bzip2=${bzip2} --prefix=$out
    make
  '';

  installPhase = ''
    make install
  '';
}
```

Here, zlib and bzip2 are explicitly listed as buildInputs. This explicitness binds the expression's output strictly to these dependencies' versions, eliminating potential hash disparities in the build artifact.

Fixed-Output Derivations

A noteworthy aspect of Nix's approach to dependency management involves fixed-output derivations. These are employed when a build process necessitates resources fetched from external or mutable locations, potentially affecting the reproducibility of builds due to changing content.

In fixed-output derivations, content integrity is ensured by specifying a fixed hash, turning mutable external input into an immutable part of the build. This mechanism is particularly useful for managing dependencies fetched from third-party repositories or URLs, imposing both integrity verification and determinism:

```
{ stdenv, fetchurl }:

stdenv.mkDerivation {
  name = "resource";
  version = "1.0";

  src = fetchurl {
    url = "https://example.com/resource-1.0.zip";
    sha256 = "1c9aIY7pOcqf1K7La8EYHyzbpuruYFfntFkK9pE3IdQ=";
  };

  buildPhase = ''
    unzip ${src}
  '';

  installPhase = ''
    mkdir -p $out/contents
    cp -r * $out/contents/
  '';
}
```

The inclusion of SHA256 hashes ensures every download's content remains unaltered across builds, confronting mutability issues head-on. If upstream changes the resource, a new hash is computed and declared, maintaining traceable and reproducible builds.

Pinning Dependencies with Nixpkgs

The nixpkgs repository, Nix's central package collection, evolves constantly, incorporating new packages and versions. While it ensures modern libraries and tools, this fluidity may lead to non-reproducibility due to unnoticed changes in newly pulled package versions.

Pinning a specific nixpkgs commit allows binding to package sets, freezing the entire dependency graph. Pinning ensures future builds derive from the same stable base, eradicating accidental derivations from newly introduced packages.

Consider:

```
let
  pinnedPkgs = import (fetchTarball {
    url = "https://github.com/NixOS/nixpkgs/archive/ad52c4d1d11b8.zip";
    sha256 = "0kxjzq34kbsnmphv79syc3kjv3gf0lp5zkdwy1f59kzfh4032gij";
  }) {};
in
pinnedPkgs.stdenv.mkDerivation {
  /* derivation specifics */
}
```

Pinning down nixpkgs at a chosen commit or hash allows for reproducibility across team members cloning the infrastructure, even months later. This practice is indispensable in multi-developer settings and long-lasting projects.

Dependency Version Compatibility and Overrides

Nix also supports the introduction of overrides within the dependency management process. Overrides provide customization control over nixpkgs, adjusting existing packages' attributes to meet specific project needs, ensuring compatibility while maintaining reproducibility.

By using overrides, developers may fine-tune dependencies' build inputs or phases, thereby introducing proprietary patches or configuration adjustments in response to upstream changes.

Override example:

```
let
  customPkgs = pkgs // {
    gcc = pkgs.gcc.override {
      enableFortran = true;
    };
  };
in
customPkgs.stdenv.mkDerivation {
  /* derivation specifics */
}
```

Employing overrides, developers integrate individual project needs without more substantial deviations from central, commonly-used packages. This strategy reinforces consistent, reproducible builds by carefully managing any customization beyond the base package definitions.

Ensuring Dependency Integrity and Security

Security forms an indispensable aspect of reproducibility, and managing dependencies underpins this by ensuring every component incorporated has been verified. Nix's functional model facilitates verifications like hash checking for URL downloads, while signed materials and reproducible build reviews can extend these rigorously.

Organizations can impose more stringent checks or focus on Nix's reproducibility aspects for standardizing verification. Practices such as Git cryptographic verification alongside statistical reproducibility audits differentiate inputs malleable threats:

1. **Checksum Verification**: Cross-verify Internet sources and tari Materials. 2. **GPG Verifications**: Third-party source auditing, relying on signature integrity. 3. **Rebuilding and Conclusion**: Independently rebuilt software with custom CI/CD tooling for stochastic differences.

Conclusion on Dependency Management

Mastering dependency management is the cornerstone for achieving reproducible builds. Nix extends a meticulous and command-driven interface that empowers developers to harness explicit, repeatable, and customizable environments over time. This approach fundamentally transforms development, enabling a transition from environment disputes into software, focusing on creative solution-seeking. By embracing explicitness, pinning, and robust overrides, dependency management catalyzes reproducibility while embracing both flexibility and security.

12.5 Building and Verifying Reproducibility

A cornerstone of reliable software development lies in the ability not just to build but also verify reproducibility. Ensuring that software builds are replicable across different systems or over time is paramount. Nix's architecture emphasizes reproducibility, drawing from its functional paradigm to manage dependencies and builds. This architecture aligns each build with targeted reproducibility protocols, fostering a system where developers and users can unambiguously trust software integrity and authenticity.

Guaranteed deterministic builds with Nix:

Nix employs a purely functional paradigm, where the build result is a function of the inputs specified in a Nix expression. This concept inherently assures the same input will always yield the same output, foundational for reproducibility. Crucially, the hash that determines a package in Nix's /nix/store encapsulates every aspect of the build's inputs, from the compiler and its flags to the libraries and their precise configurations.

Let's illustrate with an example using Nix's package definition language, building a simple C application:

```
{ stdenv, lib }:

stdenv.mkDerivation {
  pname = "helloC";
  version = "1.0";

  src = ./hello.c;

  buildInputs = [ ];

  buildPhase = ''
    gcc ${src} -o hello
  '';

  installPhase = ''
    mkdir -p $out/bin
    cp hello $out/bin/
  '';
}
```

Executing this with:

```
nix-build
```

This places an artifact with a unique hash corresponding to every element influencing the build process. Re-executing nix-build will provide an identical hash, an assurance of reproducibility directly owing to the immutability and deterministic nature of the inputs.

Verifying build outputs:

One critical aspect of reproducibility is not just deterministic builds but verifiable outputs. Verifying output ensures the resulting binaries or artifacts correlate correctly with the source code and dependencies.

Verification involves hash comparisons across multiple builds. To achieve comprehensive verification, Nix utilizes binary reproducibility checks, ensuring the resulting binary is bit-for-bit identical across different systems.

- **Hash Comparison:** Use tools to calculate the hash of build outputs. By comparing hashes from different build instances, developers ensure consistency.
- **Nix Verifications:** Nix automatically links build derivations to their hash-specific directory, fetching inputs consistently across environments. Tools like nix-store –verify check derivation dependencies, augmenting integrity checks.

Sandboxed builds and isolation:

Nix employs sandboxing tools to ensure builds are unaffected by existing host environments, spanning kernel-level isolation where supported. Sandboxing enforces strict derivation conditions, ensuring builds reference only explicit buildInputs, thus preventing external system dependencies.

To activate sandboxing in Nix, set:

```
sandbox = true
```

within /etc/nix/nix.conf. This ensures environmental constraints hold during builds, fostering consistent outcomes across different platforms or configurations.

Beyond bit-for-bit reproducibility: Diverse outputs:

While exact binary reproducibility stands as an ideal, achieving it universally can be constrained due to varied compiler toolchains, time-sensitive metadata, or system-specific modifications. Nix encourages moving beyond bit-for-bit reproducibility, focusing equally on functionality and behavioral retention.

- **Functional Consistency:** Evaluate tools and applications qualitatively for expected outputs or operations, ensuring system context variations don't hinder software behavior.
- **Behavior Constraints:** Parameters constraigned within build scripts ensure intended behavior, encompassing test executions and output result matches irrespective of minutiae like differing timestamps.

For edge cases, leveraging reproducibility tests allows deterministic behaviors without strictly identical binaries.

Practical tools and approaches for verification:

In the ecosystem of reproducible builds, cross-verification tools augment the assurance of consistent artifacts. Applying these alongside Nix further strengthens the reliability:

- **Binary Diff Tools:** Methods like diffoscope extend hashes by offering human-readable binary comparisons, identifying divergences directly.
- **Signature Checks:** Cryptographic signatures—and augmentation by tools like Gitian—authenticate builds against known good signatures, aligning reproducibility within secure thresholds.
- **Challenger Builds:** Cross-verifying builds by different, independent parties helps identify non-deterministic patterns or inconsistencies across environments, facilitating audit transparency.

Nix in continuous integration:

In continuous integration (CI) pipelines, reproducibility strengthens confidence at each build stage. Incorporating Nix within CI:

- **Consistent CI Environments:** Through executors aligned with pinned nixpkgs, CI builds can maintain exactness with developer environments, preventing "works on my machine" debug cycles.
- **Artifact Validation:** Automated multistep build verification compares hashes and binary differences across multiple CI runtimes, reconfirming alignment.
- **Version Traceability:** Using Nix's precise derivation mapping expedites audits, letting developers reference exact dependencies or sources post-deployment.

CI integration promotes reproducibility as a maintained condition, fostering traceable, transparent build iteration.

Challenges in verification processes:

Despite robust solutions, nuanced challenges persist around reproducibility verification, often entailing:

- **Opaque Toolchains:** Variations within closed-source or vendor-provided binaries resist bitwise reproducibility due to unobtainable compilation dynamics.
- **Temporal Dependencies:** Path or timestamp insertion within intermediate artifacts requiring upstream modifications to accommodate deterministic outcomes.
- **Shared Resources:** Shared services or endpoints in cloud architectures invite nondeterministic outcomes, reliant on mitigation strategies embracing offline or local reproducibility.

To confront these, Nix communities continuously adapt; employing tooling updates, alternative strategies, or nuanced community practices supporting shared learning and resource opaqueness.

Building and verifying reproducibility is a sophisticated but achievable centerpiece in today's fast-paced software landscapes. Nix's functional model exemplifies these ideals, emphasizing deterministic inputs and sandboxed builds while supporting independent verification through traceability, alignment, and consistency. Through adept utilization, reproducibility becomes not only a tool of veracity but also a platform of trust, enhancing confidence across development tiers and production landscapes.

12.6 Challenges and Solutions for Reproducible Builds

In the pursuit of reproducible builds, developers encounter distinct challenges due to the inherent complexity and variability of modern software systems. These challenges arise from diverse sources including toolchain diversity, environmental variability, and divergent platform-specific implementations. Overcoming these challenges requires both strategic planning and technical measures, allowing the consistent reproduction of build artifacts from specified source inputs irrespective of variation in external factors.

- **Common Challenges in Reproducible Builds**

- Non-Deterministic Toolchains: Compilers or build tools might introduce nondeterminism in several forms. Variations in optimization levels, inherent randomness in code generation, or version discrepancies could yield differing binaries across environments.

- Timestamp and Metadata Variability: Timestamps injected during the compilation process are notorious for disrupting reproducibility. Additionally, differing file metadata, such as ownership or mode bits during package tarball creation, could encumber reproducibility efforts.

- Uncontrolled Dependency Versions: Unpinned library or tool dependencies from package managers often update, introducing unintended variations. These changes must be adequately managed.

- Platform-Specific Variations: Disparate behavior induced by platform-specific features or different operating system configurations complicate achieving consistent build outputs across systems.

- Dynamic or Ephemeral Resources: Dependencies pulled in dynamically during the build from network resources introduce variability as they might change or become unavailable over time.

- **Strategic Solutions and Techniques**

Addressing these challenges effectively extends beyond a single paradigm and involves a multiplicity of strategies, heavily relying on solid tooling support and disciplined project management.

Deterministic Toolings Toolchains and compilers must be configured or replaced with options built for determinism. Tools like GCC and Clang, with specific flags, promote deterministic builds:

- Use -frandom-seed, -ffile-prefix-map, or -funroll-loops, among others, to standardize compilation paths and data across runs.

Moreover, consider adopting explicitly built deterministic tool suites or toolchains designed for reproducible builds, supported by initiatives like the Reproducible Builds project which seeks compiler verification, patches, and improvements.

Temporal Stability One profound method of achieving timestamp uniformity is embracing SOURCE_DATE_EPOCH. This environment variable standardizes timestamps across builds. Enhance build scripts or makefiles by incorporating the epoch variable, ensuring consistent timestamps by injecting:

```
export SOURCE_DATE_EPOCH=$(date +%s)
```

Binary embedding with consistent, calculable dates underpins dual goals of reproducibility and traceability. Tools like strip-nondeterminism can further sanitize artifacts as post-processing cleanup: stripping variable timestamps or other ephemeral metadata.

Environmental Isolation and Control Sandboxing implements one fundamental strategy to manage systematic build environments. By confining builds to strict, known states, non-deterministic externalities can be controlled:

- Utilize Nix's native sandboxing mechanisms; set sandbox = true within /etc/nix/nix.conf.
- Explore containerization with tools like Docker, albeit recognizing abstraction layer complexities and potential overheads.

These approaches hedge builds against unintended host system interactions, aligning outcomes with controlled, deterministic patterns.

Pinning and Checking Dependencies Pinning dependencies restricts variability due to upstream library changes. Employ hash-based locks or commit pinning in dependencies managers, ensuring dependency consistency across builds:

- Nix language eases derivation pinning via explicit hash references:

```
let pinnedPkgs = import (fetchTarball {
    url = "https://github.com/NixOS/nixpkgs/archive/avcdef123456.zip";
    sha256 = "0zacdefgh456ijm789012klmopqrstu34567vwx8z99911z20zyx";
}) {};
in ...
```

Additionally, automate verification routines to systematically compare fetched dependency hashes against known signatures, employing tools or scripts to enforce any discrepancies discovery across deployments.

Cross-Platform and Systematic Analysis Analyzing build processes across platforms facilitates early discovery of aberrance in packages or code segments with system-specific outcomes. Engage CI systems in cross-platform builds, ensuring errors or discrepancies surface within parallel executions, starving cascading.

Through systematic analysis enhance reproducible processes:

- Regularly update test suites, verifying identical outcomes across extracted test cases.
- Implement divergence endpoint checks within build pipelines, reporting or logging all emergent irregularities for auditing detail.

Immutable Artifact Management Managing artifacts as immutable essentials across bins or package repositories prevents references from unanticipated updates. Configure CI/CD to leverage immutable container tags or hashed content/source distributions, ensuring distributed packages reflect properly managed, approved builds.

- **Advanced Collaboration and Community Tools**

The reproducible builds community regularly contributes valuable resources addressing broad challenge matrices. Community toolings such as diffoscope dissect binary differences serving detailed insight into reproducibility errors. Additionally, orchestrating collaborations with project resources like Reproducible Builds upstream initiatives enables repositories with thorough patch management, toolchain alterations, and policy adaptations.

More recently, cryptographic assurance via credible signatures links source history with verified built artifacts. Extending reproducibility audits via chain-of-trust principles fosters public confidence across rolling deployments or releases, incentivizing reliable adoption and consumer assurance.

The synthesis of reproducible builds into infrastructural norms bridges robust practice with transparent, comprehensive, and repeatable software lifecycles. Although current challenges demand nuanced engagement strategies across development landscapes, forward-thinking solutions equip builders with scalable benefit real impacts downstream software reliability. Artifacts become conduits, cross-referencing not only integrity but ensuring vast scalable growth potentials across shared, trusting codebases. Collaborative global efforts continuously usher in refinements, accommodating varied need matrices, strengthening both core ideals and community—rooted reproducibility pursuit.

12.7 Case Studies of Reproducible Builds with Nix

Examining real-world case studies of reproducible builds presents practical insights, illustrating how the principles and solutions discussed manifest in diverse industries and applications. By evaluating and reflecting on instances where Nix has been effectively harnessed to achieve deterministic builds, developers and organizations can better understand the benefits and challenges inherent in adopting reproducible practices.

Case Study 1: A Computational Research Environment

In computational research, particularly within the domain of data science, reproducibility is paramount. Ensuring that complex data analyses and computational experiments can be precisely reproduced is not only a scientific necessity but also a requirement for academic integrity and transparency. One case study involves a research group in bioinformatics utilizing Nix to ensure the reproducibility of their computational experiments.

Challenges Faced

The research group faced several challenges in reproducibility:

- **Complex Software Stack**: The computational environment comprised numerous specialized libraries and software, each with specific version requirements.
- **Evolving Codebases**: The analytical code and tools used evolved over time, necessitating environment consistency.
- **Cross-Platform Execution**: Experiments needed to run across different operating systems and hardware.

Solution with Nix

By employing Nix, the research group described their entire software stack using Nix expressions. Each tool, library, and dependency was pinned to a specific version, captured within a deterministically generated environment.

A part of the Nix environment file:

```
{ pkgs ? import <nixpkgs> {} }:

pkgs.mkShell {
  buildInputs = with pkgs; [
    python39
    r
    pandoc
    jupyter
    bioconductor
  ];

  shellHook = ''
    export LC_ALLC.UTF-8
  '';
}
```

Furthermore, the group isolated their environments by evaluating Nix expressions within Docker containers, enhancing cross-platform consistency without overheads or variances introduced by native host environments.

Executing on different systems involved commands within the Dockerfile as follows:

```
FROM nixos/nix

COPY . /workspace
RUN nix-build /workspace/research-env.nix
CMD ["nix-shell", "/workspace/research-env.nix"]
```

Outcomes and Reflections

Reproducibility was achieved with precision, enabling fellow researchers to replicate experiments systematically. The Dockerized implementation allowed external collaborators to run identical environments, ensuring the validity of shared computational findings.

The research group also documented a marked improvement in the ease of managing updates and dependencies, resulting in more robust collaboration and dissemination of results. This case illustrates the potential for reproducible builds to enhance reproducibility, accountability, and collaborative potential across computational sciences.

Case Study 2: Enterprise Software Deployment

For software enterprises, achieving reproducible builds is essential to ensure continuous integration pipelines deliver consistent, reliable deployments to production environments. One leading software company adopted Nix for system-wide application deployment across international data centers.

Challenges Faced

Several reproducibility challenges surfaced:

- **Global Deployment Consistency**: Disparate regional data centers experienced discrepancies in package versions and dependency configurations.
- **Integration with Legacy Systems**: Ensuring new build processes harmonized with existing CI/CD infrastructure.
- **Security and Compliance**: Complying with industry regulations demanded demonstrable integrity and provenance of software builds.

Solution with Nix

Nix was integrated into the company's CI/CD pipeline. System environments were defined using Nix expressions that captured build dependencies, configurations, and tooling versions in a unified and reproducible format.

A simplified module for part of the production environment:

```
{ stdenv, nginx, openssl, nodejs, ... }:

stdenv.mkDerivation {
  name = "enterprise-app";
  src = ./src;

  buildInputs = [ nodejs ];

  buildPhase = ''
    npm install
    npm run build
  '';

  installPhase = ''
    mkdir -p $out/app
    cp -r dist/* $out/app/
```

```
";
  nginx.setupServerBlock $out/app;
}
```

For deployments, the CI/CD system invoked Nix to ensure deterministic builds, monitoring outputs across distributed systems for alignment. Hash checks were embedded within deployment processes, instantly recognizing any discrepancies.

Outcomes and Reflections

By necessitating Nix across their build processes, the software enterprise achieved stringent control over deployments. Discrepancies diminished significantly, leading to a reduction in post-deployment issues and service outages attributed to mismatched environments.

The enhanced reproducibility also supported security protocols, enabling traceability and auditability essential for regulatory compliance. This case evidences how enterprise-scale projects can leverage Nix not only for day-to-day operational consistency but as a broader guarantee of security and reliability.

Case Study 3: Open Source Developer Collaboration

The collaborative nature of open-source development magnifies the need for reproducible builds, offering developers a common baseline upon which to build and test code.

One prominent open-source development project facing reproducibility hurdles switched to Nix, seeking easy integration across various developer environments and operating systems.

Challenges Faced

- **Diverse Developer Tools and Environments**: Contributing developers employed heterogeneous systems and toolchains.
- **Regression Testing Diversity**: Varying build outputs caused challenges in asserting test validity.
- **Community Onboarding and Adoption**: Simplifying contributor setup without extensive manual configuration.

Solution with Nix

Project maintainers created a foundational default.nix, dictating necessary development environments, libraries, and tools for both contributors and automatic CI tests:

```
{ pkgs ? import <nixpkgs> {} }:

pkgs.mkShell {
  buildInputs = [
    pkgs.gcc
    pkgs.python38
    pkgs.git
    pkgs.cmake
  ];

  shellHook = ''
    echo "Welcome to the project environment!"
  '';
}
```

Instructions within the project's README guided developers to initialize nix-shell, immediately creating shared environments aligning setups apparent across builds, tests, and local development activities.

Outcomes and Reflections

Achieving consistency across developer contributions improved codebase integrity and ease of maintenance. New contributors onboarded seamlessly, experiencing reproducibility as a foundation rather than an obstacle.

Project maintainers noted improved confidence in integration tests' results and cross-platform targeting with thoroughly synchronized builds, test expectation alignment, and straightforward debugging. This case highlights how open-source ideals converge with reproducible builds fostering steady, inclusive, and transparent collaboration.

Reflections on Reproducibility Journeys

Across academia, enterprise, and open-source landscapes, reproducible builds through Nix introduce not only consistent environments and outcomes but also foster environments of trust, verifiability, and robustness. While challenges remain, these case studies underscore the profound impacts reproducible practices can have on collaboration, deployment fidelity, and systemic reliability.

The successful application of reproducibility, particularly with Nix, represents a collective step forward in addressing modern development's complexities and sharing best practices for global adoption and adaptation. Through continuous iteration and sharing experiences, reproducible builds stand prepared to transcend current limitations, contributing to breakthroughs in software engineering and practice worldwide.

Chapter 13

Nix and Containerization

Nix and containerization combine to enhance software deployment and isolation, utilizing Nix's reproducibility to create consistent, reliable container images. By employing Nix in building containers, users benefit from its precise dependency management and immutable build outputs, ensuring that containers run identically across different environments. This integration simplifies multi-stage builds and facilitates the management of complex dependencies, allowing for efficient orchestration and scalability. Leveraging Nix's capabilities in containerization provides a powerful tool for applications requiring consistent behavior and streamlined updates within containerized deployments.

13.1 Basics of Containerization

Containerization is an essential technology in the realm of modern software deployment, allowing developers to encapsulate an application's code along with its dependencies, configurations, and system libraries into a single unit called a container. This isolation ensures the software runs consistently across various environments, from development to production, without the traditional headaches of configuration discrepancies. In this section, we delve deeper into the foundational principles of containerization, investigate the underlying technologies, and explore practical scenarios with illustrative examples.

At the core of containerization is the concept of lightweight virtualization, which contrasts with traditional virtual machines (VMs). While VMs emulate entire operating systems along with their hardware abstraction layers, containers share the host OS's kernel and thus require fewer resources. This advantage leads to faster start-up times and a higher density of application instances on the same physical hardware. A typical container workflow involves designing a container image, a static snapshot or blueprint that includes everything needed to run a piece of software.

A container engine, such as Docker, Podman, or containerd, manages the lifecycle of containers on a host system, utilizing the capabilities of Linux kernel features such as namespaces and cgroups for isolation and resource allocation. Namespaces provide isolated views of system resources, like process trees, network, and inter-process communication, while cgroups enable limitation and prioritization of CPU, memory, block I/O, and network resources of containers.

Containers are built from images, which are composed of layers. Each layer represents a change or addition to the file system relative to the layer beneath it, allowing efficient caching and reuse of common parts across different images. This layered architecture is beneficial when multiple containers run similar applications, as they can share the same read-only layers while maintaining their unique writable layer.

```
# Pulling an official Ubuntu image from Docker Hub
docker pull ubuntu:latest

# Running a container interactively with the pulled Ubuntu image
docker run -it ubuntu:latest /bin/bash

# Stopping a running container
docker stop <container_id>

# Removing a stopped container
docker rm <container_id>
```

The command 'docker pull ubuntu:latest' downloads an Ubuntu image tagged with 'latest' from Docker Hub, which serves as a repository for container images. 'docker run' then instantiates a container from this image, starting an interactive Bash session inside it. The 'docker stop' and 'docker rm' commands manage the lifecycle by stopping and removing containers, respectively. Identifying containers is typically done using their auto-generated or user-specified IDs.

Containers provide not only process isolation but also file system isolation. However, containers can interact with the host environment and other containers through network interfaces. Docker, for instance, automatically creates a bridge network for containers, enabling out-of-the-box interconnectivity. To expose container services to the host or external clients, port mappings must be explicitly defined.

Applications inside containers typically adhere to the '12-factor app' methodology, ensuring the encapsulated software is stateless, with configuration stored in environment variables, logs managed as event streams, and backing services treated as attached resources. This methodology enhances portability and agility by maximizing the compatibility between development and production environments.

One of the key aspects of containers is the 'Containerfile', or Dockerfile, when using Docker as a container engine. This file comprises a series of instructions to automate the image-building process. By defining how an image is constructed, from the base image selection to the application environment setup, developers ensure consistency and reproducibility.

```
# Use an official Node.js runtime as a parent image
FROM node:14

# Set the working directory in the container
WORKDIR /usr/src/app

# Copy the package.json files and install dependencies
COPY package*.json ./
RUN npm install

# Bundle the app source code inside the Docker image
COPY . .

# Make the application port available
EXPOSE 8080

# Define the command to run the application
CMD [ "node", "index.js" ]
```

In this Dockerfile, 'FROM node:14' specifies a Node.js base image version 14. The 'WORKDIR' command sets the working directory for subsequent instructions, and 'COPY package*.json ./' followed by 'RUN npm install' manages Node.js dependencies. The 'EXPOSE' command marks the application's listening port, and 'CMD ["node", "index.js"]' instructs the container to execute 'index.js' upon start.

Containers are particularly beneficial in microservices architectures, where applications are divided into smaller, loosely coupled services. Each microservice operates independently in its container, scaling and deploying in isolation without affecting others. This modularity enhances resilience and facilitates continuous deployment practices.

Security is a critical component of containerization. Containers inherently improve security boundaries by separating applications; however, configurations must be correctly implemented to avoid misconfigurations. Best practices include running containers with least privilege, using signed images from trusted sources, and consistently applying security patches. Moreover, advanced security mechanisms, such as setting resource limitations and employing network-level security controls like VM security groups for containers, help mitigate risks.

The proliferation of container orchestration platforms, such as Kubernetes, has further extended the operational capabilities of containers. These platforms manage automated deployment, scaling, monitoring, and lifecycle management of containerized applications across large-scale, clustered environments. Within Kubernetes, workloads are abstracted into Pods, representing one or more containers that share network and storage resources, facilitating orchestration through declarative configurations.

```
apiVersion: apps/v1
kind: Deployment
metadata:
  name: webapp-deployment
spec:
  replicas: 3
  selector:
    matchLabels:
      app: webapp
  template:
    metadata:
      labels:
        app: webapp
    spec:
      containers:
      - name: webapp-container
        image: webapp:latest
```

```
    ports:
    - containerPort: 8080
```

In this Kubernetes deployment configuration, a web application is orchestrated across three replicas for robustness and high availability. The configuration specifies the container image, the application label as part of the Pod template, and the container's port exposure, aligning with the Dockerfile definition.

As organizations increasingly adopt container-based solutions, the container ecosystem evolves with enhanced tools for storage management, network overlays, and CI/CD pipeline integration. This evolution fosters an environment where isolated, reproducible, and scalable application deployment becomes integral to software development lifecycles. By establishing a consistent method across the environments—from developer workstations to cloud-native infrastructures—containers support ubiquitous computing challenges, paving the way for hybrid and multi-cloud strategies.

This section's exploration of containerization fundamentals affirms its pivotal role in modern computing and the strategic value it delivers across development and operational domains. Through intelligent use of container technologies, enterprises can realize greater deployment velocity, resource efficiency, and system reliability.

13.2 Integrating Nix with Docker

Integrating Nix with Docker presents a powerful synergy that combines the advantages of Nix's reproducible build systems with Docker's efficient, isolated execution environments. This integration leverages the strengths of both Nix and Docker to create and manage environments that are consistent, scalable, and highly portable. In this section, we explore the mechanisms of using Nix to build Docker images, detailing the steps and techniques involved, as well as the unique benefits this integration provides.

Nix is a purely functional package management system that enforces reproducibility by declaring software environments through build scripts. These scripts specify the exact versions of dependencies, leading to deterministic builds. Docker, on the other hand, encapsulates applications in containers that run consistently regardless of the host system. By using Nix to construct Docker images, developers can ensure that the software stack within each image is precise and immune to drift over time.

The integration process involves using the Nix package manager to define the dependencies and environment configuration required by an application, and then utilizing this configuration to construct a Docker image where the application can run. This methodology enhances both the build process's transparency and the Docker image's immutability.

```
{ pkgs ? import <nixpkgs> {} }:

pkgs.dockerTools.buildImage {
  name = "my-nix-docker-image";
  tag = "latest";
  contents = [ pkgs.hello ];
  config = {
    Cmd = [ "${pkgs.hello}/bin/hello" ];
  };
}
```

The above Nix expression illustrates how to create a Docker image using Nix. The expression starts by importing the Nix Packages collection (‘<nixpkgs>‘) to access the available packages. The function ‘pkgs.dockerTools.buildImage‘ is then invoked to define an image. Within this configuration, the ‘contents‘ attribute specifies the software to include—in this case, the ‘hello‘ package. The ‘config‘ attribute defines runtime parameters like ‘Cmd‘, which specifies the command to execute when the container starts.

Nix constructs this Docker image by resolving the entire dependency closure for the specified packages, ensuring all its components are derivable from exact versions defined in the Nix package collection. This guarantees a high degree of reproducibility that simplifies both the collaboration among development teams and the migration across different computational platforms.

The integration of Nix into Docker also introduces the possibility of establishing multi-layered builds whereby each layer is deterministic, contributing to efficient image caching and minimized rebuild times. Nix's dependency graph construction lends itself to creating minimal, optimized Docker images where unnecessary packages and runtime components are excluded. This results in leaner images with reduced attack surfaces and quicker deployment times.

```
# Build the Docker image using Nix
nix-build my-docker.nix

# Load the resulting Docker image
docker load < $(nix-build my-docker.nix --no-out-link)
```

The process starts with 'nix-build', a command that initiates the build process specified in a provided Nix expression file, 'my-docker.nix'. Upon successful build completion, the resulting Docker image is stored as a tarball, which can be loaded into Docker using the 'docker load' command. This separates the concerns of image construction from image execution, enhancing both the build process' clarity and the final image's reliability.

Additionally, the use of Nix precludes the issues surrounding Docker's ordinary build context, where unnecessary files might inadvertently be included, leading to bloated images and potential security vulnerabilities. Nix's precise specification prohibits such errors, ensuring that only explicitly defined dependencies are present in the final image.

The integration also supports the transition between various environments, such as development, staging, and production, without the typical hassles associated with environment-specific configurations. Nix's philosophy of treating configuration as code makes reproducibility deterministic, allowing developers to swap environments effortlessly, focusing purely on furthering application functionality and business logic.

```
# Base image constructed using Nix
FROM my-nix-docker-image:latest

# Set environment variables if necessary
ENV MY_APP_SETTING=production

# Expose application ports
EXPOSE 8080

# Specific command overrides can be articulated if needed
CMD ["custom-entrypoint.sh"]
```

The above Dockerfile serves as an extension to a Docker image built via Nix, illustrating how developers might specify additional run-time configurations and environment variables. By decoupling image construction from runtime execution configurations, teams can systematically address distinct deployment scenarios, such as development and production, with minimal friction and zero redundancy.

As organizations adopt DevOps practices and transition towards Continuous Integration and Continuous Deployment (CI/CD) pipelines, the ability to seamlessly bridge system configurations becomes paramount. By facilitating automated and reproducible builds, Nix aligns with these objectives, supporting workflows involving automated testing and deployment within containerized environments. The benchmark accuracy and consistency Nix provides positions it as a key enabler of modern software development processes, blending infrastructure as code with immutable deployment strategies.

In closing, the integration between Nix and Docker harmonizes the precise dependency management of Nix with the flexible packaging model of Docker. This combination facilitates efficient leverage of both Nix's functional paradigm and Docker's orchestration capabilities, representing a best-of-both-worlds approach to software packaging and deployment. By embracing this integration, developers gain the ability to navigate complex dependencies without encountering the common pitfalls associated with environmental inconsistencies, enabling more productive cycles of development and deployment.

13.3 Nix as a Tool for Building Immutable Containers

Nix emerges as a formidable tool in the creation of immutable containers by leveraging its robust system of declarative package management and reproducible builds. The concept of immutability in containers entails that the containerized environment—and all its dependencies—remain unchanged throughout its lifecycle, from development through to deployment. This unchanging nature provides predictability and reliability by ensuring that all system components remain consistent across different stages.

The foundational principle behind Nix is its ability to manage dependencies in a way that ensures precise environment reproduction, governed by functional programming paradigms. This yields significant benefits in containerized environments where immutability is highly valued. Such benefits include consistent deployments, facilitated debugging, and an assurance of security, since the composition of containers is strictly controlled and verified.

Nix builds containers by aggregating all necessary software components—including libraries, configurations, and scripts—defined within a Nix expression. This expression precisely declares the desired state of the environment, establishing a blueprint that doesn't mutate over time. By utilizing Nix, developers can construct Docker images or OCI-compatible containers that function as immutable artifacts, ideal for cloud-native ecosystems and deployments within orchestrated platforms such as Kubernetes.

```
{ pkgs ? import <nixpkgs> {} }:

let
  myEnv = pkgs.buildEnv {
    name = "immutable-container-env";
    paths = with pkgs; [
      coreutils
      curl
      git
      nginx
    ];
  };
in
pkgs.dockerTools.buildImage {
  name = "my-immutable-container";
  tag = "1.0";
  contents = [ myEnv ];
  config = {
    Cmd = [ "${myEnv}/bin/nginx" ];
    Env = [ "NGINX_VERSION=1.21.3" ];
  };
}
```

In this excerpt, a Nix expression is defined to build an immutable container image. A custom environment myEnv aggregates necessary packages using the pkgs.buildEnv function. Each of these packages is a derivation—a build product in Nix's terminology—compiled in isolation to ensure its purity and immutability. The Docker image is then constructed using pkgs.dockerTools.buildImage, which encapsulates the defined environment and specifies runtime commands and environmental variables.

The immutability realized through Nix ensures that each derivation and, by extension, each Docker layer corresponds explicitly to a defined set of inputs. This determinism underpins the reliability of immutable containers, circumventing the conflicts or discrepancies typically encountered with standard package management systems that involve global state and side effects.

Applying Nix within the context of container creation offers substantial advantages. Primary among them is the ability to achieve guaranteed reproducibility—an immutable container crafted through Nix will be identical whether built today or several months later, providing the build process has not changed. Nix thus minimizes the surface area for bugs resulting from dependency drift or unintentional updates, which are common in mutable package environments.

The notion of immutability extends beyond the assured state of a single container to include the broad aspect of configuration management. By harnessing the power of nixpkgs—the extensive collection of packages and modules maintained by the Nix community—administrators can declaratively establish infrastructure requirements as code. This paradigm makes it feasible to replicate or scale identical environments seamlessly, immortalizing the container state as code.

Furthermore, with immutability comes enhanced security. Since no mutation is allowed within the container once it is instantiated, the attack surface remains narrow. Adverse modifications are simply disallowed, thus protecting the container from a spectrum of infiltration tactics that exploit mutable systems. Immutable containers, as produced by Nix, can be further hardened by excluding non-essential binaries and setting non-root execution defaults.

```
# Build the Nix expression and generate the Docker image
nix-build my-immutable-container.nix

# Load and run the generated immutable Docker image
docker load < $(nix-build my-immutable-container.nix --no-out-link)
docker run --rm -p 80:80 my-immutable-container:1.0
```

Executed from the command line, the nix-build command compiles the Nix expression into a Docker image. The resulting binary artifact is an immutable Docker image, which is loaded and deployed using standard Docker commands. The immutability ensures that the environment instantiated by docker run is guaranteed to match the definition in the Nix expression—any deviation flags a failure during the build phase.

The transformational capabilities offered by Nix find further utilization in CI/CD pipelines where the need for scalable, immutable infrastructure predominates. By using Nix to define all components and settings, developers embed best practices for immutability directly into the build process. This lock-step methodology extends consistency across deployments, aligning CI/CD workflows with immutable infrastructure ideals and enabling straightforward rollback processes by virtue of predefined, reproducible environments.

Nix also integrates seamlessly with modern version control systems to synchronize environment definitions, effectively tying commits with environment declarations. As developers work collaboratively on codebases, environments can be rebuilt effortlessly through the same Nix expressions modified within the repository, resulting in identical containers that reflect any updates made to both code and configuration.

In building immutable containers via Nix, organizations foster a culture of operational excellence where each deployment acts as an exact repeatable unit, paving the way for increased efficiencies throughout the development lifecycle. This operational paradigm highlights the strategic advantage of adopting Nix: the agility to deftly manage environments amidst a landscape characterized by evolving operational demands and emerging architectural challenges.

Through comprehensive integration strategies and an immutable container framework, the interplay of Nix in containerized infrastructures leads to improved business outcomes, amplifying the capacity for innovation while lowering systemic risks and conventional limitations associated with mutable infrastructures. Ultimately, Nix equips architects and developers with the concrete tools to implement and sustain immutable infrastructures in a rapidly changing technological world.

13.4 Managing Multi-Stage Builds with Nix

Managing multi-stage builds with Nix provides a sophisticated approach to containerized application development by optimizing the build process, minimizing container sizes, and enhancing security. Multi-stage builds involve using multiple base images in a single Dockerfile, where each stage can utilize the build artifacts from previous stages. This method is particularly relevant in the context of Nix, as it allows for lean and efficient production images that incorporate only necessary runtime components.

Nix, known for its deterministic build environments, complements the multi-stage build strategy effectively. By defining precise environments and dependencies through Nix expressions, developers can consolidate the compilation and packaging processes into distinct stages. This results in a clear separation of build and runtime concerns, akin to Docker's approach to multi-stage builds, but further enhanced by Nix's reproducibility.

The following points establish a comprehensive understanding of managing multi-stage builds using Nix:

- Stage Definition: Multi-stage builds operate on the principle that different stages can be constructed independently within a single build process. Each stage starts from a defined base, which could be a base operating system or a custom Nix environment.
- Separation of Concerns: By compartmentalizing the build process into stages, it becomes easier to manage complexities and dependencies. Each stage performs a specific role, like compiling the application or assembling the final runtime environment. Unnecessary dependencies remain in intermediate stages and do not bloat the final image.
- Layer Optimization: In conjunction with Nix, multi-stage builds can leverage caching and layering optimizations, where redundant layers are eliminated, leading to efficient use of storage and faster build times.
- Security Enhancement: Each stage can be hardened to restrict permissions and access, ensuring that only the essential tools and libraries are present in the eventual production build, thereby reducing the attack surface.

To illustrate how Nix manages a multi-stage build, consider an application where a Go binary is compiled in a builder stage and later incorporated into a lean runtime image:

```
{ pkgs ? import <nixpkgs> {} }:

let
  # Define the builder stage environment
  buildStage = pkgs.stdenv.mkDerivation {
    name = "build-stage";
    buildInputs = with pkgs; [ go ];

    # The Nix expression for building the Go application
    buildPhase = ''
      go build -o /tmp/myapp ./src
    '';
  };

  # Define the runtime stage environment
  runtimeStage = pkgs.buildEnv {
    name = "runtime-stage";
    paths = [ "/tmp/myapp" ];
  };
in
pkgs.dockerTools.buildImage {
  name = "nix-multi-stage-build";
  tag = "1.0";
  contents = [ runtimeStage ];
  config = {
    Cmd = [ "/run/current-system/sw/bin/myapp" ];
  };
}
```

In this example, a Nix expression outlines the multi-stage build. The 'buildStage' is tasked with compiling the Go application using the Go toolchain ('pkgs.go') within a defined Nix derivation. The output binary is stored temporarily, and its path is referenced in the subsequent 'runtimeStage'. The 'runtimeStage' collects only the compiled binary, omitting the development tools and libraries from the final image build, thus creating a minimalistic runtime environment.

Let us further enrich this illustration by exploring how multi-stage builds can incorporate both Nix and traditional Dockerfile instructions where applicable:

```
# Stage 1: Build application with Nix
FROM nixos/nix as builder

COPY . /src
WORKDIR /src

# Run the Nix build command to produce the binary
RUN nix-build my-app.nix
```

```
# Stage 2: Create lean runtime image
FROM scratch

# Copy only the binary from the previous stage
COPY --from=builder /src/result/bin/myapp /myapp

# Define execution command
CMD ["/myapp"]
```

Here, a Dockerfile leverages Docker's multi-stage builds with Nix acting as the builder. The first stage executes the Nix build process, resulting in a cleaned binary. The second stage establishes a minimalist runtime environment ('scratch'), highlighting best practices by transferring only the necessary executable.

In essence, the orchestration of multi-stage builds via Nix achieves optimization through compartmentalization, enhances traceability by restricting artifact scope, and promotes secure and manageable container images. By adopting these strategies, developers embrace a paradigm where development efficiency meets operational excellence, reducing build complexity and fostering scalable deployments.

The aggregation of tasks into distinct, managed stages underlines the importance of Nix in continuous integration and delivery pipelines. Multi-stage builds empower teams with the flexibility to introduce incremental improvements through configuration adjustments, and ensure those changes propagate through predictable, immutable builds designed for production-grade applications.

Furthermore, managing multi-stage builds with Nix facilitates seamless integration with security policies. By leveraging Nix's inherent ability to derive dependencies strictly declared, teams can implement compliance and audit mechanisms directly within application builds. This level of integration helps organizations maintain high standards of security and operational control, even as they deploy across diversified, hybrid cloud infrastructures.

Ultimately, the synergy between Nix and multi-stage builds extends beyond technical benefits. It articulates a vision where software delivery processes adopt more rigorous, automated, and reliable forms, assert best practices in DevOps operations, and align implementations with business goals through efficient resource utilization, secure builds, and fast-paced iterations. The strategic adoption of Nix as a principal tool for managing multi-stage builds embodies the culmination of modern techniques in containerization, converging towards optimal software lifecycle management models.

13.5 Container Orchestration with Nix

Container orchestration with Nix offers an innovative approach to managing and deploying containerized applications across diverse environments. By utilizing Nix's declarative package management and configuration language, organizations achieve unparalleled consistency and control over their containerized workloads. Nix provides a robust foundation for orchestrating containers, leveraging its deterministic build environments to ensure reproducibility and immutability throughout the development and deployment processes.

Container orchestration is the automated arrangement, coordination, and management of containerized applications across multiple hosts. It involves various tasks such as deployment, scaling, networking, and distribution of application components. Nix enhances this orchestration by applying its functional paradigm to the configuration and deployment mechanisms, ensuring predictable and repeatable operations.

- **Declarative Configuration**: Nix's approach to specifying environments and applications in a purely declarative manner lends itself well to container orchestration. This declarative configuration is akin to Kubernetes manifests but goes further by natively integrating the build and deployment processes.

- **Immutability and Reproducibility**: By creating immutable and reproducible Docker images or OCI containers, Nix ensures consistent deployments across various stages of the software lifecycle, from development to production.

- **Seamless Integration with Orchestration Tools**: Nix serves as an excellent prelude to orchestrators like Kubernetes, Docker Swarm, or Nomad. It enables users to prepare their environments precisely using Nix expressions before deployment, ensuring all Kubernetes Pods or similar constructs operate with identical configurations.

Exploring the orchestration process begins with defining containerized services using Nix expressions. These encapsulate all dependencies and resources, ensuring the runtime environment is consistently producible.

```
{ pkgs ? import <nixpkgs> {} }:

let
  # Define the service environment for the container
  serviceEnv = pkgs.buildEnv {
    name = "web-service-env";
    paths = with pkgs; [
      nginx # Primary service application
      curl # Auxiliary tool for health checks
    ];
  };
in
pkgs.dockerTools.buildImage {
  name = "web-service-container";
  tag = "v1.0";
  contents = [ serviceEnv ];
  config = {
    Cmd = [ "${pkgs.nginx}/bin/nginx" ];
    ExposePorts = [ 80 ];
    Env = [ "ENV=production" ];
  };
}
```

This Nix expression constructs a Docker image encapsulating a basic web service. The service environment ‘serviceEnv‘ bundles ‘nginx‘ for HTTP serving and ‘curl‘ for monitoring purposes. The Docker image is built with predefined execution commands and environmental configurations, forming a consistent artifact deployable through various orchestrators.

The orchestration process advances as the constructed Docker images or containers are deployed onto a container orchestration platform. Taking Kubernetes as a common choice for orchestration, Nix-generated images can easily integrate, ensuring specifications match across environments.

To deploy the above-defined container in a Kubernetes cluster, one would typically create a Kubernetes deployment manifest, directing the orchestration layer to manage lifecycle operations for Pods based on the Nix-managed container image:

```
apiVersion: apps/v1
kind: Deployment
metadata:
  name: web-service-deployment
spec:
  replicas: 3
  selector:
    matchLabels:
      app: web-service
  template:
    metadata:
      labels:
        app: web-service
    spec:
      containers:
      - name: web-container
        image: web-service-container:v1.0
        ports:
        - containerPort: 80
```

By integrating with Kubernetes, this configuration efficiently manages multiple instances of the 'web-service-container', overseeing their scaling, self-healing, and updates. Through the declarative nature of both Nix and Kubernetes configurations, teams ensure a seamless translation of infrastructure as code principles from build scripts to deployment orchestration.

Moreover, Nix's synergy with orchestration platforms extends beyond Kubernetes. When using Docker Swarm or Nomad, similar advantages manifest as Nix guarantees consistent image generation. Nix's ability to output identical images irrespective of build environment differences ensures these containers can move from one orchestrator to another without requiring modifications.

The strategic benefits of integrating Nix into orchestration workflows are numerous. Nix ensures:

- **Security**: By locking configurations during the build phase, Nix minimizes runtime drift, ensuring deployment behaves as anticipated without unsuspected vulnerabilities.
- **Efficiency**: Efficient container builds lead to more rapid deployments with smaller image sizes, contributing to resource savings and reduced bandwidth overhead.
- **Reliability**: The ability to rebuild environments from a single source of truth aligns configurations with desired operational

states, avoiding inconsistencies between development and production.

In reality, orchestrating containers with Nix introduces a depth to the DevOps toolkit that supports rapid iteration cycles. As organizations shift towards microservices architectures, wherein small components require precise interdependencies, Nix offers critical tooling to manage complexity and maintain application integrity.

Consider an example wherein a Nix expression defines a multi-service architectural setup, displaying orchestration complexity addressed by Nix:

```
{ pkgs ? import <nixpkgs> {} }:

let
  # Backend service environment
  backEndEnv = pkgs.buildEnv {
    name = "backend-service-env";
    paths = with pkgs; [ python38 postgresql ];
  };

  # Frontend service environment
  frontEndEnv = pkgs.buildEnv {
    name = "frontend-service-env";
    paths = with pkgs; [ nodejs ];
  };

  # Build Docker images for both services
  backendImage = pkgs.dockerTools.buildImage {
    name = "backend-container";
    contents = [ backEndEnv ];
    config = {
      Cmd = [ "${pkgs.python38}/bin/python" "app.py" ];
      ExposePorts = [ 5000 ];
    };
  };

  frontendImage = pkgs.dockerTools.buildImage {
    name = "frontend-container";
    contents = [ frontEndEnv ];
    config = {
      Cmd = [ "${pkgs.nodejs}/bin/node" "start.js" ];
      ExposePorts = [ 80 ];
    };
  };
in {
  inherit backendImage frontendImage;
}
```

This configuration outlines both a backend and frontend container. Nix constructs separate environments for each, managing dependencies such as a Python application backend and a Node.js frontend. Coordinated through Docker orchestration, these containers provide a comprehensive microservices solution demonstrating Nix's ability to handle nuanced multi-service architectures.

Incorporating Nix into container orchestration strategies not only maximizes build efficiency and deployment reliability but also aligns modern infrastructure provisioning with best practices for repeatability and security. As organizations democratize cloud-native practices and scale across complex networks, Nix emerges as a remarkable asset: a guarantor of consistency, a simplifier of complexity, and a pillar of DevOps excellence. By orchestrating containers with Nix, teams charter a path toward informed architecture planning and optimal resource utilization that aligns development practices with strategic business objectives.

13.6 NixOS Containers: System-Wide Consistency

NixOS containers represent an evolution in achieving system-wide consistency across computing environments by leveraging NixOS's declarative configuration management and immutable infrastructure principles. As a Linux distribution built on top of the Nix package manager, NixOS enables users to define their entire system configuration, leading to highly consistent and reproducible environments. When extended into the realm of containers, NixOS provides unparalleled advantages in terms of maintaining system uniformity, ensuring predictable deployments, and simplifying multiservice orchestration.

Central to NixOS is its approach to describe systems through modules that articulate every aspect of a system's configuration. This encompasses everything from package dependencies to service configurations and even systemd units, all captured in a Nix configuration file. This unified configuration model extends naturally into containers, where it underpins the creation of containerized environments that behave identically regardless of the host system.

```
{ config, pkgs, ... }:
```

```
{
  containers.simpleContainer = {
    autoStart = true;
    config = { config, pkgs, ... }: {
      environment.systemPackages = [ pkgs.hello ];
      services.nginx.enable = true;
      networking.firewall.allowedTCPPorts = [ 80 ];
    };
  };
}
```

In this NixOS configuration, called a NixOS module, a container named 'simpleContainer' is defined. Within this container, a 'hello' package and the 'nginx' web server are installed, and network port 80 is configured to be open. What is particularly powerful about this configuration is its declarative nature; changes can be tracked, reviewed, and replicated precisely, fulfilling an assurance of system-wide consistency.

The utilization of NixOS containers can radically simplify deployment strategies, especially in heterogeneous environments requiring the same software stack. The promise of system-wide consistency is realized through a few key properties inherent in NixOS:

- **Reproducibility**: NixOS ensures that given any configuration description, replicating an identical container is a non-trivial task. Variability due to environmental factors is virtually eliminated. This guarantees that developers and operations teams are on the same page regarding software and service versions, configurations, and runtime behaviors.
- **Transactional Upgrades**: One of NixOS's standout features is its support for transactional system upgrades and rollbacks. This principle carries over to NixOS containers, permitting rapid upgrades and seamless rollbacks, reducing downtime and mitigating the risk of upgrade-induced outages.
- **Immutable Infrastructure**: NixOS containers benefit from immutable infrastructure tenets, meaning once a container is rolled out with a configuration, it does not change unless explicitly updated. Any configuration drift from the intended state can be detected and rectified effortlessly.
- **Configuration as Code**: Storing system configurations in version control enables detailed auditing, collaborative iteration,

and well-documented infrastructure, with every change captured and annotated within a single repository of truth.

Given these properties, NixOS containers shine particularly in large-scale deployments and situations demanding high assurance levels of environmental fidelity. The process of generating and managing these containers can be further exemplified through leveraging the NixOS module system to configure complex services:

```
{ config, pkgs, ... }:

{
  containers.complexContainer = {
    autoStart = true;
    bindMounts = {
      "/data" = { hostPath = "/var/lib/app-data"; isReadOnly = false; };
    };
    config = { config, pkgs, ... }: {
      imports = [ <nixpkgs/nixos/modules/services/web-apps/gunicorn.nix> ];
      environment.systemPackages = [ pkgs.python38Full pkgs.postgresql ];

      services.gunicorn = {
        enable = true;
        appRoot = "/srv/myapp";
        environment = "PYTHONPATH=/srv/myapp";
      };

      users.users.appuser = {
        createHome = true;
        home = "/home/appuser";
        isSystemUser = true;
        extraGroups = [ "wheel" ];
      };

      networking.firewall = {
        enable = true;
        allowedTCPPorts = [ 8000 5432 ];
      };
    };
  };
}
```

This more detailed configuration introduces bind mounts for data persistence, integrates a Gunicorn service for Python-based web applications, and manages user accounts with access configurations. Each aspect, from installed packages to user permissions and service settings, is described declaratively. By doing so, these NixOS containers ensure a thoroughly consistent runtime environment.

The seamless compatibility of NixOS containers with container orchestration platforms further enhances their utility. Applications wrapped within NixOS containers can be deployed into Kubernetes clusters, Docker Swarm setups, or any other container orchestration system with supported integration. This marriage of NixOS consistency and orchestration flexibility allows enterprises to establish reliable CI/CD pipelines across any cloud infrastructure:

```
apiVersion: apps/v1
kind: Deployment
metadata:
  name: complex-service-deployment
spec:
  replicas: 5
  selector:
    matchLabels:
      app: complex-service
  template:
    metadata:
      labels:
        app: complex-service
    spec:
      containers:
      - name: complex-service
        image: nixos-container:latest
        ports:
        - containerPort: 8000
```

Deploying the 'complexContainer' as a Kubernetes-managed service exemplifies the practical deployment of NixOS containers within orchestrated environments. By specifying 'nixos-container:latest' as the image, the Kubernetes orchestration engine coordinates deployment, scaling, and lifecycle management.

The systemic consistency rendered by NixOS containers promotes stable and predictable deployments, fulfilling the operational requirements for advanced distributed systems. For enterprises navigating complex microservices architectures, these containers deliver assurances of system uniformity, dramatically reducing the friction commonly associated with development-to-production transitions.

NixOS containerization endows developers and system administrators with the tools needed to establish infrastructure configurations that match software deployments line-for-line. The practice of using NixOS containers for system-wide consistency fosters environments where software experimentation can safely coexist with guaranteed production reliability, accelerating innovation without compromising operational integrity.

In summary, NixOS containers realize the vision of a synchronized infrastructure, where every service is precisely represented in its defined state. By leveraging the unique configuration management capabilities offered by NixOS, organizations achieve an unparalleled benchmark of operational consistency that meets the modern demands of scalable, reliable, and secure software deployments.

13.7 Challenges and Solutions in Nix-based Containerization

Nix-based containerization, while providing significant benefits in terms of reproducibility, consistency, and efficiency, presents its own set of challenges that developers and operations teams must address to realize its full potential. This section explores the common obstacles faced in adopting Nix for containerization and presents solutions and best practices to overcome these hurdles, ensuring smooth integration into modern development workflows.

- **Challenge 1: Learning Curve and Adoption**

  One of the primary challenges is the steep learning curve associated with Nix and its functional programming-based approach. Nix requires a solid understanding of its declarative language, build expressions, and ecosystem, which can be daunting for those new to functional package management.

  Solution:

  Investing in comprehensive training and onboarding programs is essential for successful Nix adoption. Starting with straightforward tutorials and gradually advancing to more complex scenarios helps bridge the knowledge gap. The Nix community also provides valuable resources, documentation, and forums that can be leveraged for support. Furthermore, integrating Nix into existing workflows gradually, with pilot projects, allows teams to adjust to its paradigms without disrupting ongoing operations. Mentorship programs pairing Nix-savvy developers with newcomers can accelerate learning and foster collaborative problem-solving.

- **Challenge 2: Complex Dependency Management**

  Nix's deterministic dependency management is a double-edged sword. While it ensures reproducibility, managing the myriad dependencies of modern applications can become complex, especially when integrating third-party libraries or dealing with non-standard setups.

  Solution:

  Employing best practices in dependency declaration and isolation is crucial. Developers should aim to package dependencies into self-contained expressions that maintain clear boundaries. Additionally, using nix-shell or nix-shell -p allows immediate, ephemeral environments for experimentation without affecting globally shared Nix expressions. For complex dependencies or proprietary codebases, creating custom Nix expressions or overlays can manage intricate dependency networks.

```
self: super:

{
  customPackage = super.callPackage ./custom-package.nix {
    inherit (super) dependency1 dependency2;
  };
}
```

In this overlay example, a custom package defined within custom-package.nix utilizes existing dependencies from the super environment, allowing modifications specific to project needs without altering upstream packages.

- **Challenge 3: Build Times and Computational Overheads**

  Lengthy build times and computational requirements for Nix derivations can be problematic, especially in resource-constrained environments or CI/CD pipelines where time efficiency is critical.

  Solution:

  Implementing binary cache systems (like the official Nix binary cache) can significantly reduce build times by storing pre-built binaries, which are then shared across projects and teams. Introducing dynamic cache population strategies, using tools like cachix, allows caching during continuous integration processes, thereby reducing redundant builds and conserving computational resources. Additionally, optimizing Nix expressions by minimizing non-essential rebuilds and exploiting build parallelism further enhances performance.

```
# Install cachix client
nix-env -iA cachix -f https://cachix.org/api/v1/install

# Push builds to the cachix cache
cachix push mycache
```

- **Challenge 4: Debugging and Diagnostics**

  Nix's functional approach and abstraction layers can obscure traditional debugging workflows, rendering established diagnostic strategies less effective.

  Solution:

  Adopting a systematic approach to debugging in Nix requires familiarity with its tools and logs. Utilizing nix log provides insights into individual derivation build steps, while nix repl offers an interactive environment to evaluate expressions. Enhanced logging and custom hooks can also be implemented to capture additional diagnostic information. Moreover, implementing step-in and step-out practices with nix-build alternatives can segment and scrutinize complex build processes incrementally.

```
# Rebuild with debug symbols enabled
NIX_DEBUG=1 nix-build my-expression.nix
# Access and analyze the derivation logs
nix log /nix/store/xyz-mybuild-log
```

- **Challenge 5: Ecosystem Integration**

  Integrating Nix into broader tech stacks, especially those with existing infrastructure paradigms, may encounter compatibility issues or technical resistance due to differing operational models.

  Solution:

  To facilitate seamless integration, it's necessary to strategically utilize Nix's interoperability features. Employing Dockerized Nix environments eases certain constraints, allowing Nix-created images to fit into existing containerized environments. Developing API bridges and scripting interfaces can integrate Nix with established tools like Prometheus or Grafana for enhanced monitoring. Establishing ongoing dialogues with teams responsible for infrastructure management encourages collaborative adjustments to procedures and policies, promoting mutual understanding of benefits and trade-offs.

- **Challenge 6: Security Considerations**

  The use of Nix-based containers can inadvertently introduce security vulnerabilities if not designed with comprehensive security policies in mind. Ensuring that containers remain immutable and protected is vital.

  Solution:

  To address security, implementing strict access controls and permissions within Nix expressions is essential. The use of Nix sandboxing isolates build environments, restricting unauthorized changes. Incorporating security-focused build practices, such as using signed derivations and consistently employing security audits, further mitigates risks. Automated vulnerability scanning tools integrated into CI/CD pipelines can detect and flag potential security concerns in real-time, ensuring proactive management of security obligations.

```
{ config, pkgs, ... }:

{
  security.sudo.wheelNeedsPassword = true;
  users.extraUsers.deploy = {
    isNormalUser = true;
    home = "/home/deploy";
    extraGroups = [ "wheel" ];
  };
  system.stateVersion = "21.05";
}
```

In this secure NixOS configuration snippet, system version enforcement and user privilege adjustments reflect conscious policy tailored to maintain robust security postures.

Nix-based containerization, although faced with specific challenges, offers a range of innovative solutions that align with modern development paradigms. Through adopting effective educational strategies, fine-tuning build processes, integrating seamlessly with existing tech stacks, and implementing robust security frameworks, organizations can leverage the full potential of Nix-based containerization. This allows for more reliable deployments, greater operational efficiency, and the realization of software consistency and version control that matches modern demands for secure and scalable infrastructure development.

Chapter 14

Security and Isolation with Nix

Security and isolation with Nix are achieved through its functional approach, which promotes immutability and dependency purity. Nix's use of sandboxing during builds ensures that environments are isolated and secure from external interference. By managing dependencies explicitly and cryptographically verifying them, Nix mitigates potential vulnerabilities and enhances system integrity. The deterministic builds further reduce security risks by ensuring consistent outputs. This robust framework not only delineates clear boundaries for application interactions but also facilitates secure, reproducible software configurations essential for maintaining high-security standards.

14.1 Security Principles in Nix

In the domain of package management and system configuration, security principles form the foundation upon which secure, reliable, and reproducible systems are built. The Nix package manager exemplifies a paradigm shift towards a highly secure system by emphasizing immutability and reproducibility. These concepts enhance security by fundamentally altering how software packages are constructed, deployed, and managed. The building blocks of Nix—its declarative nature, its purely functional approach, and its unique handling of package dependencies—collectively contribute to a framework designed for minimal risk and maximal integrity.

Immutability, as a core tenet, refers to the unchangeable nature of data once it has been created. In a traditional package manager, files and binaries are subject to updates which can lead to inconsistencies, broken dependencies, or even introduce vulnerabilities post-installation. Nix avoids such pitfalls by treating all package artifacts as immutable entities. This is achieved through content-addressable storage, where packages are stored based on a hash of their contents. As such, an update does not overwrite a package; rather, it results in a new package. This versioning by immutability allows systems to revert to any previous state effortlessly, thereby establishing a reliable point-in-time security assurance.

To further expound on the concept of content-addressable storage, consider the following operations in Nix:

```
nix-store --add-path /path/to/file
```

This command stores the file or directory in the Nix store, generating a new path based on its hash. Accessing a previous version of a package is a mere matter of referring back to its specific hash. This mechanism underpins the reproducibility model of Nix, ensuring that once a package's integrity is validated, it remains unchanged, eliminating the security risks associated with mutable states.

Reproducibility in Nix is another strength in its security proposition. It implies that given the same inputs, the build process will yield the same results every time. Deterministic builds are realized through the specification of dependencies and build instructions in a declarative manner via the Nix expression language. This guarantees consistency and predictability, thereby minimizing the potential attack surface for adversaries seeking to exploit anomalies or vulnerabilities that might arise from inconsistencies typical of non-reproducible environments.

Examining a simplified Nix expression:

```
{ stdenv, fetchurl }:
```

```
stdenv.mkDerivation {
  name = "example-package-1.0";
  src = fetchurl {
    url = "http://example.com/source.tar.gz";
    sha256 = "0v1h2grjZc...";
  };
  buildInputs = [ ];
  meta = {
    description = "An example package";
    license = "public-domain";
  };
}
```

This expression specifies exactly how the software is to be built and what sources are involved, alongside a cryptographic hash of the source code to ensure its integrity. Any deviation from the expected hash during fetching results in failure, thus ensuring that maliciously modified sources do not get introduced into the build environment. Through such stringent controls, attacks such as source code substitution are effectively muted.

The Nix paradigm extends security benefits into the runtime through isolation mechanisms. Process and data isolation in Nix is primarily achieved using sandboxing. During the build phases, Nix ensures that each package is built in an isolated environment. This prevents unauthorized access to the host system and mitigates the risk of contamination between build environments—addressing both confidentiality and integrity at the system level.

To activate sandboxing in Nix, typically, the configuration is adjusted through the following method:

```
sandbox = true;
```

This ensures even stricter control over the build environment, leveraging Unix namespaces and kernel facilities to simulate a minimal and isolated root environment for each build process. Consequently, packages are constrained to explicit dependencies and must declare their entire operational environment beforehand, hence prohibiting unforeseen access or dependency creep post-halting environment leaks.

From the perspective of cognitive security, Nix's prominent feature follows a model of "least privilege", wherein operations and permissions are strictly constrained to enable only what is necessary to achieve a given function. This paradigm adheres closely to the principle of least authority, ensuring comprehensive protection across different system layers.

Importantly, Nix incorporates state-of-the-art cryptographic mechanisms to validate trust in both content and environments. The use of digital signatures allows packages to be verified cryptographically, instilling an assurance of provenance. For instance, by incorporating GPG keys to verify the authenticity of Nix expressions or binary caches, system administrators or DevOps professionals can institute a chain of trust that spans the entirety of their infrastructures.

The command example to verify an imported package using a GPG key might proceed as follows:

```
nix-store --verify-path /nix/store/10abc... --key /path/to/public.gpg
```

Trust is reinforced not only at distribution levels but extends to seamless integration with other paradigms such as continuous integration/-continuous deployment (CI/CD) pipelines. In CI/CD, Nix's reproducibility and immutable deployments guarantee that such pipelines remain robust and intrinsically secure—allowing safe rollbacks and reproducible builds even in distributed systems.

The inherent advantages of integrating Nix into security frameworks appeal to sectors where failure is not permissible. Critical systems, financial services, and healthcare sectors, to name a few, can harness these principles and reduce risk significantly. The certainty that failure—in terms of data integrity or consistency—can be quickly mitigated while system recovery is assured elevates Nix beyond conventional package management systems.

Brief attention is due to the security-oriented developers who construct the Nix ecosystem. Ensuring security principles align with the flexibility of the system requires continuous vigilance. The security model does not terminate at package oversight; it extends into robust community practices, including continuous audits and transparent development processes. Bug bounty programs, code reviews, and extensive documentation collectively enhance both situational awareness and system defenses against potential threats.

Nix thus represents a fusion of functional programming paradigms with security-conscious systems architecture. Its incorporation of immutability and reproducibility provides users with advanced assurance capabilities, aligning system operations with stringent security postures requisite for modern computational challenges. Hence, moving aggressively from theory into practice, Nix continues to carve a distinguished path toward emergent needs in the landscape of secure, manageable software environments.

14.2 Package Isolation and Sandboxing

In Nix's architecture, package isolation and sandboxing are pivotal components ensuring that build processes are secure, consistent, and devoid of unintended interactions. These mechanisms protect the build environment from unauthorized access and interference, thereby maintaining a clean separation between individual build environments. At the core, isolation and sandboxing safeguard the integrity and consistency of bi-directional interactions between the software packages and the system.

The concept of package isolation in Nix manifests through its functional package management approach, where each package is treated as an independent entity. The packages are stored in a unique directory in the Nix store, identified by a hash that represents the specific dependencies and conditions under which they were built. This aspect of isolation ensures that modifications to any package do not affect other packages, thus maintaining stability and reliability across the system.

Consider an example of building a package in Nix:

```
nix-build '<nixpkgs>' -A hello
```

This invocation results in the creation of an isolated environment where the package hello is built, preventing any unintentional modification to the package's environment or dependencies.

Moving from isolation to sandboxing, we see an enhancement in security posture. Sandboxing provides a controlled execution environment where packages can be built or run with minimal risk to the host system. The sandbox constricts the environment to only include explicitly declared dependencies and access points, minimizing unforeseen interactions with the broader system. In this context, Nix leverages Linux features such as user namespaces, chroot environments, and bind mounts to implement its sandboxing strategy effectively.

Sandboxing in Nix is typically enabled by setting the configuration option as follows:

```
sandbox = true;
```

When sandboxing is enabled, it results in a multitude of enhancements to the environment:

- Each build process is confined to a filesystem subtree isolating it from other parts of the filesystem.
- The processes within the sandbox run with reduced permissions, typically as an unprivileged user, to thwart potential privilege escalation attacks.
- Network access is restricted to ensure that builds cannot fetch resources unless explicitly specified.
- The build environment is deterministic, depending only on the specified inputs in the Nix expression.

An illustrative build process confined to a sandbox can be analyzed thus:

```
nix-build --option sandbox true '<nixpkgs>' -A coreutils
```

Here, the coreutils package is built within the sandbox, ensuring that the build utilizes only the actions and resources defined by its build script and declared inputs.

Stepping deeper into the evaluation of sandboxed environments, each sandbox enforces a segregation of build phases, preventing resource interchange between builds without explicit configuration. This segregation plays a crucial role in maintaining functional purity across callbacks and dependencies. The side effects of individual builds are relegated solely to their respective sandboxed hierarchies, thereby diminishing the global impact of build failures and ensuring traceability back to specific, reproducible conditions.

Sandboxing also has performance implications, as each sandbox incurs a setup overhead through isolation, albeit providing consistency. Striking a balance, Nix's architecture optimizes sandbox creation and teardown to ensure that the consistency and integrity brought by sandboxing outweigh its performance costs.

Critical to understanding package isolation and sandboxing in Nix is the security model rooted in explicitness. Nix expressions force package maintainers to declare all dependencies explicitly, rendering invisible dependencies barren. This explicitness prevents undeclared, potentially harmful, dependencies from being added dynamically during the build phase, thus averting the classic "it works on my machine" problem often faced in diverse environments.

To exemplify a simple Nix expression that adheres to absolute dependency specificity:

```
{ stdenv, fetchurl, glibc }:
stdenv.mkDerivation {
  name = "minimal-package";
  src = fetchurl {
    url = "http://example.com/source.tar.gz";
    sha256 = "0dsfh98sh...";
  };
  buildInputs = [ glibc ];
  meta = {
    description = "A minimal package";
  };
}
```

This derivation restricts inputs to only those necessary, effectively encasing the build within a well-defined sandbox.

By virtue of this detailed isolation and sandboxing, Nix widens its applicability across multi-tenant systems and developer environments where dependency creep and the sprawl of environment-related bugs can be detrimental. The fundamental paradigm of isolated builds fosters a culture of continuous integration and deployment that remains verifiably safe. This ensures that systems can scale while maintaining security and reliability standards often unattainable with traditional package management systems entrenched in mutable state.

Furthermore, Nix's sandboxing can interoperate with containerization technologies, presenting another layer of defense and utility. Containers such as Docker or Podman, when combined with Nix-based build paradigms, allow holistic validation of images and workflows, establishing intricate chains of trust derived from reproducible builds. This architecture supports not only isolated deployment but also scalable production environments underpinned by sanctified integrity and compliance.

Despite its advantages, sandboxing does demand an evolutionary approach from developers accustomed to easier, non-restricted performance environments. To facilitate this transition, Nix's logging and debugging hooks permit careful monitoring of build processes, highlighting dependency import issues or missed declarations effectively. This transparency in monitoring and auditing forms another security layer by design.

In encapsulation, package isolation and sandboxing in Nix converge towards achieving unique safety, consistency, and repeatability guarantees. They serve to bridge developer operations with operational clarity, operational oblige, and quiescence in deployments. The resultant ecosystem presents as the collective summation of reproducibility, operational flexibility, integrity assurance, and expanded security harnessed from concept to practice.

14.3 Managing Dependencies Securely

In any complex software system, managing dependencies securely is paramount to ensure the integrity, reliability, and security of the final application. Nix adopts a declarative and purely functional approach to managing dependencies, fundamentally transforming the landscape of package management by incorporating rigorous security practices and establishing immutable foundations for dependency management.

A cornerstone of Nix's capability to manage dependencies securely is its purely functional package management model. Each package specification, or derivation, within Nix clearly articulates the exact dependencies required. These dependencies are specified using the Nix expression language, allowing for precise and reproducible environments across builds. This not only minimizes the risk of dependency drift but also ensures that every package build is consistent and repeatable.

Consider a basic derivation example, specifying tailored dependencies for a mock package:

```
{ stdenv, lib1, lib2, fetchFromGitHub }:
stdenv.mkDerivation {
```

```
  name = "example-package";
  version = "1.0.0";
  src = fetchFromGitHub {
    owner = "example";
    repo = "example-package";
    rev = "v1.0.0";
    sha256 = "0v1h23j...";
  };
  buildInputs = [ lib1 lib2 ];
  meta = {
    description = "An example package with secure dependencies";
    license = "MIT";
  };
}
```

In this derivation, each dependency like lib1 and lib2 is explicitly declared. The source code is fetched from a deterministic location, using both a specific version tag and a cryptographic hash to verify its integrity. This ensures that any malicious modification in the source repository can be detected instantly, aborting the build if an integrity breach is identified.

A deeper exploration into the cryptographic guarantee involves checksums and hashes provided through SHA-256 or similar cryptographic algorithms. These hashes assure that the downloaded content has not been tampered with, serving as an indispensable facility in the Nix ecosystem. Should the hash verification process fail, the build halts until the discrepancy is resolved, typically culminating in the acquisition and verification of a lawful source.

Beyond verifying the authenticity of source code, Nix extends cryptographic veracity to all artefacts managed in its store. Each store path incorporates a cryptographic hash of all inputs influencing the derivation. Consider, for example, the Nix store path /nix/store/xy12...-example-package-1.0.0. The path's prefix is a hash representing the package's build inputs, system architecture, and Nixpkgs channel, implying inherent security and preventing unforeseen alterations post-build.

The introduction of fixed-output derivations augments this security model by mandating that all derivations with network dependencies verify external sources via hashes. This verification is essential, granting confidence in the immutability and resilience of remote dependencies once acquired.

Nix also provides robust mechanisms for handling dependency trees and mitigating nested dependencies. Through the use of dependency graphs, developers can visualize and assess the attack surface represented by indirect dependencies, opening a pathway to rationalizing dependency management and enforcing minimal privilege principles.

Another dimension of managing dependencies securely lies in the handling of binary caches. Binary caches store pre-built binaries that contribute to efficiency, reducing build times. However, relying on external binaries introduces an element of potential insecurity. Nix addresses this by allowing for custom binary caches that are signed using GPG keys. This approach ensures the binary artefact's provenance and integrity are validated securely:

```
nix-build --option binary-caches "https://my-cache.example.com" --option trusted-
    public-keys "example-key.gpg"
```

The ability to establish trust in binary artefact providence imparts a scalable model that can be tailored to specific industrial requirements, as seen in environments demanding stringent compliance such as finance or healthcare sectors.

Integrating Nix within a continuous integration and deployment (CI/CD) pipeline exploits immutable deployments and deterministically managed environments. This ensures that the build artifacts within the pipeline are identical across all stages—from development to production—contributing decisively to the security of build environments.

Furthermore, the Nix ecosystem contributes to an integrated approach for remediating vulnerabilities across dependencies. By fostering PINNED dependencies, the build ecosystem remains insulated from sudden updates that could introduce fragile states or vulnerabilities. Assessing dependency vulnerabilities emanates from community- and technology-standard vulnerability assessment tools that are transparently integrated with Nix expressions.

Underpinning Nix's dependency model is a powerful community engagement in maintaining an evolving tree of trusted package definitions. An open strawman proposal collectively reviewed ensures that package dependencies remain updated, patched against known vulnerabilities, and evolving with the latest security policies or cryptography trends.

For example, specific to software projects leveraging Nix, automated system checks can be harmonized with vulnerability databases, inviting automatic alerts and patches flowing from the community or trusted third-party audits.

In reconciling security with flexibility, Nix provides development and deployment through a model that remains resilient without compromising functional expressivity or efficiency. It extends to secure bootstrap workflows where initialization and ongoing operation are corroborated through a security-conscious practice of derivation definitions, ensuring dependency checks extend from development phases to continuous operational lifecycle stages.

Ultimately, managing dependencies securely using Nix devolves into a basket of practices ranging from constant evaluation of security postures, meticulous deliberation on dependencies, and a foundational trust mechanism ensuring integrity and auditability. Following these principles, Nix accomplishes an adept balance of reproducibility, security assurance, and transparent operational environments, continuously fostering the evolution of software delivery standards.

14.4 Immutable Infrastructures with NixOS

The concept of immutable infrastructures represents a departure from traditional mutable environments towards systems that epitomize consistency, control, and predictability. NixOS, a Linux distribution built atop the Nix package manager, concretizes this paradigm by leveraging immutability to enforce robust security principles and operational stability. This model ensures that system configurations and states remain consistent over time, reducing the likelihood of faults induced by configuration drift and unanticipated changes.

At the core of NixOS is a declarative configuration model that allows the entire system to be described through a single configuration file. Through this configuration file, known as /etc/nixos/configuration.nix, users can define their desired system state, including packages, services, hardware configuration, and any system settings. This file functions as a precise blueprint of the system's intended state, ensuring that changes are predictable and repeatable.

A simplified example of a configuration.nix file is illustrated below:

```
{ config, pkgs, ... }:

{
  imports = [ ];

  boot.loader.grub.device = "/dev/sda";

  fileSystems."/".device = "/dev/disk/by-label/nixos";

  networking.hostName = "nixos";
  networking.useDHCP = false;
  networking.interfaces.enp0s25.useDHCP = true;

  services.sshd.enable = true;

  environment.systemPackages = with pkgs; [
    vim
    wget
    git
  ];

  users.users.alice = {
    isNormalUser = true;
    extraGroups = [ "wheel" ];
  };
}
```

In this configuration, essential components of the infrastructure are declaratively defined. Services like SSH are enabled, users are provisioned with necessary permissions, and a selection of system packages, such as vim, wget, and git, are included. This holistic clarity rendered by the configuration ensures that rebuilding or replicating the environment is both reliable and accurate.

The principle of immutability in NixOS is further realized through versioned packages and configurations. By using atomic upgrades and rollbacks, NixOS maintains a catalog of previous system states. This feature means that any upgrade, once initiated, does not alter the current running environment until confirmed, providing a safe haven to revert to a known working state if discrepancies or failures arise during an upgrade.

To apply configuration changes, one would execute:

```
nixos-rebuild switch
```

Here, NixOS evaluates the configuration.nix system file, building and activating any necessary changes while retaining the prior environment state in the form of generations. These generations are selectable through the system's bootloader, GRUB, by default, allowing for seamless transitioning between system states.

The immutable characteristic of NixOS extends into highly secure systems operation—a key benefit is the mitigation of unintended configuration changes leading to drift. Immutable infrastructures ensure that once the infrastructure is provisioned, it does not change unless deliberately updated and approved. This operational rigidity guarantees all nodes defined within a distributed architecture reflect the desired state without deviation.

This design confers several advantages in scenarios requiring high uptime and reliability. For instance, environments dealing with regulatory compliance and audits can leverage NixOS to provide undeniable proofs of system configurations at precise historical snapshots. This concept aligns well with industries demanding intrinsically secure infrastructures, such as financial services and healthcare.

Operationalizing security through immutability in NixOS also complements comprehensive monitoring to detect and alert to unauthorized attempts to modify system states. As configurations cannot drift spontaneously, any deviation alarms can be investigated as potential security incidents, offering an additional layer of protection.

Moreover, NixOS supports reproducibility by eliminating configuration inconsistencies across development, testing, and production environments. The same configuration that describes a developer's workstation can equivalently serve in a production ecosystem, whereby promoting software pipeline assurance from development to deployment. This reproducibility ensures that software artifacts tested in one environment function identically across all environments, supporting agile practices and reducing or eliminating the "it works on my machine" dilemma prevalent in heterogeneous configurations.

In further deepening the immutable infrastructure purview, NixOS integrates adeptly with containers and virtualization solutions. While containers furnish application-level isolation and efficiency, NixOS governs system-level configuration integrally with container orchestration. This collaboration not only promotes minimized overhead but also enhances administrative grip over the entirety of infrastructure, supporting complex delivery systems with multiple layered services and dependencies.

A hypothetical integration for a container service might appear through:

```
services.docker.enable = true;

virtualisation.docker.containerd.enable = true;
virtualisation.docker.rootDir = "/data/docker";
```

This configuration not only enables Docker as a service but also specifies the root directory for its operations, showcasing how NixOS manages container systems within its immutable structure.

At scale, immutable infrastructures necessitate automation for rollback procedures, upgrades, and audits, which NixOS handles ingeniously through built-in tooling like NixOps. NixOps provides an orchestrative overlay allowing scalable deployment, holistic system updates, and deployment state verification, all derived from the declaratively defined states in NixOS configurations.

In essence, adopting immutable infrastructures with NixOS presents a paradigm that efficiently addresses contemporary operational challenges such as inconsistency, unplanned changes, and administrative overhead, while ushering a tightly controlled, deeply secure ecosystem beneficial for scaling trustworthy infrastructure deployments.

14.5 Implementing System Security Policies

System security policies are imperative for maintaining the integrity, confidentiality, and availability of information within a computing environment. NixOS provides a robust framework for implementing and managing these security policies, offering a structured approach to enforcing system access controls and other security measures. By leveraging the declarative capabilities of NixOS, administrators can encode security policies directly into the system configuration, ensuring that security configurations are explicit, versioned, and reproducible.

At the heart of managing security policies in NixOS lies the configuration management model. The /etc/nixos/configuration.nix file acts as a pivotal point for defining system-wide policies expressed cohesively alongside other system configurations. This integrative approach ensures that policy enforcement is automatic and consistent across system reboots or upgrades.

Consider a configuration snippet that enforces a set of security policies:

```
{ config, pkgs, ... }:

{
  # System lock screen and sleep inactivity settings
  services.xserver.displayManager.autoLock.enable = true;
  services.xserver.displayManager.autoLock.sleep = 900;

  # Network firewall configuration
  networking.firewall.enable = true;
  networking.firewall.allowedTCPPorts = [ 22 80 443 ];
  networking.firewall.allowedUDPPorts = [ ];

  # Secure Shell (SSH) daemon settings
  services.openssh.enable = true;
  services.openssh.permitRootLogin = "no";
  services.openssh.passwordAuthentication = false;

  # AppArmor system protection
  security.apparmor.enable = true;
}
```

In this configuration, policies encompass user session management, network access control, secure shell (SSH) practices, and mandatory access control (MAC) via AppArmor. This multi-faceted policy implementation exemplifies how diverse security policies can be consolidated within the NixOS framework.

Starting with user session management, setting autoLock enforces an autolock on the user session after 15 minutes of inactivity, a crucial policy for preventing unauthorized physical access to unattended systems. This configuration is often supplemented with additional policies for password complexity and expiration, which can be controlled through PAM (Pluggable Authentication Module) settings.

Network security policies are addressed through the NixOS firewall capabilities. By specifying allowed TCP and UDP ports explicitly, we limit network exposure strictly to necessary services, effectively reducing the attack surface. Unused services are closed by default, adhering to the principle of minimum privilege.

SSH security is bolstered with several key settings: disabling root login, forbidding password-based authentication, and allowing only key-based login. These practices mitigate brute-force attacks and unauthorized access attempts.

The introduction of AppArmor enhances system security through MAC, providing profiles that restrict programs' capabilities based on assigned policies. Enabling AppArmor proactively prevents processes from making unauthorized changes to the system, thereby placing another layer of defense against potential exploits.

System audits and logging are intrinsic elements of security policy realization. NixOS allows detailed configuration of the logging subsystem, providing granular access to system events, which are vital in post-incident analysis and forensic investigations:

```
services.journald = {
  enable = true;
  settings = {
    SystemMaxUse = "500M";
    RuntimeMaxUse = "250M";
  };
};
```

This configuration specifies journaling limits to prevent log overflow, maintaining the balance between detailed auditing requirements and system resource constraints.

Furthermore, security policies extend beyond configuration into regular updates and patch management. The atomic update capability of NixOS facilitates seamless security patches without jeopardizing existing system state integrity. Regular updates ensure that known vulnerabilities are promptly patched, crucial in safeguarding against zero-day exploits.

Automating policy deployment and configuration management can be achieved through NixOps or other deployment tools, which support scaling these carefully defined policies across multiple systems in a datacenter or cloud environment. This automation ensures consistency and simplifies compliance audits by generating verifiable state descriptions.

Intrusion detection and prevention are integral parts of a comprehensive security policy infrastructure in NixOS. Tools such as AIDE (Advanced Intrusion Detection Environment) can be configured to run regular checks against filesystem integrity, identifying unauthorized modifications to the system's hierarchy:

```
security.aide.enable = true;
security.aide.options = [
  "--check_atime"
  "--check_nlink"
];
```

This configuration setup triggers AIDE checks to monitor specified file attributes, ensuring system integrity through ongoing vigilance.

To encapsulate security best practices, administrators can also establish a security baseline framework, derived from industry standards such as CIS (Center for Internet Security) benchmarks. These frameworks provide a structured approach to configuring operational security controls, which can be translated into NixOS declarations, creating a reproducible, standards-compliant security environment.

Education and training play a crucial role in the effective implementation of system security policies. System administrators and developers should be regularly updated on emerging threats and updated NixOS security features through focused learning and workshops. Consider creating company-wide security teams tasked with regular policy reviews and updates, ensuring proactive risk management.

Ultimately, implementing system security policies within NixOS not only enhances the technical defenses of a platform but also constitutes a cultural shift toward a security-first mindset. By aligning security implementations closely with the core principles of declarative, immutable configurations, NixOS fosters an environment where policy enforcement is automatic, repeatable, and auditable, significantly reducing the risks associated with misconfigurations and latent vulnerabilities.

14.6 Nix and Trusted Computing

Trusted Computing is a technology designed to provide secure computing environments through hardware and software components working in tandem to ensure system integrity. It leverages special hardware elements, such as Trusted Platform Modules (TPMs), to enable robust security functionalities including measured boot, cryptographic operations, and secure storage. When combined with Nix's functional and reproducible package management model, Trusted Computing presents a formidable approach to constructing and maintaining trustworthy computing platforms.

The foundation of Trusted Computing lies in the integrity measurement and attestation processes, typically enforced by TPMs. The TPM is a dedicated microcontroller designed to secure hardware through integrated cryptographic keys. In practice, it measures early boot code and system configurations, storing hashes in Platform Configuration Registers (PCRs) for integrity validation. The integration of TPM enhances Nix-managed systems by ensuring that each boot and application deployment corresponds to a trusted state.

Integrating Nix with Trusted Computing platforms requires configuring NixOS to leverage TPM to guard system boot processes and sensitive operations. A typical configuration block to enable a TPM module and associated services in NixOS might look like this:

```
services.tpm2.enable = true;
services.tpm2-tss = {
  enable = true;
  extraParams = "--logLevel debug";
};
```

Given the presence of a TPM, this enables foundational security features like key management and secure storage, which can be advanced further using Nix's immutability advantages, ensuring that all software environments are secure and reproducible.

An important aspect of trusted computing is Secure Boot, which leverages TPM to verify and authorize all software loaded during the boot process, guarding against boot-time malware attacks. Integrating Secure Boot with NixOS ensures that only digitally signed and verified bootloaders and kernel modules can execute. This trust chain can be configured with Secure Boot keys, extending the security assurance from hardware through to application layers.

A potential NixOS configuration for Secure Boot, applied to GRUB as a part of the bootloader, might involve:

```
boot.loader.grub.efiSupport = true;
```

```
boot.loader.grub.enable = true;
boot.loader.grub.efiInstallAsRemovable = false;
boot.loader.grub.device = "nodev";
boot.loader.efi.canTouchEfiVariables = true;
```

Ensuring secure boot processes aligns with the core philosophy of Nix by providing deterministic end-to-end bootstraps, bolstering system integrity and folding in cryptographic guarantees into the operational posture.

A distinctive capability of Nix is its integration with attestation processes, such as those espoused by the TPM. Attestation refers to the process by which a system's current state can be verified against a known good state, often cryptographically, through TPM measurements. This capability enables systems to autonomously verify their trustworthiness or report system integrity status over a network, building seamless trust bridges in networked environments.

NixOS's elaborate tooling means users can script attestation workflows, embedding cryptographic properties in routine administrative tasks using TPM2 tools aligned to specific needs for system and data integrity checks. For example, integrating TPM-based disk encryption seamlessly with NixOS configuration can render hard drive contents immutable against unauthorized access:

```
networking.wireguard.interfaces = {
  wg0 = {
    address = [ "10.0.0.2/24" ];
    privateKeyFile = "/etc/wireguard/privatekey";
    listenPort = 51820;
  };
};
```

Here, exemplifying a WireGuard interface, the use of stored encryption keys in TPM adds a secondary verification layer to the secure processing of network encryption workflows, underscoring a symbiotic relationship between network and system security.

Moreover, as trusted computing extends into high-assurance environments requiring sensitive data handling, administrators can leverage the platform integrity features to ensure applications and datasets operate within an officially sanctioned environment. Through meticulously defined Nix expressions, they ensure consistent verification of trusted software chains, whose integrity checks are enforced through trusted computing principles.

The intersection of Nix with trusted computing reflects profound industrial relevance, especially within finance, healthcare, and public infrastructure. As these sectors necessitate demanding compliance and audit standards, implementing verified builds, measured deployments, and cryptographic assertions on the software environment significantly elevates organizational security maturity.

Integrating Nix with trusted computing practices fosters agility and resilience in cloud deployments. By ensuring that orchestration tools, such as NixOps, provision trusted computing environments that harness public key infrastructures (PKI) and TPM-backed credentialing, net new deployments inherit security guarantees necessary for robust service delivery over cloud fabrics.

The approach goes beyond the mundane and establishes a future-forward view, where automated, trusted software pipelines contribute an unyielding infrastructure security base. Nix empowers organizations to institute immutable distributed systems that seamlessly verify and attest operational security, incorporating built-in safeguards honored across geographical and jurisdictional boundaries.

In closing, the harmonious integration of Nix with Trusted Computing paradigms supplies a rich tapestry of security orchestration through combined assurance commitments. It stands as a lighthouse for building secure boot routines and cryptographically verified software environments with transparency. In stride towards the future, Nix's pairing with Trusted Computing environments portends a defining blueprint for achieving security and operational excellence against adversarial evolutions in a dynamic threat landscape.

14.7 Addressing Security Vulnerabilities

Addressing security vulnerabilities within software systems is a critical task that involves identifying, mitigating, and responding to potential threats. The Nix ecosystem, particularly within NixOS, provides a unique approach to managing vulnerabilities due to its functional and declarative nature. Leveraging reproducibility and immutability, Nix ensures that vulnerabilities can be addressed systematically and securely, decreasing the likelihood of detrimental impacts across systems and services.

The first line of defense in addressing security vulnerabilities relies on an efficient mechanism for identification. Within NixOS, systems are primarily defined and deployed through configuration.nix, ensuring that each deployment matches an exact state and thereby enabling precise vulnerability scans. Through centralized vulnerability assessment tools, one can automate the scanning of software packages and configurations against known vulnerability databases such as the Common Vulnerabilities and Exposures (CVE) list.

For instance, the integration of automated scanners like OpenVAS or custom scripts can be coordinated through Nix expressions to flag outdated or vulnerable packages:

```
{ config, pkgs, ... }:

pkgs.stdenv.mkDerivation {
  name = "security-scanner";
  src = pkgs.fetchurl {
    url = "https://example.com/scanner.tar.gz";
    sha256 = "1shx9g...";
  };
  buildInputs = [ pkgs.nmap pkgs.openssl ];
}
```

This setup demonstrates how to fetch and integrate a security scanner into the environment, ensuring that the tool itself is securely sourced and its integrity verified.

Beyond identifying vulnerabilities, it is imperative to adopt effective mitigation strategies. One of NixOS's notable attributes is its capability for atomic updates and rollbacks. These features are indispensable when addressing vulnerabilities as they enable system administrators to apply patches without fear of introducing new, potentially destabilizing elements. Should an update result in unforeseen issues, the entire system can be reverted to its previous secure state within moments.

To execute an update, administrators utilize:

```
nixos-rebuild switch --upgrade
```

This command synchronizes the system state with the latest definition from the Nix channels, applying relevant patches and updates from the Nixpkgs repository while ensuring minimal disruption and downtime.

Another approach to mitigating vulnerabilities is achieved by encapsulating packages within sandboxed environments, thereby restricting the potential impact of a compromised package. NixOS enforces sandboxing during package builds, corroborating the immutability principle by curtailing unauthorized access and limiting exposure. This containment minimizes the spread and influence of vulnerabilities beyond the direct scope of an affected package.

To further tighten security, administrators can employ restrictive runtime policies using seccomp, AppArmor, or SELinux, which provide granular control over application capabilities and interactions. These extensions can limit not only what applications can execute but also dictate permissible resource access levels, effectively reducing the attack surface an adversary might exploit.

For example, integrating security modules in NixOS configurations can be articulated thus:

```
security.selinux.enable = true;
security.selinux.policy = "/path/to/custom/policy";
security.apparmor.enable = true;
```

These settings enable system-level enforcement of security modules to curtail unauthorized activity, providing an additional layer of run-time integrity protection.

In the face of a newly emerged threat or zero-day, NixOS benefits from its vibrant community and rapid update cycle. The decentralized and transparent nature of its package repositories means security patches and updates are speedily propagated once a vulnerability is reported. As a participant in the open-source community, swift collaboration and immediate dissemination of security advisories allow users to react promptly.

In addition to systems controls, vigilance through continuous monitoring and alerting is paramount in vulnerability management. NixOS supports comprehensive logging and monitoring frameworks, capable of detailed security exception reporting and alerting for anomalous behaviors indicative of compromise. Betrayal of system integrity or unauthorized access attempts can be reported using tools like Prometheus and Grafana, ensuring security events are promptly detected and remediated.

To setup monitoring, administrators might define a NixOS service extension for Prometheus:

```
services.prometheus = {
  enable = true;
  dataDir = "/var/lib/prometheus";
  scrapeConfigs = [
    {
      job_name = "nixos";
      static_configs = [{ targets = ["localhost:9090"] }];
    }
  ];
};
```

This service will track and aggregate key metrics, offering real-time insights into potential security disturbances and allowing for timely interventions.

Last but not least, integrating routine audits and compliance checks guarantees that vulnerabilities do not slip through the net amidst routine operations. Formulating compliance baselines and leveraging built-in frameworks to enforce security standards can help discern policy violations before they grow into substantial threats.

With these elements working in concert, NixOS facilitates a robust, secure environment whereby addressing vulnerabilities is not merely reactive but a proactive art, enfolding detection, mitigation, and prevention strategies into everyday administrative activities. Through the elegance of paradigms such as immutability and reproducibility, NixOS breeds systems that are inherently secure, flexible, and competently positioned to contend with an evolving threatscape, ensuring defenders remain a step ahead in the battle for system integrity.

Chapter 15

Troubleshooting and Best Practices in Nix

Troubleshooting and best practices in Nix focus on effectively addressing challenges and optimizing system configurations. Understanding common errors and leveraging debugging tools are key to resolving issues quickly. Utilizing Nix's logging and diagnostic capabilities provides insights into build processes and system behaviors. Adopting best practices such as consistent use of version pinning, efficient dependency management, and proper use of overlays can enhance performance and reliability. Engaging with the Nix community and staying informed about updates and tooling improvements further supports maintaining robust, high-performing systems.

15.1 Common Issues and Error Messages

When working with Nix, users may encounter a variety of issues that manifest as error messages. Understanding these messages requires comprehension of both the underlying structure of Nix expressions and the environment in which they execute. This section aims to elucidate common issues and error messages encountered in Nix, providing not only the cause but also strategies to address them.

The Nix expression language, while powerful, has its intricacies that can lead to misconfigurations or syntax errors. Consider the following common error message:

```
error: attribute 'foo' missing
```

This message often occurs when attempting to access an attribute that does not exist in the current scope. Attributes in Nix, similar to keys in a dictionary, must be defined before they can be referenced. Errors of this nature can usually be resolved by ensuring that the attribute is declared as expected. Consider a scenario where the Nix file is expected to define 'foo':

```
{ pkgs ? import <nixpkgs> {} }:

pkgs.mkDerivation {
  name = "example";
  src = ./source;
  foo = "bar"; % Attribute should be defined here
}
```

If 'foo' is never defined, referencing it later in your Nix expression will trigger the aforementioned error. Checking the scope and ensuring all attributes are properly initialized mitigate this issue.

Another frequent issue arises from type mismatches:

```
error: cannot coerce a list to a string
```

This type of error highlights an attempt to implicitly cast or use a value as a different type, not supported in Nix. This typically happens when trying to combine strings and lists, or passing arguments in a way Nix does not handle automatically. Consider the following incorrect example:

```
{ pkgs ? import <nixpkgs> {} }:

let
  myList = ["a" "b" "c"];
in
pkgs.mkDerivation {
  name = "example";
  src = ./source;
  command = builtins.concatStringsSep " " myList + " additional command";
}
```

The issue here is with the use of operators across incompatible types. The correct approach involves proper type conversion or concatenation mechanisms:

```
{ pkgs ? import <nixpkgs> {} }:

let
  myList = ["a" "b" "c"];
  extra = "additional command";
in
pkgs.mkDerivation {
  name = "example";
  src = ./source;
  command = builtins.concatStringsSep " " myList + " " + extra;
}
```

By cautiously managing types within Nix expressions, such errors can be efficiently resolved.

Dependency resolution errors frequently occur, often resulting in the following message:

```
error: package 'xyz' not found in the context
```

This error indicates that the specified package cannot be located within the specified channels or configured overlays. This can often be due to a missing or incorrect channel configuration or package name typo. Ensuring that the Nix configuration is up-to-date with the appropriate channels can alleviate this issue. Verify the channel configuration and package availability using:

```
nix-channel --list
nix-channel --update
```

There is also the possibility of a derivation failure, resulting from a build system error or environmental instability:

```
error: builder for '/nix/store/...-package.drv' failed with exit code 1
```

The ensuing diagnosis involves examining the build log to pinpoint the source of failure, often available via a command such as:

```
nix log /nix/store/...-package.drv
```

This command provides insights into what went awry during the build phase. Common issues include dependency mismatches, missing dependencies not listed in the 'buildInputs', or misconfigured environment variables. Adding verbosity to the build process through 'NIX_-DEBUG' can provide further intelligence on the problem.

Understanding and managing environmental constraints is equally critical, which is illustrated by the following error:

```
error: unable to create directory '/nix/store/...': Permission denied
```

Such permission-oriented errors are indicative of Nix requiring root or proper user permissions to write to directories. Solutions involve either granting appropriate permissions or running commands as a privileged user:

```
sudo <package-management-command>
```

Ensuring the user has the requisite permissions to access or modify system paths can prevent these hindrances.

Civilizing complex expressions and managing adequately complex constructs mitigate parsing errors, commonly exemplified thus:

```
error: unexpected end of file
```

This often relates to improperly structured bracket, brace, or indentation syntax. Nix expressions should be carefully validated for completion of every syntactical symbol, ensuring that each opening brace or parenthesis corresponds with a closure. Employing editor syntax-highlighting features aids in visually verifying matched pairs.

```
{ pkgs ? import <nixpkgs> {} }:

let
  examplePackage = pkgs.callPackage ./my-package {};
in
pkgs.mkShell {
  buildInputs = [ examplePackage ];
}
```

It is recommended to employ thorough code review processes, especially for larger expressions, to eschew syntactical oversights.

These errors exemplify a subset of issues encountered when engaging with Nix. By grasping these commonplace challenges and their resolutions, users gain the capability to navigate the intricacies of Nix with increased proficiency and insight. Restarting the Nix daemon or clearing

'.cache' directories in ambiguous situations can also resolve persistent issues by circumventing cached misconfigurations or artifacts.

Diagnosing and addressing commonplace error messages in Nix fortifies one's proficiency in managing Nix-based systems. It is this adeptness that cultivates the confidence to experiment and expand further on the robust capabilities that Nix provides.

15.2 Debugging Techniques for Nix Expressions

Debugging Nix expressions is a critical skill for ensuring that configurations work as intended and that build processes complete without errors. This section delves into strategies and tools available for debugging Nix expressions, facilitating the identification and resolution of errors within builds and syntax.

The Nix language provides features to assist in understanding how expressions are evaluated. One effective method of debugging involves the use of the nix repl, an interactive Read-Eval-Print Loop environment. This allows for direct interaction with Nix expressions, making it easier to evaluate portions of code in isolation:

```
$ nix repl '<nixpkgs>'
```

In the REPL environment, users can test and evaluate expressions as they would in their Nix files, gaining immediate feedback on expression evaluation. For instance, verifying the availability of a specific package and its attributes:

```
nix-repl> :b hello
```

The result provides details about the derivation, its attributes, and any potential issues with the specified package. This can illuminate incorrect package references or missing attributes in expression files.

Another significant technique involves utilizing the built-in functions provided by Nix, such as trace. The trace function outputs a message to standard error without disrupting the flow of execution, allowing for diagnostic print statements embedded within expressions:

```
{ pkgs ? import <nixpkgs> {} }:

let
  inputValue = "Hello, Nix!";
in
pkgs.mkShell {
  buildInputs = [
    trace "The input value is: ${inputValue}" pkgs.hello
  ];
}
```

This code snippet helps display the value of variables at runtime, greatly assisting in understanding expression flows and identifying misconfigured values.

Environment-specific debugging can be accomplished by leveraging the nix-instantiate command. It allows dry runs of builds, essentially evaluating derivations to pinpoint potential failures in the instantiation phase without performing a full build:

```
$ nix-instantiate default.nix
```

Analyzing the output of nix-instantiate reveals expression errors in terms of non-existent paths, invalid derivations or syntax errors. It can be especially useful to add –show-trace when running this command to receive a more detailed error trace:

```
$ nix-instantiate default.nix --show-trace
```

Incorporating logging is another potent debugging technique. While Nix itself does not support extensive runtime logging due to its declarative nature, enabling bash or shell script logs within buildPhase or installPhase derivation attributes can surface real-time insights:

```
{ pkgs ? import <nixpkgs> {} }:

pkgs.stdenv.mkDerivation {
  name = "example-logger";
  src = ./source;

  buildPhase = ''
    echo "Starting the build process" > $out/log.txt
    ./configure
  '';
}
```

In this example, messages are logged during the phases of a derivation, giving context to the progression and diagnostics at each step, crucial for understanding issues when a derivation fails to build as expected.

Debugging also involves inspecting the purity and determinism of expressions, core principles in Nix's operational philosophy. Ensuring that Nix expressions refer only to dependencies and paths known at instantiation is vital. Unchecked references to user environment paths or mutable state often lead to instability. When debugging, reviewing expressions for unnecessary non-deterministic elements is critical:

```
{ pkgs ? import <nixpkgs> {} }:

pkgs.stdenv.mkDerivation {
  name = "non-deterministic-example";

  buildInputs = [ pkgs.gcc ];

  buildPhase = ''
    date >> $out
  '';
}
```

The example above illustrates using the date command, which introduces non-determinism. Scrutiny of such expressions aids in maintaining the reproducibility that Nix promises.

Spatially complex expressions can become difficult to read and debug. Refactoring them into simpler, more modular components enhances both readability and debuggability. Using let bindings and modular files serves to organize code such that errors become apparent through reduction of cognitive load:

```
{ pkgs ? import <nixpkgs> {} }:

let
  buildGcc = pkgs.runCommand "buildGcc" { } ''
    ${pkgs.gcc}
  '';

in
pkgs.mkShell {
  buildInputs = [ buildGcc ];
}
```

This approach, combined with commentary within the code, fosters clear indication of each module's role, lessening the opacity during debugging.

Further sophistication in debugging involves the systematic use of Nix's language-specific testing tools. nix-build with test targets or phases can simulate and validate expected outcomes in isolated environments, more so under sandboxed conditions:

```
$ nix-build default.nix --check
```

– Maintaining isolation ensures no side effects from implicit environment variables or user-specific states intervene with observability.

In-depth understanding of the result paths and environment variables employed within builds also supports debugging efforts. Examining environment variable files .drv during the process elucidates variable usage and name conflicts, which can be instructive in remedying configuration discrepancies.

By adeptly applying these debugging techniques, developers working with Nix can ascertain the configuration integrity and operational efficiency of their systems. Mastery over such practices reduces build errors and amplifies the predictability of environment setups. By ensuring expressions are deterministic, modular, and well instrumented for diagnostics, the robust nature of Nix environments comes to fruition, empowering developers to tackle complex package and configuration management tasks with confidence and precision.

15.3 Effective Use of Nix Logs

Utilizing logs generated during the operation of Nix builds and evaluations is crucial for diagnosing issues and gaining insights into the behavior of expressions and derivations. The logging system in Nix provides valuable information regarding the flow and outcome of package builds, assisting users in troubleshooting, performance tuning, and validating configurations.

Internally, Nix logs consist of stdout and stderr outputs captured during the execution of derivation phases. These logs offer a comprehensive view into what transpires during the various stages of building a package. One primary method for accessing Nix logs is through the 'nix log' command. This functionality permits the inspection of logs associated with specific derivations, aiding in identifying build failures or warnings.

To effectively leverage logs, users should begin by locating the derivation path. A typical command to initiate this process is:

```
$ nix-build -K some-package.nix
$ nix log /nix/store/...-some-package.drv
```

The '-K' flag ensures that the build logs and intermediate results are preserved, even if the build completes successfully or fails. This practice is vital for post-mortem analysis of environmental conditions or build inputs that may contribute to issues.

Inspecting logs involves analyzing several key phases such as fetch, unpack, configure, build, and install. Each phase provides relevant messages that could include compilation errors, missing dependencies, or misconfigured build scripts. For example:

```
configuring
configure: error: Package requirements (libpng >= 1.2.9) were not met
```

In this instance, the log entry elucidates the absence of a required library, highlighting a dependency issue. Thorough examination and understanding of the function of each phase in your build process are indispensable in isolating the root cause of errors.

An advanced feature is augmenting logs' verbosity to obtain a greater level of detail. Adjusting the verbosity provides more profound insights, especially regarding complex expressions or multi-stage build processes:

```
NIX_DEBUG=installs nix-build some-package.nix
```

Setting the NIX_DEBUG environment variable to different values, such as derivations, installs, or fetches, can increase the level of reporting, generating a more verbose output in the logs. By correlating detailed debug output with stages of the build process, developers can dissect multifaceted build problems more effectively.

Another contentious area lies in the configuration section of builds. Often misconfigurations or default configuration assumptions lead to failures that can be systematically addressed by examining configuration log outputs:

```
checking for gcc... no
checking for cc... no
configure: error: in '/build/xyz-1.2.3':
configure: error: no acceptable C compiler found in $PATH
```

The above log snippet indicates the absence of a crucial build dependency—namely, a C compiler—which is pivotal in many package builds. Systematically addressing these omissions, typically through the inclusion of missing packages in nativeBuildInputs or buildInputs, resolves such issues:

```
{ stdenv, gcc }:

stdenv.mkDerivation {
  name = "example";

  nativeBuildInputs = [ gcc ];

  src = ./source;
  configurePhase = ''
    ./configure
  '';
}
```

Clear and precise integration of required build tools into Nix derivations enhances the success rates of expression evaluations and builds, obviating the need for extraneous debugging subsequent to log analysis.

For more intricate configuration issues, creating custom shell scripts to encapsulate environment variables or configuration states provides further clarity. Encapsulation allows logs to reflect a more determinable state:

```
{ pkgs ? import <nixpkgs> {} }:

pkgs.stdenv.mkDerivation {
  name = "example-script";

  buildInputs = [ pkgs.coreutils ];

  buildPhase = ''
    echo "Running build phase"
    ./configure > $out/configure.log 2>&1
  '';
}
```

By redirecting output to a log file, the developer gains an encapsulated view of a derivation state effectively and reliably, particularly for phases generating extensive output.

Understanding and utilizing log rotation, particularly for significant builds, further enhances the effective use of logs. For long-running or intensive build operations, logs can become exceptionally large. Consider using system or user-level log management practices to handle log size and retention, ensuring that vital diagnostic information is maintained while curating storage efficiency.

Differentiation between infra-level logs and build command output further segments the potence of Nix logs. Build-time execution logs pertain to individual package processes, whereas environmental and infrastructure logs may cover system-wide issues affecting builds:

```
nixos@host:~$ journalctl -u nix-daemon.service
```

For instance, if build caching or network-related issues are suspected, broader system logs provide context regarding daemon state, connectivity, or filesystem accessibility, extending beyond an individual package's build scope.

Certain packages or expressions might necessitate more granular deconstruction—debugging individual steps through versatility in logging approach. Dependencies between packages occasionally result in recreation of derivation paths; logs help differentiate between direct build errors and downstream propagation or cascading failures within interconnected builds:

```
$ nix-build default.nix --rollback
```

A methodical approach involves tailoring logging practices to align with specifics of build mechanics, phasing, and systematic deduction of resolution paths. This enhances the effectiveness of logs as a data source for troubleshooting while maintaining environment soundness.

Custom scripts in distinct phases also allow simulations of component states, facilitating controlled log generation and analysis. Interaction with users, particularly those in development environments, encourages leveraging automated and repeatable logging, offering a measurable cadence in system diagnostics.

In encapsulating all these facets, effective use of Nix logs necessitates an intricate dance between build mechanics, configuration knowledge, and environmental understanding. By adopting systematic log practices, developers strengthen their capability to diagnose, analyze, and rectify underlying build and expression issues with greater efficacy, expediting troubleshooting efforts while bolstering confidence in Nix's comprehensive package and configuration management capabilities.

15.4 Versioning and Compatibility Practices

Managing package versions and ensuring compatibility within Nix environments are crucial tasks for maintaining stable, consistent, and reproducible builds. As systems evolve and software projects undergo updates, it becomes imperative to implement robust versioning and compatibility strategies to prevent disruptions caused by incompatible dependencies or inadvertent updates. This section explores best practices for handling package versions and compatibility constraints effectively in Nix-based systems.

One fundamental aspect of versioning with Nix is the concept of "pinning." Pinning involves fixing the version of a specific package or an entire package set to a known, stable state. By doing so, users can prevent unexpected changes caused by upstream updates that might introduce breaking changes or regressions. Pinning is typically achieved using specific Git commits or tags when importing 'nixpkgs', for example:

```
{ fetchTarball }:

let
  nixpkgs = import (fetchTarball {
    url = "https://github.com/NixOS/nixpkgs/archive/<commit-hash>.tar.gz";
  }) {};
in
nixpkgs.mkShell {
  buildInputs = [ nixpkgs.hello ];
}
```

This example demonstrates pinning the 'nixpkgs' repository to a specific commit, ensuring that all packages are drawn from a consistent, vetted state. Pinning can extend beyond the 'nixpkgs' repository to include other Git repositories housing custom packages or overlays, enhancing reproducibility across environments.

For applications with multiple dependencies, managing versions can swiftly become complex. A robust strategy is the use of overlays, which allow for the customization of package definitions and the specification of version requirements inline with the base 'nixpkgs'. Overlays provide flexible mechanisms to override package versions or attributes:

```
{ pkgs ? import <nixpkgs> {} }:

let
  myOverlay = self: super: {
    myPackage = super.myPackage.overrideAttrs (old: rec {
      version = "2.0";
      src = super.fetchurl {
        url = "https://example.com/my-package-2.0.tar.gz";
        sha256 = "...";
      };
    });
  };
  pkgs = import <nixpkgs> { overlays = [ myOverlay ]; };
in
pkgs.mkShell {
  buildInputs = [ pkgs.myPackage ];
}
```

Using overlays ensures that specific versions are used without altering the global state of the package set. This precise control promotes build consistency across different team members or deployment environments.

Compatibility issues often arise from incompatible dependencies. In Nix, utilizing options such as allowBroken, allowUnfree, or preferNative, and setting them explicitly in configurations, can aid in resolving or acknowledging compatibility problems:

```
{ pkgs ? import <nixpkgs> {
    config = {
      allowBroken = false;
      allowUnfree = false;
      preferNative = true;
    };
  }
}:

let
  myApp = pkgs.runCommand "myApp" { } ''
    echo "Example application" > $out
  '';
in
pkgs.mkShell {
  buildInputs = [ myApp ];
}
```

These configurations provide a way to tailor the evaluation process, ensuring a balance between stability and functional flexibility. Employing allowBroken and related options requires careful consideration, as enabling broken or unmaintained packages can introduce additional uncertainties.

Additionally, embracing semantic versioning (SemVer) principles when maintaining custom packages can significantly enhance version clarity and dependency management. Utilizing SemVer mandates clear definitions of major, minor, and patch version differences, fostering greater predictability and comprehension of API changes across updates.

To facilitate compatibility across different system architectures, leveraging platform expressions in derivations supports cross-compilation efforts or the utilization of architecture-specific optimizations:

```
{ stdenv, fetchurl }:

stdenv.mkDerivation {
  pname = "crossExample";
  version = "1.0";

  src = fetchurl {
    url = "https://example.com/cross-example.tar.gz";
    sha256 = "...";
  };

  meta = {
    platforms = stdenv.lib.platforms.linux;
  };
}
```

Defining supported platforms within the derivation metadata ensures that packages are only built on compatible architectures, reducing errors related to unsupported operations or features.

As software ecosystems progress and evolve, maintaining compatibility can necessitate utilizing multiple versions of the same package. Nix's capabilities allow the inclusion of multiple version branches through custom derivations or layered overlays, maintaining separate namespaces:

```
with import <nixpkgs> {};

let
  stable = pkgs.callPackage ./stable-version.nix {};
  latest = pkgs.callPackage ./latest-version.nix {};
```

```
in
pkgs.mkShell {
  buildInputs = [ stable latest ];
}
```

For workflows where different projects rely on dissimilar versions, maintaining segregated dependency trees or using specialized shell environments ensures each project operates with its prescribed version dependencies.

Lastly, adopting a routine update and review process for pinned dependencies and versions facilitates the timely incorporation of crucial security patches and features while avoiding technical debt buildup. Utilizing scheduled clean-up and updating procedures keeps packages aligned with upstream improvements and patches without compromising the stability of pinned software systems.

Systematically applying these versioning and compatibility practices safeguards the operational integrity of deployments, minimizing downtime and inconsistency across development and production environments. By leveraging pinning, overlays, metadata configuration, and intentional version management strategies, users can build reliable, reproducible, and future-ready systems that withstand the velocity of modern software delivery paradigms.

15.5 Optimization and Performance Tuning

Optimization and performance tuning in Nix involve strategies focused on improving the speed and efficiency of both package builds and the Nix environment as a whole. This section details various approaches to streamline Nix operations, optimize resource utilization, and reduce build times, ultimately enhancing the developer experience and system performance.

A fundamental strategy in optimizing Nix is leveraging the power of reusable binary caches. By default, Nix utilizes binary caches from trusted sources, such as the official 'nixos.org' server, to speed up package installations by reusing precompiled binaries rather than building from source. Configuring additional binary caches can further accelerate builds, especially in environments with custom or frequently updated packages. This is achieved by specifying cache URIs in 'nix.conf':

```
substituters = https://cache.nixos.org https://my.custom.cache
trusted-public-keys = cache.nixos.org-1:ABCDEFG... my.custom.cache-1:HIJKLMN...
```

The presence of custom binary caches ensures rapid deployments by providing pre-built binaries tailored to organizational or project-specific requirements.

Another optimization technique involves the exploitation of build parallelism. Nix effectively utilizes concurrency by distributing build tasks across multiple CPU cores. Users can adjust the number of concurrent jobs via the '–cores' option or configure it system-wide in 'nix.conf':

```
$ nix-build --cores n my-package.nix
```

Setting 'cores' to the maximum available (e.g., the number of logical processors) enables Nix to exploit parallel architecture for faster builds. Explicitly configuring this in 'nix.conf' applies it universally for all Nix operations:

```
max-jobs = 8
```

Maximizing resource utilization by adjusting the concurrency level based on available system resources balances build speed with other workload demands.

Caching build inputs, such as source files or intermediate results, serves as another effective optimization to enhance Nix's build performance. Employing '–reuse-build' or enabling optional layer outputs prevent redundant recomputation, speeding up consecutive builds involving unchanged inputs:

```
$ nix-build --reuse-build my-package.nix
```

Intermediary caching is pivotal, particularly in iterative development or testing processes, by enabling components to be rebuilt only when necessary, reducing unnecessary computation and redundant resource consumption.

An additional technique for performance tuning involves minimizing derivation sizes by trimming unnecessary inputs and outputs. Identifying and excluding superfluous build dependencies or intermediate outputs not essential for the final package reduces disk space requirements and transfer times:

```
{ pkgs ? import <nixpkgs> {} }:

pkgs.stdenv.mkDerivation {
  name = "optimized-package";
  src = ./source;

  buildInputs = [ pkgs.libpng ]; % Include only necessary dependencies

  installPhase = ''
    mkdir -p $out/bin
    cp program $out/bin/
  '';
  meta.outputsToInstall = [ "bin" ]; % Exclude other non-vital outputs
}
```

This tailored approach to defining inputs and outputs efficiently manages resource allocation and aligns package size to essential contents.

Optimizing the Nix store is another pivotal aspect of performance tuning. Frequent builds can lead to an accumulation of outdated or redundant data. Regularly executing garbage collection commands maintains the store's cleanliness and ensures optimal storage usage:

```
$ nix-collect-garbage --delete-old
```

Pairing this with 'nix-store –optimise' compacts the store, reclaiming space and reducing unnecessary redundancy, while also enhancing read and write performance due to reduced store fragmentation.

For high-performance use-cases or resource-constrained environments, custom compiler flags plugged into Nix derivations can enhance runtime performance or shrink binary sizes. Adjusting 'CFLAGS', 'LDFLAGS', and analogous environment variables allows fine-tuning of package builds to meet stringent performance requirements:

```
{ stdenv, fetchurl }:

stdenv.mkDerivation {
  pname = "performance-tuned";

  src = fetchurl {
    url = "https://example.com/software.tar.gz";
    sha256 = "...";
  };

  buildPhase = ''
```

```
    export CFLAGS="-O3 -march=native"
    export LDFLAGS="-Wl,-O1"
    make
  '';
}
```

'-O3' optimizes for speed and '-march=native' tailors the compilation to the current processor, augmenting performance by leveraging CPU-specific optimizations.

For systems reliant on deterministic builds or reproducibility under diverse conditions, enabling sandbox builds reinforces consistency by isolating build processes from environmental contaminants. Although pugilistic in enforcement, sandboxing ensures that performance tuning efforts are reproducible across builds and environments:

```
sandbox = true
```

In some cases, exploiting lighter configurations or adjusting service levels reduces overhead. Eliding debug symbols from release builds or turning off opulent logging can expedite final production builds:

```
{ pkgs ? import <nixpkgs> {} }:

pkgs.stdenv.mkDerivation {
  pname = "lightweight-package";
  version = "1.0";

  src = ./source;
  buildInputs = [ ];

  releaseBuild = true; % Omit debug symbols

  buildPhase = ''
    make release
  '';
}
```

Incorporating these facets to turning strategies into operations invigorates sustainable optimization practices, whether by refining derivations or through adept application cache management, thereby strengthening Nix's capacity to efficiently manage both development and production workloads.

15.6 Maintaining and Updating Nix Environments

Maintaining and updating Nix environments requires a blend of strategic planning, vigilant monitoring, and leveraging the powerful tools provided within the Nix ecosystem. As Nix environments underpin the predictability and consistency of deployments, this process is essential in ensuring that systems remain secure, updated, and efficiently managed. The following section explores methodologies and best practices for managing and upgrading Nix environments effectively.

Central to the maintenance of Nix environments is the concept of declarative configuration management. By defining the system state in a series of Nix expressions, users can recreate exact software environments across various machines. This is achieved using tools such as 'nixos-rebuild', which apply configurations from a single source of truth:

```
$ nixos-rebuild switch --flake <nix-system-config>
```

By employing flakes, the configuration and software dependencies are hashed, ensuring quick and reliable rebuilds by referencing known stable states. An integral part of this maintenance is the use of strong version control practices, underpinning clear documentation and tracking of changes to configurations.

To maintain security and ensure compliance, consistently updating environments to include recent patches and software updates is imperative. Periodic updates using channels, such as 'nixos-unstable', provide access to the latest package versions. However, care should be taken to test these updates in sandbox environments to avoid incompatibility or unforeseen behaviors.

```
$ nix-channel --update nixos && nixos-rebuild switch
```

The '–update' operation synchronizes your local copies of Nix channels with their upstream versions, refreshing available package listings and updates to system configurations.

To mitigate the effects of updates, the adoption of pinning practices, as previously discussed, is paramount. By locking dependencies to specific versions within 'nixpkgs', developers ensure that environments do not inadvertently shift due to upstream changes. Reassessing pinning as part of routine audits alleviates version drifts, allowing specific changes to be evaluated systematically and safely integrated:

```
{ pkgs ? import <nixpkgs> { overlays = [
  (self: super: { inherit (super) foo-bar v1; })
]; } }:

let
  pinnedPackage = pkgs.foo-bar "1.2.3";
in
pkgs.mkShell {
  buildInputs = [ pinnedPackage ];
}
```

Such pinning is foundational to maintaining predictable environments while permitting incremental, controlled updates.

For larger environments with numerous packages and complex dependencies, the incorporation of CI/CD (Continuous Integration/Continuous Deployment) frameworks becomes indispensable. Nix seamlessly integrates with CI/CD tools, offering automated testing and deployment pipelines that swiftly adopt and deploy changes across environments.

```
pipelines:
  - name: Nix Build
    steps:
      - label: ':nix: Build Nix Packages'
        command: 'nix-build && nix-env -qaP'
      - label: ':nixos: Deploy changes'
        command: 'nixos-rebuild switch'
```

Incorporating such pipelines infuses deployments with strength by emphasizing automated testing and rollback capabilities, ensuring the resilience and reliability of each update.

Garbage collection in Nix plays a key role in maintaining a clean and efficient environment. As derivations and builds evolve, unused artifacts can accumulate, leading to potential storage-related issues. Regularly scheduled garbage collection routines effectively purge unneeded elements, reclaiming storage resources:

```
$ nix-collect-garbage -d
```

Running ‘nix-store –gc‘ removes out-of-reach store paths from the Nix store, economizing on space. Complementing this, the ‘-d‘ option eradicates old generations of user and system profiles, fostering a cleaner system state.

Overlay management emerges as another powerful tactic in environment maintenance. Introducing overlays can customize or override default package configurations, enabling experimentation with different software versions or configurations without disrupting stable environments. Effective overlay management entails clear version control and a sophisticated understanding of dependencies, reducing potential conflicts as newer version branches are introduced:

```
let
  customOverlay = self: super: {
    foo = super.foo.overrideAttrs (old: {
      version = "1.2.3";
    });
  };
  pkgs = import <nixpkgs> { overlays = [ customOverlay ]; };
in
pkgs.mkShell {
  buildInputs = [ pkgs.foo ];
}
```

Besides direct software management, evaluating and adjusting non-software dependencies or system configurations—like storage quotas, network rules, or scheduling policies—is crucial. Continuously monitoring these elements maintains optimal system resource allocation, contributing to an overall efficient operational state.

Furthermore, engaging with the vibrant Nix community offers access to shared knowledge, insights, and best practices. Community-driven forums, wikis, and mailing lists serve as reservoirs of collective intelligence, providing assistance with troubleshooting, advanced configuration strategies, and the exploration of new features or tools.

The maintenance and update processes in Nix require a measured and proactive approach to ensure environments remain robust, consistent, and devoid of obsolescence. This involves adhering to best practices, such as declarative configuration, comprehensive version control, integration of CI/CD structures, regular garbage collection, astute overlay management, and community engagement. Collectively, these strategies cultivate a perpetually optimized and secure environment suitable for the evolving demands of modern software deployment and development efforts.

15.7 Community and Support Resources

The Nix ecosystem, while inherently technical and complex, is supported by a robust and active community. Community involvement is fundamental to the growth and success of Nix, providing resources, shared knowledge, and support avenues for users ranging from novices to seasoned practitioners. This section explores the myriad of ways users can engage with the Nix community and leverage available resources to enhance their understanding and resolve challenges related to Nix environments.

One of the primary support channels within the Nix community is the official NixOS Discourse forum. This platform provides a space for users to discuss a wide array of topics, including general usage inquiries, advanced features, troubleshooting help, and development discussions. It acts as a repository of communal knowledge, with threads often containing detailed solutions to common issues:

https://discourse.nixos.org/

The structured format of Discourse allows users to search through existing conversations, often finding answers to their questions without needing to start a new thread. Participation in active discussions fosters a collaborative learning environment where new and innovative solutions often emerge.

Complementary to forums, the NixOS subreddit offers an informal venue for discussions, ranging from specific technical issues to broader philosophical debates about the nature of declarative configuration management. The Reddit community, while less structured than Discourse, can provide immediate feedback and community interaction, serving as a gateway for new users:

https://www.reddit.com/r/NixOS/

With active participation, users contribute to both problem-solving and the dissemination of Nix's potential in varied use-cases, benefiting the collective learning curve.

One of the most valuable resources is the official NixOS Wiki, which contains a wealth of information, walkthroughs, and configuration examples. This encyclopedic reference allows users to gain insights into best practices, dive deep into specific Nix features, and discover community-contributed tips or complete examples of complex configurations:

https://nixos.wiki/

New users benefit particularly from curated guides, while experienced users can extend this repository with their insights, enhancing the communal knowledge base.

In addition to static content, real-time interaction is facilitated by the community's presence on platforms like IRC and Matrix. Channels such as #nixos on libera.chat are frequented by knowledgeable contributors who can offer immediate advice and insights:

irc://irc.libera.chat/#nixos

Connecting with community members in these channels enables dynamic problem-solving and real-time collaboration, often leading to faster resolution of complex issues or exchange of ideas towards developing new features.

Furthermore, ongoing education and user engagement are supported through community-run events and conferences, such as NixCon. These events allow participants to learn new techniques, engage with thought leaders, and partake in workshops which delve into advanced aspects of Nix. To supplement community engagement, users can watch recorded sessions and keynotes from past conferences:

https://nixcon.org/

These gatherings strengthen the community through collective learning and sharing of experiences, bringing together users from various domains who contribute back to Nix's development and dissemination.

Owing to the open-source nature of Nix, users are encouraged to contribute directly to its codebase. GitHub serves as the central platform for collaboration, enabling users to propose enhancements, report bugs, or participate in discussions on ongoing issues:

https://github.com/NixOS/nixpkgs

Navigating through pull requests or issue histories often imparts valuable insight into Nix's workings, rendering users more adept at employing or troubleshooting Nix in their projects. Moreover, contributing to repositories strengthens users' ties to the project, paving the way for becoming influential voices in the community.

Mentorship opportunities further bolster community interaction, with experienced practitioners willing to guide newcomers or those transitioning to more advanced Nix usages. This is facilitated by dedicated programs and informal networks within community spaces. Cross-border collaboration in this capacity is a hallmark of open-source ethos, inclusive of a wide diversity of input and experience.

Exploratory communities like the one surrounding Nix typically thrive by welcoming diversity and maintaining an inclusive, respectful atmosphere, ensuring that each user—regardless of their background—can contribute to and benefit from communal resources. As NixOS gains traction, the expansion of community support structures remains a testament to its growing influence and adaptability.

Engaging with the Nix community and using the abundant support resources available offers invaluable opportunities for education, problem-solving, and collaboration. Whether through forums, chats, collaborative coding, events, or contributions back to the ecosystem, these interactions bolster user proficiency and forward Nix's evolution as a robust, community-driven platform. Through active participation, users not only ensure their personal success within Nix systems but also contribute to the ongoing prosperity and dynamism of the Nix project at large.

Printed in Poland
by Amazon Fulfillment
Poland Sp. z o.o., Wrocław

43045574R00233